A RESIDENCE
AT THE
COURT OF LONDON

Richard Rush was appointed American Minister in London at the end of 1817. He was born in Philadelphia in 1780, the son of a fashionable doctor, and had a sparkling political career before travelling to London to take up his appointment at the Court of St James. A passionate anglophile and interested in all manner of international affairs, Rush had never been to England before and was very interested in all aspects of the new world opening out before him.

A Residence at the Court of London is a charming and unusual memoir, and of real value as a historical document. Introduced by Philip Ziegler, author of *Diana Cooper* and *Mountbatten*, this is the first one-volume edition of Rush's three volumes of delightful memoirs.

Also published in the Century Classics

The cover shows 'Inconveniences of a Crowded Drawing Room' by G. Cruikshank

A RESIDENCE
AT THE
COURT OF LONDON

by Richard Rush

ENVOY EXTRAORDINARY AND MINISTER
PLENIPOTENTIARY FROM THE UNITED STATES OF AMERICA,
FROM 1817 TO 1825
INTRODUCTION BY PHILIP ZIEGLER

CENTURY
London Melbourne Auckland Johannesburg

First published in three volumes in 1833
© Introduction Philip Ziegler 1987

This edition first published in 1987 by Century, an imprint of Century Hutchinson Ltd, Brookmount House, 62–65 Chandos Place, London WC2N 4NW

Century Hutchinson Australia Pty Ltd
PO Box 496, 16–22 Church Street, Hawthorn, Victoria 3122, Australia

Century Hutchinson New Zealand Limited
PO Box 40-086, Glenfield, Auckland 10, New Zealand

Century Hutchinson South Africa (Pty) Ltd
PO Box 337, Berglvei, 2012 South Africa

ISBN 0 7126 1780 9

Contents entry for Chapters XXVII and XXVIII to be revised in subsequent editions. The publishers would like to apologize for any inconvenience caused to the reader.

Printed in Great Britain by
Richard Clay Ltd, Bungay, Suffolk

CONTENTS

PREFACE

Books about one's own country written by foreigners possess a curious fascination. Everything is familiar, yet seen through a glass darkly; the facts are the same but the interpretation different; details that the reader takes for granted provoke amazement in the author, yet what for the local inhabitant seems a phenomenal innovation is passed by with scarcely a mention.

When the account is written 160 years before, the distancing effect is double. London in the 1820s is at least as unfamiliar to us as it was to Richard Rush, yet the reasons for that unfamiliarity are widely different. For both reader and writer it is a voyage of discovery; the fact that the discoveries are rarely the same adds piquancy to the exercise.

Richard Rush was appointed American Minister in London at the end of 1817. He had been born in Philadelphia thirty-seven years before, the son of a fashionable doctor, and he made his career as a lawyer, being appointed Attorney General of the United States in 1814. Earlier in 1817, while John Quincy Adams was in Europe, he had served as Secretary of State and had negotiated the Rush-Bagot Agreement which limited the armaments allowed vessels in the Great Lakes. He was both anglophile and internationally minded, but had never left the United States before his posting to the Court of St James. He was sound, sensible and unassuming, inclined to be a little ponderous but filled with goodwill and passionately interested in every aspect of the new world – or perhaps more correctly Old World – which was opening up in front of him.

The timing of his appointment was not entirely happy. It was less than five years since Britain and the United States had been at war, and though the conflict had bulked far larger in the minds of the Americans – it was, after all, Washington that had been burnt, and not Whitehall – Mr Rush had to compete with a certain amount of prejudice. There were also problems left over from the war or still earlier: disputes over fishing rights, long-standing complaints about the impressment of seamen from American vessels, compensation for slaves 'liberated' by Britain during the recent war, and the north-western boundary between the United States and Canada. On the whole Rush found that the American position was treated with some sympathy by British ministers, but the relationship between the two countries was never very easy and, at times, acrimonious.

He arrived in a Britain which was beginning to recover from the worst effects of the Napoleonic Wars. The economic depression and high unemployment among discharged soldiers and sailors were by no means cured but an excellent harvest in 1817 had eased matters and trade was reviving. Lord Liverpool was in the sixth year of his long Tory administration; George III was still technically on the throne but everyone knew that his madness was incurable and that the Prince Regent was monarch in all but name.

Readers will find themselves alternately amazed at how similar things are to the present day and surprised by the differences. On his arrival Rush found that the Custom officers ransacked his carpet bags and peered within the folds of his linen, by no means an unfamiliar process to the contemporary traveller (though the temporary confiscation of his books is less regularly encountered in the 1980s). Yet at his first dinner party, where a handful of ambassadors were heavily outnumbered by British grandees, the latter talked French even among themselves. How many could do the same with comfort today, even though Britain is now a member of the European Community? The British workmen, Rush noticed, drank tea the whole time, yet the newspapers contained 'hardly a typographical error'.

Dinner parties were a particularly rich source of social observations. At dinner with Mr Planta, Under Secretary of State at the Foreign Office, Rush met Canning, who was then Foreign Secretary, Huskisson, Robinson (Chancellor of the Exchequer), Lord Granville and several other notabilities. Late in the evening Canning proposed a game of Twenty

Questions. After the due number of questions had been asked, 'Mr Canning sat silent for a minute or two; then, rolling his rich eye about, and with a countenance a little anxious, and in an accent by no means over-confident, he exclaimed, "I think it must be the wand of the Lord High-Steward!" And it was – EVEN SO.' The game, it is interesting to note, was played at the dinner table after the ladies had left; it was not till after midnight that the men moved upstairs to take coffee.

In 1818 Castlereagh, on whom Rush was calling, suggested that his guest might find it interesting to see something of the general election that was then in progress by coming down with him to the hustings in Covent Garden. Rush politely replied that he would be happy to go under such auspices. 'You might have better,' replied Castlereagh somewhat grimly. He was quite right. The ministerial candidate had been hissed and pelted with missiles the previous day and appeared with his arm tied up and a bandage over his eye. This greatly heartened the crowd, who set upon Castlereagh with equal enthusiasm as soon as he appeared. The minister took flight, ran into a shop in Leicester Square, escaped by the back door, and was eventually hounded to the steps of the Admiralty. Having reached asylum, Rush recorded, 'he turned round and with much complaisance thanked his pursuers, then close upon him, for their escort, saying that he would not trouble them to accompany him farther; which drew huzzas in his favour.'

For anyone interested in diplomatic history there is much of real importance in Rush's memoirs. He recounts in some detail the more important of his conversations with Castlereagh, Canning and other ministers, and his government's reaction to the attitudes taken by the British. He had to deal with one most explosive incident when two British subjects, Ambrister and Arbuthnot, were taken prisoner fighting with the Seminole Indians in Florida against General Andrew Jackson's invading army, condemned to death and executed. The affair was blown up by the British press into a fury of slightly synthetic indignation, and only the commonsense and restraint of Rush and Castlereagh prevented matters getting out of hand and ending in a war that would have been wasteful and destructive and might well in the long run have cost

Britain Canada. Rush's accounts of this and other controversies have been essential material for historians since they
were first published in 1833.

But for most people it is the social background that will
prove above all appealing. Rush in London society played the
innocent provincial to perfection. Wide-eyed, ingenuous,
slightly over-awed yet vigorously keeping up his end as the
representative of a proud sovereign republic, he observed
everything with eager interest and recorded it in a prose that is
the more telling for being without sophistication or literary
frills. There is nothing else quite like these memoirs, and they
more than deserve the wider readership that this edition is
bound to give them.

Philip Ziegler 1987

TO THE READER

When I first took the pen to prepare the following sheets for the press, it was with the intention of going through the full term of my mission; but finding them run on to their present number in using the materials of little more than a year, I have, for the present, given over that intention. I am the more admonished to this course, as Miss More, in noticing Pope's precept that the greatest art in writing is 'to blot,' says that there is still a greater – *the art to stop.*

The contents of the chapters may startle at first; but I trust only at first. I am as deeply sensible of the impropriety of making an ill use of the incidents of private life, as it is possible any one can be, and flatter myself that what I have said in this connexion will be clear of all exception. I would otherwise burn the sheets. I would burn them, if I thought they contained a line or word to create a moment's uneasiness in any one person whose name is mentioned. In giving an account of conversations other than official, I have drawn upon my notes sparingly; not that I heard things improper, had all been told; but that a thousand things pass in conversation, not adapted to print, any more than intended for it. Reports then or narratives, given under restraints from which I never could be free, may be found meagre; and in such cases I am the one to blame, desiring always to err on the side of abstinence, where indulgence would be criminal. Doubtless also there has often been a falling-off in my limited reports of what was said by others, from the better manner in which it was said by the persons themselves. Here, too, I am the one responsible. In many instances I have been happy to render acknowledgments for the kindest hospitalities received in England. Should the work be continued, this list would be much enlarged by names not hitherto reached.

There are questions involved in the negotiations I have

recorded, of the deepest prospective interest to both the United States and Great Britain. If I have explained these so that they may be rightly understood, and send them into the world under a companionship that may add to the chances of their being at all read in both countries, I believe that I shall not have written altogether in vain. When I say in *both*, I confess that I chiefly mean Britain; for with all the power of intelligence and information in that country upon public as all subjects, I am satisfied that the American questions are less generally inquired into than many others, and less generally understood than in this country. I have written in the spirit of good feeling towards Britain, which may be cherished by every American compatibly with his superior love for his own country, and which I believe few Americans fail to cherish who stay there as long as I did. A residence of nearly eight years corrected many erroneous impressions I had previously taken up; as a residence of like time in this country by Britons almost invariably imbues them with totally different feelings and opinions respecting the United States from those adopted by their hasty, and too often uninformed and uncandid travellers who come among us. Enough has been written and said on both sides to irritate. My desire is, and such my effort, to soothe. President Jackson, in his last annual message to Congress, has spoken of the value of a good understanding between two countries *'cemented by a community of language, manners, and social habits, and by the high obligations we owe to our British ancestors for many of our most valuable institutions, and for that system of representative government which has enabled us to preserve and improve them.'*

In publishing negotiations which I conducted for my country, and other official communications, it is proper I should say, that I violate no duty. It is known to be as well the practice as the principle of the Government of the United States, to publish such documents for general information: and in fact I publish nothing that has not heretofore had publicity in this manner, though piece-meal and at detached intervals. . . .

I might have thrown into separate works the parts official and parts personal. But I preferred their junction. No public man, whatever the extent or magnitude of his duties, leads a purely official life, detached from personal scenes and feelings interwoven with it. Some view of these may even serve on occasion to elucidate better the true movement of official acts, by exhibiting the latter in a broader connexion. I have also thought, that it might not be wholly unacceptable to the American community to know something of the personal reception of their Minister in England in virtue of the trust he bears; not simply that which awaits him in the common forms when he first arrives, but more generally afterwards. The same motive will open to his countrymen some views, imperfect indeed and few, but still some views of the social tone prevailing in classes amongst which his public trust necessarily, and, if his residence be protracted, largely throws him.

Brief reflections which I may now and then have hazarded on the institutions and character of England, are of little moment. They will pass only for what they are worth, with those who may be at the trouble of reading them. Far from my purpose has it been to scan all her institutions and character, (a mighty task!) but rather to speak cursorily of portions falling under my own immediate observation in some among the many spheres of her society and population. Other portions have been abundantly described by her own and foreign writers. . . .

Of current politics I have said nothing. Who looks for party spirit therefore in these pages, will not find it. They are merely intended to be historical and descriptive, if, in very humble ways, they may at all lay claim to such characteristics. It will scarcely be supposed that, even as far as they go, they embody all the scenes, social or official, of my mission. Of the first, there are only occasional notices; and of the second, only such have been selected as are decidedly national, and not all these. The whole business of private claims, requiring appeals to the British Government, I have of course passed by; with a great variety of incidental duties. These are of constant recurrence in countries between which there is so large and active a commerce as the United States and Great Britain. The Consuls take charge of many of them in the first instance; but the cases are still numerous in which they find their way to the Minister.

I went to England again on a short visit in 1829. An interval of but four years had elapsed; yet I was amazed at the increase of London. The Regent's Park, which, when I first knew the west-end of the town, disclosed nothing but lawns and fields, was now a city. You saw long rows of lofty buildings, in their outward aspect magnificent. On this whole space was set down a population of probably not less than fifty or sixty thousand souls. Another city, hardly smaller, seemed to have sprung up in the neighbourhood of St. Pancras Church and the London University. Belgrave Square, in an opposite region, broke upon me with like surprise. The road from Westminster Bridge to Greenwich exhibited for several miles compact ranges of new houses. Finchley Common, desolate in 1819, was covered with neat cottages, and indeed villages. In whatever direction I went, indications were similar. I say nothing of Carlton Terrace, for Carlton House was gone, or of the street, of two miles, from that point to Park Crescent, surpassing any other in London, or any that I saw in Europe. To make room for this new and spacious street, old ones had been pulled down, of which no vestige remained. I could scarcely, but for the evidence of the senses, have believed it all. The historian of the Decline and Fall of the Roman Empire remarks, that the description, composed in the Theodosian age, of the many stately mansions in Rome, might almost excuse the exaggeration of the poet; that Rome contained a multitude of palaces, and that each palace was equal to a city. Is the British metropolis advancing to that destiny? Manchester, Liverpool, Birmingham, and other provincial towns that I visited, appeared, on their smaller scales, to have increased as much.

In the midst of it all, nearly every newspaper that I opened rang the changes upon the distress and poverty of England. Mr Peel's bill banishing bank-notes under five pounds from circulation, had recently passed. There was great clamour – there is always clamour at something among this people. Prices had fallen – trade was said to be irrecoverably ruined, through the *over-production of goods*. I have since seen the state of things at that epoch better described perhaps, as the result of an *under-production of money*. Workmen in many places were out of employ; there were said to be fourteen thousand of this description in Manchester. I saw portions of them walking along the streets. Most of this body had struck for wages. I asked how they subsisted when doing nothing. It was answered, that they had laid up funds by joint contributions among themselves whilst engaged in work. In no part of Liverpool or its extensive environs did I see pauperism; the paupers for that entire district being kept within the limits of the poor-house; in which receptacle I was informed there were fifteen hundred. I passed through the vale of Cheshire; I saw in that fertile district, in Lancashire, Staffordshire, Derbyshire, Leicestershire, Warwickshire, Worcestershire, appearances of widespread prosperity, in the lands, houses, canals, roads, public works, domestic animals, people – in every thing that the eye of the merely transient traveller took in. I stopped at Kenilworth, and Warwick Castle; enchanting spots, which English litera- ture has almost rendered classic. I had invitations to Trentham Hall, Apthorpe, Hagley, Ockham, Landgewin, Grange Park, Digswell; from going to which I was prevented by objects confining me to the metropolis. But I seize this opportunity of marking my sense of the kindnesses intended me by the proprietors of those beautiful seats. Nor can I let it pass without comprehending in my grateful acknowledg- ments my valued American friends, George Marx and Joshua Bates, Esquires, who with their amiable families, kept London from being a dull place to me during the autumn and part of the winter, by their warm-hearted hospitalities. I have to say the same of my friend of longer date, Colonel Aspinwall, Consul of the United States for London, then residing with his amiable family at Highgate.

I cannot close these preliminary lines without the remark, that, since the volume was written, events have transpired in our own country calculated at first to give uneasiness to those who dearly love it. But may we not hope that all danger is past; and that the UNION, which made and can alone preserve us a nation, will derive from them new strength and glory?

R. R.

Sydenham, near Philadelphia,
April 1833.

CHAPTER I

VOYAGE, AND ARRIVAL AT THE ISLE OF WIGHT

On the 19th of November 1817, I embarked at Annapolis in the Franklin seventy-four, as Envoy Extraordinary and Minister Plenipotentiary from the United States to the Court of London. The ship was new, built at Philadelphia, and ordered round to Annapolis to take me and my family on board. The anchors were weighed to the sound of music. We were three days in getting down the Chesapeake, and on the 23rd found ourselves at sea. The evening sun shone upon the light-house as we left the capes, which jut out towards each other, looking, from the ocean, like a fine natural gateway to the entrance of this part of our country.

I will not stop to describe the minute occurrences of the voyage, though a large man-of-war abounds with them, as they strike upon the observation of a person who has never before been at sea. The crew consisted of upwards of seven hundred men. The ship was of two thousand tons, and, although rated a seventy-four, mounted ninety guns. If silence and cleanliness be proofs of discipline, the ship's company was entitled to that praise. We had one storm, a severe one; so it seemed to a landsman. As it was coming on, the sails were taken in, even whilst it raged, the top-gallant yards sent down, and masts struck, with a quickness that appeared wonderful. '*Call a hundred men aft,*' said the officer on the quarter-deck to a midshipman, when something urgent was to be done. In a moment, a hundred men were there. Occasionally the trumpet was used; the straining of the voice through which, amidst the roaring of the winds, had a hideous sound.

When the storm began to abate, I fell into conversation with Commodore Stewart. We were holding-on to one of the guns that had been run into the cabin. 'Commodore,' said I, 'this is a new scene to me; what could you do if we were at war and an enemy of equal force hove in sight?' – '*Chase him,*' he said, gravely. – 'What then,' I replied; 'you could not engage, I suppose? for ten hours your ship has been tempest-tost; all your exertions seem to have been required to resist the storm.' – 'True,' he said, 'but we could keep the enemy in sight.' – 'But certainly you could not fight him,' I again remarked. – 'We could not,' he rejoined, 'now; but we should watch each other, and go to it when the storm was over.' – 'What! all exhausted with the labour it has cost, all dismantled as your ship is!' – 'Yes, as quick as possible,' he answered, 'there would be no time to lose; the rigging must go up faster than it came down.' Such is war. The elements cannot stop it. Their very raging seems akin to it. This was no vain boasting. The Commodore was a modest, unassuming man; but faithful to his duty in the battle or storm.

An incident occurred that may be worth mentioning from its possible bearing upon the theory of the currents along our coast. We left the capes of Chesapeake on a Sunday, steering for England. On the following Friday, to the surprise of all on board, we saw land. It proved to be the Island of Bermuda. But how came we there? Our Captain had no intention of running down to that latitude. From the first few hours after leaving the capes, the winds had been light, chiefly from the north and north-west, and the weather thick. No accurate observations could be taken. We were aware that the ship had fallen to the south before entering the gulf-stream, but had counted upon its current, which sweeps from south to north, bringing us sufficiently back again. It happened that, when we entered it, the wind freshened, and carried us across very fast, dying away soon afterwards. Thus the current had but little time to act, in drifting us again to the north. This seemed to be, in part, the way of accounting for the situation of the ship. Yet the fact was strange that she should be so far south, as no very strong winds had blown from the north, or any quarter. . . .

On the evening of the 28th, after having had Bermuda in view for a few hours, and noticing some signals made to us, the wind springing up, we gladly bade it adieu, and laid our course for England. It was on the Sunday following that we had the storm. From that time the ship went swiftly onward under boisterous winds. On the 14th of December we were in the Channel. The nights were long and dark; the days gloomy.

We could get no good observation from the sun or stars. We spoke no vessels, saw none; nor any sign of a pilot. The New England pilot boats and those of the Chesapeake, our officers said, would run out to sea twenty and thirty miles to look for vessels; but here, in the English Channel, such a high-way for vessels, no pilots were to be seen, and at a season when most wanted. It was somewhat remarkable, that neither the Commodore, who had been twenty years in the navy, nor any of his Lieutenants, though seven in number, and some like himself familiar with almost all seas, had ever before been up the English Channel; nor had the sailing-master, or mate. Cowes or Portsmouth was the port we desired to make. Our midshipmen, two, in particular, whose names I remember, young Powell of Virginia and Cooper of New York, would climb up to the truck of the mainmast; but neither land, nor light-house, nor pilot-boat, nor any thing could be descried. All was a dreary waste. Throughout the 14th and 15th the Commodore's anxiety was very great, especially by night, for the weather was rough, and he believed we were close to the coast. The ship was chiefly steered by soundings; her situation being ascertained from the appearances of the soil which the lead brought up; a resource when other guides of navigation fail, but tedious, and apt to prove deceptive.

At length, early in the morning of the 16th, all uneasiness was dispelled. The first gleams of light disclosed land. It was a long blue-looking ridge rising out of the water. A gun was fired, which brought a pilot. We learned, as he stepped on board, that the land before us was the Isle of Wight, and that we were near Cowes. All eyes were upon him as he passed along the deck. The first person that comes on ship-board after a voyage seems like a new link to human existence. When he took his station at the helm, I heard the Commodore ask how the Needles bore. 'Ahead north,' he answered. – 'Do you take the ship through them.' – 'Ay.' – 'Does the wind set right, and have you enough?' – 'Ay.' This closed all dialogue, as far as I heard. He remained at his post, giving his laconic orders. In good time we approached the Needles. The spectacle was grand. Our officers gazed in admiration. The very men, who swarmed upon the deck, made a pause to look upon the giddy height. The most exact steering seemed necessary to save the ship from the sharp rocks that compress the waters into the narrow strait below. But she passed easily through. There is something imposing in entering England by this access. I afterwards entered at Dover, in a packet, from Calais; my eye fixed upon the sentinels as they slowly paced the heights. But those cliffs, bold as they are, and immortalized by Shakespeare, did not equal the passage through the Needles. There was a breathless curiosity also in the first approach augmenting its intrinsic grandeur.

In a little while we anchored off Cowes. If the Needles were a grand sight, the one now before us was full of beauty. Castles, cottages, villas, gardens, were scattered on all sides. When we left our own country, the leaves had fallen, and the grass lost its green; but now, although the season was more advanced and we had got to a higher latitude, a general verdure was to be seen. This was doubtless the effect in part of exquisite cultivation, and in part of the natural moisture and mildness of the climate of this part of England. As we looked all round after so immediately emerging from the gloom of the ocean, it seemed like enchantment. Boats came off from the shore to look at our ship; the persons in them, their dress, countenances, the minutest thing, fixed our attention. Our Consul at Cowes came on board, and some officers of the port. Three pilots also came. Between these and our pilot words were soon heard. The cause was remarkable. It turned out that our pilot was in fact *no pilot*. He had been one, but his branch was taken away for habitual drunkenness. Continuing to own his boat, he sailed about this part of the Channel at his pleasure, like the old man of the sea. Hearing our gun, he came on board, and, making the most of our being a foreign ship, cunningly resorted to the exercise of his old craft. The disappointed pilots declared, and our Consul rather confirmed what they said, that at the moment of their dispute he was in a state of intoxication; so that we were then first made acquainted with the fact of having been brought through the Needles by a drunken steersman! It appeared singular that such an occurrence should have happened in the English Channel; yet so it was. It was hinted that he had so good a tact in his business, and knew that part of the coast so well, that he would generally steer right even when drunk. Such was the lucky accident in our case, and, being ignorant, we were not uneasy. His drunkenness taking the form of taciturnity, he escaped detection in the eyes of strangers, though his sulkiness had not been unnoticed. The others stoutly denied his right to any fees; but as the fact of service performed was in his favour, and no one else could claim on that ground, the Commodore did not think that it rested with him to settle points of law. *Our* Palinurus certainly had the advantage in alertness over the sleepy set who would have robbed him of his reward.

      _____ 'Cassio, I *forgive* thee;
But never more be officer of mine.'

CHAPTER II

LANDING AT PORTSMOUTH AND JOURNEY TO LONDON

I stayed on ship-board two days waiting the proper order from London, for which the Consul had written, to have my baggage passed. During this interval the surrounding scene lost none of its interest; it was further enlivened by visitors coming on board the ship. We got the London newspapers wet from the press. It is a remark of Humboldt, that no language can express the emotion that a European naturalist feels when he touches for the first time American land. May not the remark be reversed by saying, that no language can express the emotion which almost every American feels when he first touches the shores of Europe? This feeling must have a special increase, if it be the case of a citizen of the United States going to England. Her fame is constantly before him. He hears of her statesmen, her orators, her scholars, her philosophers, her divines, her patriots. In the nursery he learns her ballads. Her poets train his imagination. Her language is his, with its whole intellectual riches, past, and for ever newly flowing; a tie, to use Burke's figure, light as air, and unseen; but stronger than links of iron. In spite of political differences, her glory allures him. In spite of hostile collision, he clings to her lineage. Walking the deck with two of our lieutenants, while sounding up the Channel, 'Think,' said one of them, '*that we may be in the track of the Armada*;' and they talked of the heroine queen at Tilbury. These are irrepressible feelings in an American. His native patriotism takes a higher tone from dwelling on the illustrious parent stock. Places and incidents that Englishmen pass by fill his imagination. He sees the past in conjunction with the present. Three thousand miles, said Franklin, are as three thousand years. Intervention of space seems to kindle enthusiasm, like intervention of time. Is it not fit that two such nations should be friends? Let us hope so. It is the hope which every minister from the United States should carry with him to England. It is the hope in which every British minister of State should meet him. If, nevertheless, rivalry is in the nature of things, at least let it be on fair principles. Let it be generous, never paltry, never malignant.

The order for my baggage not arriving at the time expected, I landed without it. Preferring to land at Portsmouth, the boats were prepared, and on the 19th I left the ship. The Commodore and some of his officers accompanied me. A salute was fired, as on embarking; the usual ceremony when our ministers are received on board, or landed from the national ships. Approaching Portsmouth, we passed numerous vessels of war. Some were lying in ordinary, some ready for sea. There were docks, and arsenals, and store-houses, and batteries, and fortifications. The day was fair; the wind fresh. This gave animation to the harbour scene, swelling the sails of vessels in motion, and streaming out the colours of those at anchor. It was a fine naval panorama. Besides formidable rows of line of battle ships and frigates, we saw transports crowded with troops. I had before seen ports alive with the bustle of trade; but never one so frowning and glistening with features and objects of war.

When we reached the shore, *tide-waiters* advanced to take possession of my baggage. They were informed of my public character. This did not turn them from their purpose. The national ship from which I had debarked was in view; her colours flying. Still they alleged, that having received no orders to the contrary, they must inspect my baggage. I said to Commodore Stewart that, strictly, they were right, and directed my servant to deliver it. There was but little, the principal part having been left on board to await the permit of exemption. It might have been supposed that these guardians of the revenue would have satisfied their sense of duty by a merely formal examination of what was delivered so readily. Not so; carpet-bags were ransacked; the folds of linen opened, as if Brussels lace had been hidden in them; small portmanteaus peered into, as if contraband lurked in every corner. Nothing was overlooked. A few books brought for amusement on the voyage were taken possession of, and I had to go on without them. I should have been disposed to make complaint of this mock official fidelity and subaltern folly, but from an unwillingness to begin my public career with a complaint. And I remembered to have heard Mr Adams say, that when the Allied Sovereigns visited England after the battle of Waterloo, their baggage was inspected at Dover, the order for exemption having, by an inadvertence, not been sent. There is no privilege, by positive law, of a foreign minister's effects from Custom-house examination; but by universal comity, it is forborne. The exercise of such a claim with the privity of a Government would become an affront. I must add, that the order for the full delivery of all mine, with every immunity, arrived at Cowes soon after I left the ship. In the sequel the unlucky books found their way back to me.

I proceeded to the George Inn in Portsmouth, where the Commodore and his officers were to give me the favour of their company to dinner. Arrived there, we had every attention from the master, and his servants. Comfortable apartments were promptly prepared, and the ready-laid fires lighted. We found that careful anticipation of our wants, and orderly arrangement of every thing, for which we had understood English inns were remarkable.

Whilst seated round our parlour fire in the evening, fatigued by the excitements we had gone through, and waiting the summons to dinner, we heard the bells. It was a fine chime to which we all listened. My wife was especially fond of their music. Sometimes the sound grew faint, and then from a turn in the wind, came back in peals. We knew not the cause. It passed in our thoughts that the same bells might have rung their hurras for the victories of Hawke and Nelson; 'May be,' said one of the party, 'for Sir Cloudesley Shovel's too.'* Thus musing, an unexpected piece of intelligence found its way into our circle. We were given to understand that they were ringing on the occasion of my arrival; a compliment to my station to which I had not looked. We went in to our first dinner in England under a continuation of their peals. The cloth removed, we had a glass or two to our country and friends, after which we returned to our sitting-room. When all were re-assembled there, I had an intimation that 'The Royal Bell-ringers were in waiting in the hall desirous of seeing me.' They did not ask

* English Naval Commander 1650–1707.

admittance, I was told, but at my pleasure. I directed them to be shown in at once, beginning now to understand the spring to the compliment. Eight men with coats reaching down to their heels, hereupon slowly entered. They ranged themselves one after another, in a solemn line along the wall. Every thing being adjusted, the spokesman at their head broke silence with the following intelligible address. He said that they had come, 'with their due and customary respects, to wish me joy on my safe arrival in Old England as Ambassador Extraordinary from the United States, hoping to receive from me the *usual favour*, such as they had received from other ambassadors, for which they had their *book to show*.' Their book was a curiosity. It looked like a venerable heirloom of office. There were in it, the names of I know not how many ambassadors, ministers, and other functionaries, arriving from foreign parts, throughout the lapse of I know not how many ages, with the donations annexed to each. *Magna Charta* itself was not a more important document to the liberties of England, than this book to the Royal Bell-ringers of Portsmouth! I cheerfully gave to the good-humoured fraternity the gratuity which their efforts in their vocation appeared to have drawn from so many others under like circumstances. So, and with other incidents, passed my first day in England.

On the following morning, Admiral Thornborough, the admiral in command at Portsmouth, Sir James Yeo, captain in the British navy, and Sir George Grey, chief commissioner of the dock-yard, called upon me. They offered their congratulations on my arrival. The admiral said, that if Commodore Stewart required any supplies for his ship, every facility which the yard afforded would be at his command. He added, that he would be happy in the opportunity of showing him the hospitalities of the port. Sir George Grey expressed his regrets that he had not known of my intention to land at Portsmouth, saying that he would have sent the Admiralty Yacht to the Franklin to bring me, my family, and suite, on shore; the more so, as the day was blustering, and he feared we had suffered from exposure in the ship's boats, the distance being several miles from Cowes to Portsmouth. I made the acknowledgments which these courtesies demanded. If but the natural offspring of the occasion, they tended to show, that whatever had been the conduct of the subordinates of the Custom-house, those who stood higher were likely to be actuated by different feelings towards an official stranger. I estimated properly Sir George Grey's offer, but had a silent feeling that would have made me prefer under any circumstances the landing from the ship's boats, with my country's flag at the stern.

At noon I set out for London. My family consisted of my wife, four small children, young Mr Taylor, of Washington, attached to my legation, whose name I cannot mention without an allusion to his amiable and gentlemanly qualities, and three servants. As the post-chaises drew up, the master of the inn returned me his thanks for my custom. The servants also formed a line on each side of the entry, thanking us as we passed along. I am aware that this had all been paid for; still there is a charm in civility. Money owing, says the moralist of Tusculanum, is not paid, and when paid is not owing; but he who pays gratitude possesses it, and he who possesses, pays it. So, civility for the small things of life is a species of gratitude which we like. We were soon out of Portsmouth, and went as far as Godalming that day, a distance of thirty-eight miles, over roads like a floor.

I was surprised at the few houses along or near the road side. I had been full of the idea of the populousness of England, and although I must needs have supposed that this could not be the case in every spot, it had not occurred to me that along such a high road I should find the first and so remarkable an exception. We rarely met waggons, carriages, or vehicles of any sort, except stage-coaches. We did not see a single person on horseback. The stage-coaches illustrated what is said of the excellence of that mode of travelling in England. These, as they came swiftly down the hills or were met in full trot upon the plains, the horses fine, the harness bright, and the inside and out filled with passengers, not only men but women crowding the tops, had a bold and picturesque appearance. The few peasants whom we saw were fully and warmly clad. They wore breeches, a heavy shoe, which, lacing over the ankle made the foot look clumsy; a linen frock over the coat, and stout leather gloves, which they kept on while working. They were generally robust men, short, and of fair complexions. We passed a waggon of great size. It had a pole, but double shafts, with a horse in each, and a line of four horses before each shaft horse, making ten in all, of enormous size. Their tails were uncut, and the long shaggy hair hung about their pasterns. The waggon was loaded with bales pile upon pile, higher than I had ever seen. Our postilions called it the Portsmouth heavy waggon. We afterwards saw others of like size and construction, drawn by like horses, loaded with the produce of agriculture. Whilst the draft-horses were thus enormous and rough, and the stage-coach horses sleek and beautiful, our post-horses were small, gaunt, and unsightly, but with great capacity to go fast. I was looking for a favourable change in their appearance at every relay, without finding it. In good time I discovered that the principle of sub-division applied to horses, with as much strictness as to every thing else in England, there being every variety for work and luxury.

In regard to population, I had subsequent opportunities of perceiving that there were other parts of England, and of greater extent, where it was much more thin than was generally the case from Portsmouth to Godalming. London, and a circuit of twenty miles round, give more than two millions of inhabitants; Yorkshire gives one million, and Lancashire about one million. Hence these three portions of territory, so small when compared with all England, embrace nearly one third of her population. This concentration in particular districts seems to have left others relatively bare. It is difficult to believe under such facts, whatever theories we meet with, that England is at present overpeopled. Her soil, it would seem, must be open to further meliorations, which, with improved systems of policy and agriculture, and further means of internal communication, great as are already the latter, will in time not distant carry her population as far above what it now is, as it now exceeds what it was at the period of her early kings. If we take Holland as an example of successful industry and art, where a nation has been compelled to struggle against the disadvantages of a stinted soil, there are great portions of territory in England still like a desert, which after-ages may behold productive.

At Godalming, we lost our mocking-bird. We had brought it as a mark of remembrance from Mr Crawford, formerly Minister of the United States in France, to Lady Auckland, for some kindnesses received from her in England. We nursed it with all care during the voyage. It drooped, however, at sea, and the night being cold at Godalming, it died. This bird is small, and has no beauty of plumage. Its notes are as melodious as the nightingale's, and of more variety; but I doubt if they can ever be drawn out in their full extent, and richness, except in its native climates. . . .

On the morning of the 21st we proceeded on our journey. Every thing now began to wear a different aspect. The change was more decided after passing Guildford, the county town of Surrey. We saw the traces of a more abundant population, and advanced state of husbandry. The season did not show the country in its best dress; but we were enabled to see more of it by the very absence of the foliage. Farms, and common dwellings, with fields beautifully divided, and enclosed; country seats with lodges and stately gates of iron marking the entrance to them; lawns, fresh and verdant, though it was the winter solstice; parks and pleasure-grounds munificently enclosed; ancient trees in avenues, standing in copses, or shooting up among the hedges, with shrubbery tastefully arranged in gardens, and vines and flowers clustering about the houses, were among the objects that rose in succession as we passed along. We put frequent questions to the postilions, but they could tell us little. The eye was constantly occupied. None of us had ever before been in Europe. As we got nearer to London, indications multiplied of what had been effected by time, to fill up its vast environs. Unlike the approaches to Rome, some of which are said to be at the present day through partial desolation, all within our view grew more and more instinct with life: until, at length, evening coming on, at first villages, then rows of buildings, and people, and twinkling lights, and all kinds of sound, gave token that the metropolis was close by. We entered it by Hyde Park Corner, passing through Piccadilly and Bond Street, beholding the moving crowds which now the town lights revealed. Another turn brought us into Conduit Street, where rooms had been engaged for our accommodation. In a little while we proceeded to the house of Ross Cuthbert, Esq., in Gloucester Place, a Canadian gentleman, married to one of my sisters, at whose hospitable table we dined: where also it was my fortune to meet another sister, wife of Major Manners of the British army.

CHAPTER III

FIRST INTERVIEW WITH LORD CASTLEREAGH – FIRST APPEARANCES OF LONDON

December 22, 1817. I addressed a note to Lord Castlereagh, the English Secretary-of-state for Foreign Affairs, informing him of my arrival. I asked when I might have the honour of waiting on him. He immediately replied that he would be happy to see me at the Foreign-office, in Downing Street, tomorrow at four o'clock.

December 23. Went to the Foreign-office. A sentry was walking before the door. I was admitted by a porter, and shown by a messenger into an ante-room. Another messenger conducted me upstairs to Lord Castlereagh's apartment. First salutations being over, I said that I should be happy to learn at what time I might have the honour of delivering to his Royal Highness the Prince Regent my letter of credence from the President, constituting me Envoy Extraordinary and Minister Plenipotentiary of the United States, at his Royal Highness's court. I handed his Lordship a copy of the letter. He replied, that the Prince was at Brighton; that he himself was going there on the day following, expecting to be absent a week; that he did not know precisely when the Prince would leave Brighton, but was sure he would appoint an early day for receiving me, after he came to town. I said that his Royal Highness's pleasure on the occasion would be mine. His Lordship begged I would consider myself free to call upon him, immediately after his own return to town; remarking that he would consider my reception by the Prince as having taken place, if there were any subjects I desired to broach beforehand. He added, that his wish would invariably be to give every facility to the transaction of business between us, in the hope of results satisfactory to both countries; for all which I thanked him. He also said that perhaps he might wish to converse with me on matters of business before my formal reception. He made enquiries for Mr Adams, my predecessor in the mission, and President Monroe, whom he had also known in England. He spoke of the prosperity of the United States, which he said he heard of with pleasure: remarking that the prosperity of one commercial nation contributed to that of others. His whole reception of me was very conciliatory. There was a simplicity in his manner, the best, and most attractive characteristic of a first interview. It lasted about twenty minutes.

December 24. – Go through several parts of the town: Bond Street, Albermarle Street, Berkeley Square, Piccadilly, St. James's Street and Park, Pall Mall, St. James's Square, the Strand, and a few others. Well-dressed persons, men and women, throng them. In the dresses of both, black predominates. It is nearly universal. This proceeds from the general mourning for the Princess Charlotte, late heiress apparent to the throne, who died in November. The roll of chariots, and carriages of all kinds, from two until past four, was incessant. In all directions they were in motion. It was like a show – the horses, the coachmen with triangular hats and tassels, the footmen with cockades and canes – it seemed as if nothing could exceed it all. Yet I was told that the sight in Hyde Park, any day in May or June, was more striking; and that if it happened to be on the same day with the Epsom or Ascot races, which keep the roads alive for ten miles with London carriages, a stranger misses none from the Park. Sometimes with this glitter of private equipages, you saw a stationary line of hacks, the worndown horses eating out of nose-bags; and sometimes, at a slow, tugging walk, immense waggons, filled with coals, in black sacks, drawn by black horses, large and shaggy, and fat as those in the Portsmouth waggon. I am disappointed in the general exterior of the dwelling-houses. I had anticipated something better at the west end of the town; more symmetry; buildings more by themselves, denoting the residences of the richest people in the richest city in Europe. But I do not yet see these. I see haberdashers' shops, poulterers' shops, the leaden stalls of fishmongers, and the slaughtering blocks of butchers, in the near vicinity of a nobleman's mansion and a king's palace. This may be necessary, or convenient, for the supplies of a capital too large to admit of one or more concentrated markets; but the imagination at a distance pictures something different. Perhaps it is to give a hint of English liberty; if so, I will be the last to find fault. Being the day before Christmas, there was more display in the shops than usual. I did not get back until candle-light. The whole scene began to be illuminated. Altogether, what a scene it was! the shops in the Strand and elsewhere, where every conceivable article lay before you; and all made in England, which struck me the more, coming from a country where few things are made, however foreign commerce may send them to us; then, the open squares and gardens; the parks with spacious walks; the palisades of iron, or enclosures of solid wall, wherever enclosures were requisite; the people; the countless number of equipages, and fine horses; the gigantic draft horses; – what an aspect the whole exhibited! what industry, what luxury, what infinite particulars, what an aggregate! The men were taller and straighter than the peasantry I had seen. The lineaments of a race descend like their language. The people I met, constantly reminded me of those of my own country – I caught the same expression – often it glided by in complete identity – my ear took in accents to which it was native – but I knew no one. It was like coming to another planet, familiar with voices and faces – yet encircled by strangers.

December 31. The fog was so thick that the shops in Bond Street had lights at noon. I could not see people in the street from my windows. I am tempted to ask, how the English became great with so little day-light? It seems not to come fully out until nine in the morning, and immediately after four it is gone. King Charles's saying of the English climate is often brought up; that it interrupts outdoor labour fewer days in the year than any other. Did he remember the fogs, and how very short the day is, for labour, during a portion of the year?

CHAPTER IV

INTERVIEW WITH LORD CASTLEREAGH – SLAVES
CARRIED AWAY FROM THE UNITED STATES CONTRARY
TO THE TREATY OF GHENT – EQUALIZATION OF
TONNAGE DUTIES – WEST INDIA TRADE – MEMBERS
OF THE BRITISH AND AMERICAN CABINETS

January 3, 1818. Waited on Lord Castlereagh at eleven in the morning, at his private residence, St. James's Square. It was by his request, in a note received yesterday. I was shown into a room near the hall. Family portraits were on one side, books on another, and two white *bull-dogs* lying before the fire. Contradicting their looks, they proved good-natured. In a few minutes, a servant conducted me into a room adjoining, where I found Lord Castlereagh. He received me with his former courtesy, renewing his obliging inquiries for the health of my family after our winter's voyage, with the expression of a hope that the fogs of London had not alarmed us.

He informed me that he had been to Brighton, and delivered to the Prince Regent the copy of my letter of credence, and that the Prince would receive me as soon as he came to town. In the mean time he had his Royal Highness's commands to say, that I must look upon myself as already, in effect, accredited.

He proceeded to say, that if there were any subjects of business I desired to mention, he would hear me. He remarked, that it had been his habit to treat of business with the foreign ministers in frank conversations; a course that saved time, and was in other ways preferable, as a general one, to official notes. He intimated his wish to do the same with me. I replied, that nothing could be more agreeable to me than to be placed upon that footing with him.

The way being opened for business, I entered upon it. I said there were two subjects that my Government had charged me to bring to the notice of his Majesty's, without delay. The first had reference to the slaves carried off by the English ships from the United States at the close of the late war, in contravention, as we alleged, of the treaty of Ghent.* This subject, already discussed between the two Governments without prospect of an agreement, was exciting, I remarked, an interest in the United States, to be expected where the property and rights of a large class of their citizens were at stake. It had therefore been made my earliest duty to renew the proposition submitted to my Government, and believed to point to the best, if not only mode of satisfactory settlement. The proposition was, that the question be referred to a third power to be chosen as umpire between the parties. This course was recommended by the example of provisions in the treaty of Ghent as to other subjects on which differences of opinion had existed between the two nations; my Government therefore had the hope, that Great Britain would accede to it in this instance also.

His Lordship said, that he had been much on the Continent, whilst the discussions on this subject were going forward, and inquired if we had precise information as to the number of slaves carried away. I replied, not in hand, but that it would be afforded at the proper time. He next asked, if their dispersed situation would not be an impediment to restitution. This was met by saying, that the owners would look to a pecuniary equivalent. Conversation was continued on the general question. In conclusion, he promised to keep it in mind.

The next subject grew out of the commercial convention between the two countries, of the 3rd of July 1815. This convention had established a reciprocity of duties and charges of all kinds, upon the vessels of the two nations in each other's ports. Its operation was, by its terms, to begin from the day of its date. The rule of reciprocity ought therefore to have attached, practically, at that time; instead of which, each nation continued for a while to levy the duties existing before the convention, and Great Britain had not yet abolished them all. My Government desired, I said, to carry back the operation of the convention to the day of its date, and was ready to give this rule effect by retrospective measures, hoping to find a

* The treaty, negotiated and signed in Belgium, that ended the war of 1812.

corresponding disposition in his Majesty's Government.

This subject being new to his Lordship, he gave no opinion upon it, but promised, as in the other case, to seek the necessary lights for forming one. I may state that, in the end, it was adjusted to the satisfaction of both nations.

The foregoing being the only topics which it fell within my purpose to bring to his Lordship's notice at this time, he, in turn, drew my attention to a subject on which he desired information.

It related to the four articles submitted by the British Government to my predecessor for partially opening the West India trade to the vessels of the United States. His Lordship wished to know, what probability there was of my Government agreeing to them.

As this trade enters much into future negotiations between the two countries, the first mention of the subject calls for a succinct explanation of the general question.

It stands thus, according to the statement on the side of the United States. They contend for a free intercourse in their vessels with the British West India Islands, and British colonies on the continent of North America, whenever the trade to either is opened at all by Great Britain to their flag; else, they say, that, by navigation acts of their own, they will be obliged to prohibit the trade altogether. The steady policy of England has been, to secure as large an employment as possible of her own tonnage, in carrying on her commerce with the rest of the world. Her celebrated navigation acts, commenced in Cromwell's time, and adhered to in principle ever since, whatever occasional departures there may have been from them in practice, have all had this end in view. They provided that the whole trade between England and the continents of Asia, Africa, and America, should be carried on in English ships, manned by English sailors. They also embraced regulations that placed the trade between England and the European nations upon nearly the same footing. It was against the previous monopoly of Dutch tonnage that these navigation acts were levelled. What more natural, than that other nations should be unwilling to witness the same monopoly in the tonnage of England, that she objected to in that of the Dutch; more especially since the foreign and colonial dominions of the former, have swelled to an extent that could scarcely have been conceived in the time of Cromwell. The West India Islands being part of the British Empire, her right to interdict *all* trade between them and any foreign country, could not be denied; and was not. As a general rule, she did interdict it. But when, to advance objects of her own, she would throw the trade open to the United States, she confined it to her *own ships*, manned, as by law they must be, by *her own sailors*. What the United States claimed was, that, whenever the trade existed at all, it should be carried on in *their* vessels, manned by *their* sailors, as well as with the vessels and sailors of England. This was their doctrine. It had been maintained since the days of President Washington. It contemplated no interference with the colonial rights, or monopoly of Britain. It left her at full liberty to prohibit the importation into her colonies of whatever articles she thought fit from the United States; and in like manner to prohibit exportations. It only asked, that commercial intercourse, of whatever nature it might be, should be placed upon a footing of equality as to the *vessels* and *sailors* of both. This had lately been done in the trade between the United States and the European dominions of Britain, by the convention of July 1815. . . .

Britain on her part alleged, that she had the right to regulate her trade between her colonies and the rest of the world in all respects as she saw fit. This she declared it was proper she should do, not only as regarded the commodities entering into the trade, but the vessels carrying them. She said, that to assent to the basis of reciprocity in her trade between these Islands and the United States, would give to the latter inherent advantages, owing to their proximity to the Islands. That she maintained the Islands at great expense for their civil governments and military establishments, and that on these grounds, as well as that of her general sovereignty over them, not only had the right, but held it necessary to her just interests, to employ, chiefly, if not exclusively, her own vessels and seamen in the trade whenever opened, no matter to what extent, or on what inducements. Such, briefly, was the British doctrine. It will come into view again, and derives from the original Navigation Act of England, as passed by the Commonwealth Parliament in 1652. . . .

This celebrated act may be said to have changed the maritime condition of the world. It continues to this day to affect the legislation of the United States.

The four articles of which Lord Castlereagh spoke, reduced to their essence, may be described thus. The first extended to the United States the provisions of certain Free Port acts, as they were called, authorizing a trade in the articles which they enumerated, between certain specified ports of the British West Indies, and the colonies of European nations, in vessels having only one deck. The second made a special provision for the trade between the United States and the Island of Bermuda, in a larger list of articles, and without limiting the size of the vessel. The third allowed cotton and tobacco to be imported from the United States in their own vessels to Turks Island, and salt to be taken away from that island, also in their vessels. The fourth aimed at regulating the intercourse, though under many restrictions, between the United States and the British continental colonies in America, adjoining the dominions of the former.

To his Lordship's inquiry as to the probability of my Government agreeing to these articles, I replied, 'that the President, when I left Washington, had them under consideration; but I owed it to candour to say, that there was little likelihood of their being accepted, so far did they fall short of the reciprocity desired.' He afterwards inquired of what nature would be our counter projet, in the event of their rejection. I said, one that would open this trade fully, and, above all, give to British vessels no privileges of any kind whatever, direct or incidental, over the vessels of the United States. The latter were ready to grant, in their ports, to British vessels coming from the islands, all the privileges which their own vessels enjoyed; and could not be content with less to their vessels, in the ports of the islands. His Lordship here spoke generally of the colonial system of Britain. He said it was interwoven with her whole commercial code, and code of navigation; and that she owed it to interests which she believed to be important in both connexions, to adhere to the system in the main, however willing to submit to occasional or partial relaxations. I rejoined, that, with whatever reluctance the United States would adopt the policy of closing the trade altogether, in the continued absence of the reciprocity for which they contended, they would at last be compelled to adopt it, in necessary justice to their own commercial and navigating interests. I referred him to some acts of Congress already passed with that intent. He wound up by remarking, that Britain, considering the nature of her colonial system, had no right to complain of measures of that character on the part of the United States, however she might regret them; nor would she complain. She had maintained it so long, that she would find it difficult on that as well as other accounts, to change it. Such was the general outline of what fell from him.

Before I came away, he said; that the Christmas holidays had scattered the members of the cabinet; they were chiefly in the country; on the return of some of them to town he would avail himself of an early opportunity of enabling me to make their acquaintance by meeting them at dinner at his house.

I will here give the names of those who composed the Cabinet. They were as follows:- The Earl of Liverpool, First Lord of the Treasury, and Prime Minister; Lord Eldon, Lord Chancellor; the Earl of Harrowby, Lord President of the Council; the Earl of Westmoreland, Lord Privy Seal; Lord Sidmouth, Secretary-of-state for the Home department; Lord Castlereagh, Secretary-of-state for Foreign Affairs; Earl Bathurst, Secretary-of-state for the Colonial department; Mr Vansittart, Chancellor of the Exchequer; Lord Melville, First Lord of the Admiralty; the Earl of Mulgrave, Master-general of the Ordnance; Mr Canning, President of the Board of Controul for the Affairs of India; Mr Wellesley Pole, Master of the Mint; and Mr C. B. Bathurst, Chancellor of the Duchy of Lancaster. These comprehended the whole list on my arrival in England. No other officers of the Government, however high in station, were then of the cabinet. The Secretary-of-war was not, nor the Attorney-general. The absence of the former I could not well explain, although the Colonial Secretary acted in the concerns of war at cabinet councils, seeing that the navy had a stated representative in those councils. Was not the army entitled to equal consideration? I could even less explain the exclusion of the Attorney-general. No acts of government, in a free country, are independent of law. Hence, I should have inferred, that this officer would have been one of the primary advisers of the Crown. I was aware of the high legal functions of the Lord Chancellor; but in the complicated and daily workings of the machine of free government throughout a vast empire, I could still see room for the Attorney-general in the cabinet.

During my residence of more than seven years at the English court, this administration remained unchanged. There were resignations that led to new appointments, and some transpositions. . . . None of the new appointments were understood to have grown out of want of concord in the body. The policy, as the premiership of Lord Liverpool, was maintained. He was placed in that post by the Prince Regent, in 1812. The age and infirmities of the reigning monarch had led Parliament two years before to establish a regency in the person of the Prince of Wales. The Regent found, and kept, Mr Perceval at the head of affairs, until he perished by assassination. It was then that Lord Liverpool was called to the helm. History will view his administration as one of renown to England. In the exertions of Europe against Napoleon from 1812 to 1815, the part which she acted by her arms and resources is before the world. Both were directed by this ministry, until the achievement at Waterloo closed the momentous struggle. It was there that the Duke of Wellington, after numerous victories in India, in Portugal, in Spain, that had earned for him the reiterated thanks of Parliament and applauses of the nation, ascended to the pinnacle of military glory. One of the English ministers, on entering the House of Commons, bearing in his hand the Treaties of Peace which the triumphant battles of this great commander had done so much towards securing, was enthusiastically cheered by all the members. It was a spontaneous burst of public joy. Party differences were forgotten in deeds so overpowering. The same minister – it was Lord Castlereagh – afterwards declared in one of his speeches, that the '*British empire had twice dictated the Peace of Europe in the capital of France.*' The fame of such deeds naturally established in the confidence of the British public, the ministry on whose banner they were inscribed.

Lord Liverpool was not a person to lose confidence so acquired. Splendour of genius was not his characteristic; but among his talents was that of assembling able men around him. Each was made efficient in his sphere, and the power of the whole augmented. If Lord Liverpool was not the ablest man of the body, he was essentially its head. With a sound judgment improved by public affairs, he was fitted for the business of a nation. What he did not take in by promptitude, he mastered by perseverance; not that he was deficient in the former, but that he paused upon his first conclusions. Systematic and grave, educated in maxims which he conscientiously approved, however others may have dissented from them; courteous, yet inflexible; with a personal character eminently pure, and a high reputation for official probity, his influence, as it rested upon practical qualities, went on to increase; so that, during the whole term of my residence, I never heard that a change of ministry was for one moment seriously in contemplation. Such was the Premier whom I found and left in power. He enjoyed the entire confidence of his sovereign; and had the confidence of the country to an extent that made him sure of his measures in both Houses of Parliament. Such, too, was the ministry with which I was to conduct negotiations, and all other business of my mission.

It was with a full sense of responsibility that I entered upon its duties. I was sustained by remembering who were at the head of my own Government. In President Monroe his country recognized a patriot and sage. Time and long service had consecrated his virtues and talents. A chivalrous officer of the revolution, his youthful blood had been poured out on the plains of Trenton. To the careful study of history and government, he added a participation in the business of legislative halls, and that of diplomacy, at home and abroad. Perfectly acquainted with the foreign policy of the United States as with their domestic concerns; elevated in all his principles; just, magnanimous, self-controuled, few countries ever possessed a chief magistrate better qualified to administer its affairs with wisdom, or more exempt from passions to mislead. First of his cabinet, as regarded every thing foreign, stood Mr Secretary Adams; a statesman of profound and various knowledge. He had received the best education that Europe and his own country could bestow, and from early life been practised in affairs. Minister at several of the Courts of Europe, favourable opportunites were before him of studying their policy, and a superior capacity enabled him to improve his opportunities. Thus gifted and trained as a statesman, he was accomplished as a scholar, fervent as a patriot, and virtuous as a man.

For the remainder of the Cabinet of the United States, there were Mr Secretary Crawford of the Treasury department; Mr Secretary Calhoun of the War department; Mr Secretary Thompson, and afterwards Mr Secretary Southard, of the Navy department; with Mr Attorney-general Wirt; men whose abilities gave further assurance to those in the foreign service of the country, that her interests would not be overlooked. Such were the counsels whence my instructions were to flow. Of this cabinet I may add, that two of its members have since been called by the people to the high posts of President and Vice President of the United States; Mr Secretary Adams to the former, Mr Secretary Calhoun to the latter.

CHAPTER V

LONDON EAST OF TEMPLE BAR – LONDON NORTH OF OXFORD STREET

January 7, 1818. Went through Temple Bar into the *city*, in contradistinction to the West-end of London, always called *town*. Passed along Fleet Street, Ludgate Hill, St. Paul's, Cheapside, the Poultry, Cornhill, and other streets in the direction of the Tower. Saw the Bank, Royal Exchange, Lord Mayor's house, Guildhall, India House, the Excise buildings. If I looked with any feeling of wonder on the throngs at the West-end, more cause is there for it here. The shops stand, side by side, for entire miles. The accumulation of things is amazing. It would seem impossible that there can be purchasers for them all, until you consider what multitudes there are to buy; then, you are disposed to ask how the buyers can be supplied. In the middle of the streets, coal-waggons and others as large, carts, trucks, vehicles of every sort, loaded in every way, are passing. They are in two close lines, reaching farther than the eye can see, going reverse ways. The horses come so near to the foot-pavement, which is crowded with people, that their hoofs, and the great wheels of the waggons, are only a few inches from them. In this manner the whole procession is in movement, with its complicated noise. It confounds the senses to be among it all. You would anticipate constant accidents; yet they seldom happen. The fear of the law preserves order; moreover, the universal sense of danger, if order were violated, prevents its violation. I am assured that these streets present the same appearance every day in the year, except Sundays, when solitude reigns. I must notice as before the dress of the people. A large proportion were of the working classes; yet all were whole in their clothing; you could hardly see exceptions. All looked healthy; the more to be remarked in parts of the city where they live in perpetual crowds by day, and sleep in confined places. The Custom

House, and black forest of ships below London Bridge, I saw by a glimpse: that was enough to show that the Thames was choked up with vessels and boats of every description, much after the manner that I beheld Cheapside and Fleet Street to be choked with vehicles that move on land.

I went into two shops. One a silversmith's, that of Rundell and Bridge, on Ludgate Hill. Outside it is plain; you might pass by without noticing it; but on entering, the articles of silver were piled in heaps, even on the floor. Going further into the building the masses increased. In a room up-stairs, there was part of a dinner-service in course of manufacture. The cost of an entire service varied from thirty to fifty thousand pounds sterling, according to the number of pieces, and workmanship; sometimes it was much higher. A candelabra for the middle of a table, had just been finished for a customer, at fourteen hundred pounds. A dress sword for another customer was shown; the cost was four thousand guineas. Other specimens of luxury might be mentioned, including ambassadors' snuff-boxes of gold and diamonds. The proprietors were extremely civil; for I gave trouble only from curiosity. If you purchase but a pin for a few shillings, they return thanks; if you do not incline to take it away yourself, they readily send it home, no matter how far off. The other shop was Shepherd's, for cut-glass, near Charing Cross. There too I had civility from the proprietor. In place of speaking of his wares, I will relate what he said of the Emperor Alexander. His Imperial Majesty, it seems, when on his visit to England with the Allied Sovereigns, honoured his shop with a call. Pleased with his articles beyond any of the kind he had seen in Europe, he gave an order for a magnificent list for one of his palaces. The pieces arrived in St. Petersburgh. Immediately, a ukase issued, prohibiting the future importation of cut glass into Russia. Whether the Emperor most desired to encourage the home manufacture of so beautiful a ware, or enhance the gratification of his Imperial taste by keeping it exclusive, were questions that I had no right to propound.

Of all the sights, the one in the middle of the streets, bespoke to me most of causes and effects. Being afterwards in Paris, I saw more of architectural beauty, at first; more of brilliancy. The Boulevards, the Palais Royal, the Rue Rivoli, which looked into the Tuileries through golden-tipped palisades, and a few other places, were not to be matched by any thing I saw in London. But their compass was small, and soon exhausted. The space between Northumberland House and Bishopsgate disclosed more of transportation, more of the operations that proclaim circulation of capital, more of all that laid at the roots of commerce at home and throughout the world, more of all that went to the prolific sources of riches and power, than I was able to discover in going about Paris, again and again, in every direction. I am aware how much larger London is than Paris; but the bustle of business seemed to abound in the English metropolis, in a proportion tenfold greater than its superior size.

January 19 – I have taken a house. It is situated in Marylebone parish, north of Oxford *Road*, as I hear the latter called by some, probably from its having been an open road within their recollection. Now, it is a street fully built up, and among the longest and widest in London. North of this street lies a part of the town different from any I have hitherto seen. The streets cross each other at right angles. All are of good width: some a hundred feet and more. Many of them, as Harley Street, Wimpole Street, Baker Street, Devonshire Place, Portland Place, and others, present long ranges of houses built with uniformity, which gives them a metropolitan aspect. Through some, you look, as through a vista, into the verdant scenery of the Regent's Park. This commences almost at the point where the buildings, which are lofty, end; so that you seem to step at once into the country. An air of gloom hangs over these streets, from the dark brick of which most of the houses are built, or which coal smoke gives them; the case, I may add, with nearly every part of London. This part is quite secluded, if so I may speak of a town district of more than a hundred thousand inhabitants. You hear little noise beyond the rumble of equipages, beginning at two o'clock, abating in the evening, and returning at midnight. Its quietness, and the number of ready-furnished houses to be hired in it, are probably the inducements for its being much chosen by the foreign ambassadors for their residence. I found that the Russian, Austrian, and French Ambassadors, had here fixed their domiciles. Every house has its area enclosed with iron palisades. The front door-steps are all of brown stone, with iron railings topped with spikes; so that the eye traced in all directions lines of this bristling iron-work. If you add, that on the broad pavements of flag, you perhaps saw nobody before noon, unless a straggling servant in morning livery, or a butcher's boy with tray in hand issuing here and there from an area, you have the main external characteristics of this region when first I beheld it. There is another town district, a mile or two east, made-up of well-built streets about Russell Square, that had an aspect somewhat similar. It contained, I was told, another one hundred thousand inhabitants, London dissected showing these various circles. 'The entire metropolis,' says Gibbon, in his memoirs, is 'an astonishing and perpetual spectacle to the curious eye; each taste, each sense, may be gratified by the variety of objects which will occur in the long circuit of a morning walk.'

Of the part I have been describing in its external aspect, I must notice the complexion within. A great number of the houses were to let, and I went through them. From the basement to the attics, every thing had an air of comfort. The supply of furniture was full. The staircases were of white stone. The windows and beds in servants' rooms had curtains. No floor was without carpeting. In many instances libraries made part of the furniture to be rented with the houses – a beautiful part. The rents varied from four hundred to a thousand guineas a year. In some of the *squares* of the West-end, I learned, that the rent of a furnished house was sixty and sometimes eighty guineas a *week*. Houses of the first class, with the sumptuous furniture to suit, are not to be hired at all. These, belonging to the nobility or other opulent proprietors, are left in the care of servants when the owners are away. The house I took was in Baker Street, at a rent of four hundred and fifty guineas a-year. The policy of my Government being to give to its public servants small salaries, the latter act but in unison with this policy, in having their establishments small. It is not for those honoured by being selected to serve the Republic abroad, to complain. Nor, with the English, do I believe, that the consideration attaching to foreign ministers, is dependent upon the salaries they receive. However large these may be, and sometimes are, in the persons of the representatives of the

Imperial and Royal governments of Europe, they are still so much below the wealth of the home circles in London, as to be no distinction, supposing distinction to be sought on that ground. The surpassing incomes in the home circles, and habit of expenditure, with the ample accommodations by which the many who possess them live surrounded, incline their possessors to regard such official strangers as objects, rather than agents, of hospitality. It may be otherwise in capitals on the Continent; but this is the general relationship which the diplomatic corps holds to society in London.

CHAPTER VI

DINNER AT LORD CASTLEREAGH'S – THE FIRST VISIT – DINNER AT LORD WESTMORELAND'S

January 20, 1818. Dined at Lord Castlereagh's. The company consisted of Lord and Lady Castlereagh, the Earl of Westmoreland, Lord Melville, Lord Mulgrave, Mr Wellesley Pole, the Duke of Wellington, Lord Burghersh, the Ambassador of France and his Marchioness, the Austrian Ambassador, the Portuguese Ambassador and his Countess, the Minister Plenipotentiary from Bavaria, the Marquis Grimaldi of Sardinia, and a few others. Of the foregoing, some were strangers, to whom, as to myself, it was a first dinner.

The invitation was for seven o'clock. Our names were announced by servants in the hall, and on the landings. The company had chiefly assembled when we arrived. All were in full black, under the court mourning for the Princess Charlotte. I am wrong – one lady was in white satin! It would have been painfully embarrassing, but that her union of ease and dignity enabled her, after the first suffusion, to turn her misfortune into a grace. Salutations were in subdued tones, but cordial, and the hand given. Introductions took place at convenient moments. Before eight, dinner was announced. The dining-room was on the floor with the drawing-rooms. As we entered it through a door-way surrounded by a hanging curtain that drew aside, the effect was beautiful. A profusion of light fell upon the cloth, and as every thing else was of silver, the dishes covered, and wines hidden in ranges of silver coolers, the whole had an aspect of pure white. Lord Castlereagh sat at the head. On his right was the lady of the French Ambassador, with whom, in going in, he had led the way. Lady Castlereagh was on the side, half way down. On her left, was the Duke of Wellington, with whom she came in. Between the Duke and the Earl of Westmoreland, was my wife, who came in upon the arm of the latter. Opposite, was the lady of the Portuguese Ambassador. She entered with the French Ambassador, and sat next to him. I was between Lords Melville and Mulgrave. The former gratified me by the manner in which he spoke of the United States; the latter by what he said of President Monroe, who was Minister in England when he was Secretary for Foreign Affairs. He had ever found him, he said, conciliatory in business, while steadfast in his duty. Being near to these two noblemen in coming in, I paused to give place, having understood that Cabinet Ministers preceded Ministers Plenipotentiary on these occasions; but they declined it, and I went first; Lord Melville remarking, 'We are at home.' There were twelve servants; the superior ones not in livery.

The general topics related to France, and French society. The foreigners spoke English; nevertheless, the conversation was nearly all in French. This was not only the case when the English addressed the foreigners, but in speaking to each other. Before dinner, I had observed in the drawing-room, books lying about. As many as I glanced at were French. I thought of the days of Charles II when the tastes of the English all ran upon the models of France. Here, at the house of an English minister of state, French literature, the French language, French topics were all about me; I add, French *entrées*, French wines! I was unwilling to believe that the parallel to the days of Charles II held throughout. By my longer residence in England I discovered, that the enlightened classes were more ready to copy from the French what they thought good, than the same classes in France to copy from England. As regards language, the difference is striking. There is scarcely a well-educated person in England who does not speak French, whilst thousands among the best educated in France are ignorant of English. In the competition between these great nations, this gives England an advantage. It is no answer that French is the language of intercourse in Europe: the Frenchman may repose upon this, for not acquiring the English; but it cannot take from Englishmen the advantage of being at home in both tongues. Equally have the English the advantage in travel. They go in great numbers to France; while few of the French, comparatively speaking, visit England.

Soon after nine, the ladies left table. Before ten, the gentlemen followed. The company broke into knots, or loitered through the drawing-rooms. In one, was a full-length likeness of the Prince Regent, by Lawrence; in another, the celebrated portrait of Charles I by Vandyck, presenting three views of his face; scattered about in all, were articles of virtù or munificence. Of the latter, were vases of massive porcelain and other memorials, sent as presents to Lord Castlereagh by the crowned heads of Europe, after the treaties of Paris and Vienna. I had now conversation for which opportunities had not before offered. The Austrian Ambassador told me, that his court had appointed Baron Sturmer Consul-General to the United States. He said, that it was the wish of his court to cultivate amicable relations with the United States, the more, as foreign commerce had become an object with Austria. I replied that my Government would receive the information with satisfaction. This was the first public officer sent by Austria to the United States, and laid the foundation of commercial relations that had not before subsisted between the two nations. I remarked, that the commerce of Austria appeared to be doing well in the Black Sea. 'For a beginning,' he replied. I added a hope, that the flag of the United States, might find admittance into that sea; but it was a point on which he was not prepared to speak. To Lord Castlereagh I expressed the pleasure I had derived from making the acquaintance of his guests; amongst them, the Duke of Wellington's. He spoke of the Duke. He said that his achievements in war were known; but that his ability in council, his caution, his conciliation in dealing with the complicated arrangements of the Continent that had followed his battles, were not so much known; these formed not less a part of his character, and had gained for him, perhaps in a higher degree than centered in any other individual in Europe, the confidence of its cabinets and sovereigns.

Before parting, his Lordship said, that the Prince Regent would probably be in town by the middle of February, and that I might then expect my audience of reception.

At eleven, I came away. The servants were at their stations, and passed the call for my carriage, as when we were announced; forms observed towards all.

Whilst I was in England, there was entire cordiality in the

intercourse of the diplomatic corps. The period was one of peace. No acts transpired among nations, tending to abridge the harmony of private life among their representatives. . . .

The embassies of the great powers were amply provided with secretaries, and had persons attached to them in other capacities. The entire aggregate made a large body. Not large when compared with the embassies of other times. Sully brought to England a retinue of two hundred gentlemen. Bassompierre, still earlier, speaks of an *'equipage of four hundred persons'* returning with him to France. The former, on reaching London, was saluted with *three thousand* guns from the Tower. So, D'Estrades, ambassador to the States General from Louis XIV tells us, that he was met at Ryswick by the Deputies, with a train of *threescore coaches*. Compliments so profuse have wisely gone out of date.

But, in all affairs, forms prevail. Governments never dispense with them. Having mentioned the diplomatic corps, I will allude to some of the forms that regulated their intercourse. Once, the uncertainty of questions of precedence led to difficulties, even wars. The congress of Vienna, in 1815, extirpated them all. It declared that every question of that nature should be settled by the rule of time. He who has been longest at a court or government, is to be first. The relative power of the nation he represents, is to count nothing. This is a rule satisfactory to small states. It is to the praise of large ones that they established it. It applies to all intercourse where competition can arise, whether in business or ceremony; and therefore regulates visits. The member of the corps who has last arrived pays the first. The rule's propriety has commanded universal assent. Under its operation, we shall hear no more of personal rudenesses, no disturbances of the public decorum, no cutting of traces that one ambassador's coach may whip up before another.

But, as far as visits are concerned, it has turned out, that the certainty of the rule leads to its being frequently disregarded. In obedience to it, I was prepared to pay the first visit to all the members of the corps who had arrived before me. But, from several, I had the favour of calls by anticipation, as was common in other cases. Fortunate change! when the strife of courtesy has supplanted hostile strife.

The right of precedence in treaties is of a different nature. These solemn instruments are executed in double original. This gives to each nation the opportunity of being named first, and signing first, in the treaty to be deposited in its own archives. Such is the rule as between the United States and foreign powers. Formerly it was not so. In the time of President Madison, an occasion arising where the representative of a monarchy questioned the principle of coequality in the United States on the asserted ground of Republics being of secondary dignity, the rule was established, and has since been adhered to.

January 31. Dined at the Earl of Westmoreland's, at his residence, Grosvenor Square. Forms were as at Lord Castlereagh's. The party was small – Sir John and Lady Ann Becket, Mr and Mrs Patterson of Baltimore, the Danish Minister, and some of the members of Lord Westmoreland's family. The cheerful manner of his lordship promoted conversation. Much of it related to England. Duelling was spoken of. His lordship said, that among private gentlemen in England it was very rare; that if a person from this class had been engaged in a duel, and applied for admission to a club, there would be a scrutiny; and unless it appeared that he was not quarrelsome, he would be in danger of rejection; but that if he had been engaged in two, he believed he would be black-balled. His lordship did not condemn duelling. He only meant that the occasions of it in private life were so few in classes where proper restraints existed, that he whose misfortune it was to have had two duels on his hands, would find gentlemen shy of him as an associate in such institutions. It was upon this he grounded his opinion. His lordship's urbanity made the evening very pleasant. It was not until a late hour that we got home.

CHAPTER VII

INTERVIEW WITH LORD CASTLEREAGH – SLAVE
QUESTION UNDER THE TREATY OF GHENT – NORTH-
WESTERN BOUNDARY BETWEEN THE UNITED STATES
AND BRITISH POSSESSIONS – POST AT THE MOUTH OF
COLUMBIA RIVER

February 1, 1818. Had an interview with Lord Castlereagh.

He began about the slaves; expressing the readiness he would ever feel in endeavouring to bring to a satisfactory close all points in dispute between the two countries. That in this spirit he had laid before the Cabinet my proposal of the 3rd of January upon this subject; and had to inform me that it would be acceded to. But, as the treaty of Ghent had led to the proposal, the assent would be under the rules which that treaty had fixed in relation to other points. That to this end, he was prepared to give effect, substantially, to my proposal, by saying, that his Government was willing that the question about the slaves should also go before commissioners; and in the event of their not concurring, that resort should be had to an umpire, as prescribed by the fourth and subsequent articles of the treaty in reference to territorial claims. That an article between the two Governments, supplemental to the treaty, might be requisite to give the proper authority for this proceeding. That as regarded the commissioners, his Government had no objections to devolving the service upon some of those already appointed under the treaty, unless mine should wish new appointments; that, in short, the whole machinery of that instrument should be adopted, in settling the conflict of opinion about the slaves.

Finishing upon this point, he went to another. The present, he said, appeared to be a favourable time for putting in train for settlement, claims to territory, other than those comprehended in the treaty of Ghent. That it belonged to forecast, to aim at extinguishing, in a friendly way, seeds of future controversy, while the subjects were of no great present importance, but liable to become so in future. That such considerations led him to hope that the Government of the United States would not be disinclined to measures having in view the final settlement of that part of the North-western boundary line contemplated in the old treaty between the two countries of 1783; he meant, the line from the most North-western point of the lake of the woods to the Mississippi. Accordingly, he had to say, that the adoption of measures for accomplishing this object would be highly acceptable to the British Government. The treaty of Ghent, he thought, would form a guide equally convenient for fulfilling the intentions of the parties in this instance also. Should his proposal be acquiesced in, another supplemental article might be added to the treaty, to give it effect, and new commissioners be appointed; or, as before suggested, those already appointed, perform the duty.

Lastly, he came to the affair of the post at Columbia river. A despatch from Mr Bagot*, he said, had informed the British Government that the United States were about to take possession of that post, by sending out an armed ship; and he had to express the regret felt at the measure. It was to have been wished, he remarked, that, before the ship sailed, notice had been given to his Majesty's Minister in Washington of her destination, Great Britain having a claim of dominion over that territory. He proceeded to inform me, that Mr Bagot had sent in a remonstrance upon the occasion; to which, at the last dates, no answer had been received. He closed by saying, that it was the desire of his Government to submit a proposal that the question of title to this territory should, as in the two other cases, go before commissioners, and be governed in all other respects by the precedent of the treaty of Ghent; annexing to it a third supplemental article as the groundwork of contingent arbitration before some friendly sovereign.

To his proposals and remarks I made such replies as they seemed to call for; and first as to the post on the Columbia. Nothing, I told him, could exceed the concern I felt at our act being viewed in the light presented by him, and nothing could have been less expected. The grounds upon which England

* The British Minister in Washington.

claimed dominion, were unknown to me; but granting that she had a claim, was the lawfulness of the step taken by the United States to be questioned? That the post was in their possession before the war of 1812 was admitted; and also, that it had fallen by capture into the hands of Britain during the war. How then under a treaty of peace, the first article of which stipulated the mutual restitution of all places reduced by the arms of either party, was our right to restitution to be impeached? I mentioned the cases of Nootka Sound and Falkland Islands. In these, Great Britain, under circumstances far less strong, had asserted the principle of which we claimed the benefit.

His lordship admitted our right to restitution, and our claim to be in possession, when negotiations for the title were going on. But the manner of obtaining it, he said, was to be lamented, from its possible tendency to interrupt the harmony subsisting between the two countries. He sincerely hoped it would not have the effect, and added, that to forestall all risk as far as he could, he had addressed a note to the Lords of the Admiralty, and one to Lord Bathurst as charged with colonial affairs, desiring that prompt orders might be issued for preventing all hostile collision, either at the post, or with British ships in its vicinity. He took from his files, copies of these notes, and read them to me.

I said, that although it was scarcely to be expected that I could yet have received official information respecting the measure, and although, in fact, none had reached me, I was entirely confident that it had originated in no unfriendly feeling. Nor was it believed that any thing essentially due to Great Britain had been omitted. It had so happened, I remarked, that I had some knowledge myself of the intentions of my Government at the time the measure was projected, which enabled me with the less scruple to speak as I did. I left Washington, it was true, before the departure of the ship; but felt sure that there could have been no alteration in the views that had suggested her voyage to those seas; and, above all, I knew that the employment of force as a means of reinstating ourselves under the treaty, had in no wise been in contemplation.

These assurances appeared to have the proper influence in

placing the transaction in its true lights. The post came peaceably into our possession, and the case was not subsequently revived as one of complaint.

As regarded the North-western boundary line, I remarked, that this subject had no place in my instructions. An article to the effect of his proposal, had once been inserted in a convention between the two Governments, but expunged by that of the United States. The ground of objection was, that the only line that could be run in the direction proposed under the treaty of 1783, would not, as had been ascertained since the date of the treaty, strike the Mississippi; and to run it lower down would bring it through territory within the limits of the United States. Great Britain was free to renew the proposal; all that I could do, would be to transmit it to my Government, and it would be for his lordship to judge how far the past rejection, with its unchanged ground, was discouraging to another attempt.

Finally, as to the slaves. I said, that I had no authority to assent to the proposal as modified from that of my predecessor, which I had done nothing more than renew. That much anxiety continued to exist on this subject in the United States, and that the fact of each Government having adhered to its own construction of the treaty on this point, afforded little presage of a concurrence in opinion by commissioners chosen by each. Still, I had every reason to think that the President would view as friendly, the principle of the proposal; for whilst it did hold out a preliminary step of no very probable efficacy, it came at last to our own overture. I would gladly therefore transmit it for his consideration, assuming, as I did, that this subject of compensation for slaves would be acted upon by itself, in the event of obstacles being found to lie in the way of the two others.

To this his lordship did not yield his assent. He hoped that I presupposed an imaginary case, abstaining in this way from a positive refusal at first. He afterwards, in effect, embodied one in the remark, that as each Government had objects of its own in view, the three propositions ought, in his opinion, to be classed together, awaiting a common assent or rejection. I combated this doctrine. The carrying off of the slaves involved a case of palpable injury, and, as we also contended, of wrong;

one that brought loss to all, and ruin to some of the proprietors. The fundamental laws of the Union guaranteed to our Southern planters as sure a property in their slaves, as in their houses and lands; and as well might the two last be taken from them as the first. The two other propositions rested upon ancient, undefined claims; not pressing in their nature, or any of their consequences. The case of the slaves, moreover, sprang out of the treaty of Ghent, and was peculiarly entitled to the benefit of its equitable example in settling controversies. The other two subjects were wholly extrinsic. Whatever rights or expectations might even justly be coupled with them by Great Britain, it seemed proper that they should stand upon independent ground. It was so that I drew distinctions.

But I perceived no change in what were at least his lordship's first impressions, that the three questions ought to be dealt with in the same way. The interview was extended to much length, and closed by his saying, that as all the proposals proceeded from his Government, they would be forwarded to Mr Bagot for the information of mine, in addition to the communication of them made to me.

CHAPTER VIII

RECEPTION BY THE PRINCE REGENT – THE LEVEE – THE ROYAL FAMILY

February 9, 1818. Received a note from Lord Castlereagh informing me that the Prince Regent had appointed Thursday the 12th, for my reception, at Carlton House, at a quarter past two, previous to the levee.

February 12. Had my reception. A competent knowledge of the world may guide any one in the common walks of life; more especially if he carry with him the cardinal maxim of good-breeding in all countries – a wish to please and unwillingness to offend. But if, even in private society, there are rules not to be known but by experience, and if these differ in different places, I could not feel insensible to the approach of an occasion so new. My first desire was, not to fail in the public duties of my mission. The next, to pass properly through the scenes of official and personal ceremony to which it exposed me. At the head of them, was my introduction to the Sovereign. I desired to do all that full respect required, but not more: yet – the external observances – what were they? They defy exact definition beforehand, and I had never seen them. From the restraints, too, that prevail in these spheres, lapses, if you fall into them, are little apt to be told to you; which increases your solicitude to avoid them. I had, in some of my intercourse, caught the impression, that simplicity was considered best adapted to such an introduction; also, that the Prince Regent was not thought to be fond of set speeches. This was all that I could collect. But simplicity, all know, is a relative idea. Often it is attainable, in the right sense, only through the highest art.

I arrived before the hour appointed. My carriage having the *entrée*, or right to the private entrance, I went through St. James's Park and got to Carlton House by the paved way, through the gardens. Even this approach was already filled. I was set down at a side-door, where stood servants in the Prince's livery. Gaining the hall, persons were seen in different costumes. Among them yeomen of the guard, with halberds. They had hats of velvet, with wreaths round them, and rosettes in their shoes. In the courtyard, which opened through the columns of the portico, bands of music were heard. Carriages, in a stream, were approaching by this access, through the double gates that separate the royal residence from the street. The company arriving this way, entered through the portico, and turned off to the right. I went to the left, through a vestibule, leading to other rooms, into which none went but those having the *entrée*. They consisted of cabinet ministers, the diplomatic corps, persons in chief employment about the court, and a few others, the privilege being in high esteem. Knights of the Garter appeared to have it, for I observed their insignium round the knee of several. There was the Lord Steward with his badge of office; the Lord Chamberlain with his; also, gold *stick*, and silver *stick*. The foreign ambassadors and ministers wore their national costumes; the cabinet ministers, such as we see in old portraits, with bag and sword. The Lord Chancellor, and other functionaries of the Law, had black silk gowns, with full wigs. The bishops and dignitaries of the Church, had aprons of black silk. The walls were covered with paintings. If these were historical, so were the rooms. As I looked through them, I thought of the scenes in Doddington; of the Pelhams, the Bolingbrokes, the Hillsboroughs. The Prince had not left his apartment. Half-an-hour went by, when Sir Robert Chester, Master of Ceremonies, said to me, that in a few minutes he would conduct me to the Prince. The Spanish Ambassador had gone in, and I was next in turn. When he came out, the Master of the Ceremonies advanced with me to the door.

Opening it, he left me. I entered alone. The Prince was standing; Lord Castlereagh by him. No one else was in the room. Holding in my hand the letter of credence, I approached, as to a private gentleman, and said, that it was 'from the President of the United States, appointing me their Envoy Extraordinary and Minister Plenipotentiary at the Court of his Royal Highness; and that I had been directed by the President to say, that I could in no way better serve the United States, or gain his approbation, that by using all my endeavours to strengthen and prolong the good understanding that happily subsisted between the two Countries.' The Prince took the letter, and handed it to Lord Castlereagh. He then said, that he would 'ever be ready on his part to act upon the sentiments I had expressed; that I might assure the President of this, for that he sincerely desired to keep up and improve the friendly relations subsisting between the two nations, which he regarded as so much to the advantage of both.' I replied, that I would not fail to do so.

The purpose of the interview seeming to be accomplished, I had supposed it would here end, and was about to withdraw; but the Prince prolonged it. He congratulated me on my arrival. He inquired for the health of Mr Adams, and spoke of others who had preceded me in the mission, going back as far as the first Mr Pinckney. His inquiries were minute. He made others, which it gave me still more pleasure to answer – he asked if I knew the ladies from my country, then in England, who had made such favourable impressions, naming Mrs Patterson, and the Miss Catons. I replied that I did, and responded to his gratifying notice of these my fair countrywomen. A few more remarks on the climate of the two countries closed the audience.

It would be out of place in me to portray the exterior qualities of this monarch. The commanding union of them has often been a theme in his own dominions. He was then in his 56th year; but in fine health, and maintaining the erect, ambitious, carriage of early life. The Envoy extraordinary and minister plenipotentiary from Sicily and Naples, had his reception immediately afterwards.

When the Prince came from his apartment, called in the language of palaces his *closet*, into the entrée rooms, I presented to him Mr John Adams Smith, as public secretary of the legation, and Mr Ogle Taylore, as attached to it personally. Other special presentations took place; amongst them, that of the Prince of Hesse Homberg, by Lord Stewart, both distinguished in the then recent battles of the Continent. The Prince Regent moved about these rooms, until he had addressed everybody; all waiting his salutation. Doors hitherto shut, now opened, when a new scene appeared. You beheld in other rooms the company that had turned off to the

right. The opening of the doors was the signal for the commencement of the general levee. I remained with others to see
it. All passed, one by one, before the Prince, each receiving a
momentary salutation. To a few he addressed conversation,
but briefly; as it stopped the line. All were in rich costume.
Men of genius and science were there. The nobility were
numerous; so were the military. There were from forty to fifty
generals; perhaps as many admirals, with throngs of officers of
rank inferior. I remarked upon the number of wounded. Who
is that, I asked, pallid but with a countenance so animated?
'*That's General Walker*,' I was told, '*pierced with bayonets, leading on
the assault of Badajos.*' And he, close by, tall but limping? '*Colonel
Ponsonby; he was left for dead at Waterloo; the cavalry it was thought
had trampled upon him.*' Then came one of like port, but de-
prived of a leg, slowly moving; and the whisper went, '*That's
Lord Anglesea.*' A fourth had been wounded at Seringapatam; a
fifth at Talavera; some had suffered in Egypt; some in
America. There were those who had received scars on the deck
with Nelson; others who carried them from the days of Howe.
One, yes one, had fought at Saratoga.* It was so that my
inquiries were answered. All had '*done their duty;*' this was the
favourite praise bestowed. The great number of wounded was
accounted for by recollecting, that little more than two years
had elapsed since the armies and fleets of Britain had been
liberated from wars of extraordinary fierceness and duration
in all parts of the globe. For, so it is, other nations chiefly fight
on or near their own territory; the English everywhere.

Taking the whole line, perhaps a thousand must have
passed. Its current flowed through the entrée rooms, got
onward to the vestibule, and was finally dispersed in the great
hall. Those who composed it, found themselves there, by a
course reverse to that of their entrance; and went away
through the portico, as their carriages came up.

The whole ceremony lasted until past five. When it was over,
I called upon each member of the Royal Family; a mark of respect omitted by no foreign minister after being received by
the Sovereign. The call is made by inscribing your name in
books kept at their several residences. The royal family were,

* Two battles of the Revolutionary War, both fought in October 1777.

of the male branches – the Dukes of York, Clarence, (now William IV.) Kent, Cumberland, Sussex, Cambridge, and Gloucester. Of the female branches – the Duchess of Gloucester, the Princesses Augusta, Elizabeth, Sophia, and Sophia Matilda. Prince Leopold (present King of Belgium,) husband of the late Princess Charlotte, shared the same attentions; as did the Duchesses of York and Cumberland. How far it may be necessary for a distant Republic, whose genius is entirely different from the ancient governments of Europe, to exchange with them diplomatic representatives of the higher class, may be a question; but it can be none whether, when once sent, they shall offer all the appropriate marks of respect which the usages of the world accord to sovereigns and those in immediate connexion with them. To withhold or stint them would be in conflict with the purposes of the diplomatic office. It was in this feeling that, during my residence, I thought it proper never to be absent from a levee, or pretermit in any wise attentions to the royal family paid by other foreign ministers; and I will take occasion to add, that I did not find an insensibility to the just motives of such a course.

It will be in unison with my narrative to insert a copy of the letter of credence I delivered to the Prince Regent. It followed the established formulary, when the United States send ministers to foreign courts. An eminent individual in England asked me what the form was from republics to monarchies. The answer is easy. The head of a republic, however appointed or chosen, represents, for the time being, its collective power and dignity. To foreign nations, he is the visible image of its sovereignty, and speaks to monarchs, clothed with its attributes. The letter will afford at the same time a specimen of the peculiar style adopted by nations when speaking to each other through the personality centring in their executive heads. It is in these words:-

'James Monroe, President of the United States of America, to his Royal Highness the Prince Regent of the United Kingdom of Great Britain and Ireland:

Great and good Friend:

I have made choice of Richard Rush, to reside near your Royal Highness in quality of Envoy Extraordinary and

Minister Plenipotentiary of the United States of America. He is well informed of the relative interests of the two countries, and of our sincere desire to cultivate and strengthen the friendship and good correspondence between us; and from a knowledge of his fidelity, probity, and good conduct, I have entire confidence that he will render himself acceptable to your Royal Highness by his constant endeavours to preserve and advance the interests and happiness of both nations. I therefore request your Royal Highness to receive him favourably, and to give full credence to whatever he shall say on the part of the United States, and most of all when he shall assure you of their friendship, and wishes for your prosperity; and I pray God to have your Royal Highness in his safe and holy keeping. Written at the city of Washington, the thirty-first day of October, anno Domini one thousand eight hundred and seventeen. By your good friend,

JAMES MONROE

John Quincy Adams,
Secretary of State.'

The letter of credence from the King, or Prince Regent, of England, on sending a minister plenipotentiary to the United States, is the same, *mutatis mutandis*, in its formal commencement and conclusion; and substantially the same throughout.

My reception having established me in full official standing, I left cards at the houses of the cabinet ministers and diplomatic corps. The former have precedence over the latter (though in England they often wave it) because, sharing the confidence and administering the power of the Sovereign, they become indentified, so far with his dignity. I visited also the Lord High Steward, Lord Chamberlain, the Master of the Horse, and a few others personally attached to the royal household. The only one of the cabinet upon whom I had called previously, was Lord Castlereagh. Cabinet ministers in England are exempt from returning visits to foreign ministers, as to all others; nevertheless, the courtesy of Lord Castlereagh had returned mine.

It was so that I aimed at going through the obligations of ceremony, as I found them established at the English court. I may have dwelled on them the longer because they were new to me; but not too long. I do not discuss their importance. I give them as facts. The philosopher may rail at them; but, in his philosophy, he may discover, if candid, matter for raillery too. In the machinery of political as social life, the smallest parts are often those that give impulse to the greatest movements. If we visit a strange country, scan its general population, enter its farm-houses, its cottages, its work-shops, we are permitted to speak of appearances and habits that on all sides arrest the eye. May we not, with a guarded freedom, do the same of the high places of the world? In the modes of life in each, are beheld component parts of the grand whole. If, from the former, issue the springs of power, it is in the latter, under monarchies, that its agents dwell. Perhaps if the feelings that exist in each could be better known to the other, jealousies might be softened, more frequently than increased.

It may be thought that the forms I detail, are the growth only of monarchical soils. Their roots lie deeper. If none but republics existed, other forms would arise, differing in circumstance, but not in essence. In the genius of the latter governments, there is a sternness peculiarly opposed to giving up claims to outward reverence. The Roman Senate took more offence at Caesar's refusal to rise on an occasion when they intended to do him honour, than at his passing the Rubicon or seizing upon the treasury. The title of Majesty is modern, as applied to Kings. The Romans used it with peculiar fondness, says Dryden, in reference to the people – MAJESTAS POPULI ROMANI. The first treaty that Cromwell entered into with the United Provinces, had a stipulation that their ships should strike their flags in British seas, to the 'REPUBLIC' of England. We have seen, in our own day, with how prompt a sensibility President Madison, whose life has been a model of dignity as of public and private virtue, stood upon the point of form, when treaties were to be signed. Nor was he less scrupulous, when complimentary salutes were to be exchanged with the vessels or batteries of foreign powers. If the individual of just pride respects himself whilst he respects others, nations will ever be still more quick to the same feeling, and to all its external manifestations.

CHAPTER IX

ATTEMPT UPON THE LIFE OF THE DUKE OF WELLINGTON – OLD CUSTOMS ABOUT THE COURT – DINNER AT THE DANISH MINISTER'S – PRIVATE AUDIENCE OF THE QUEEN – THE DRAWING-ROOM – DINNER AT LKORD CASTLEREAGH'S

February 16, 1818. The late attempt upon the life of the Duke of Wellington in Paris is a topic. He went there on business relating, as is believed, to the evacuation of France by the Army of Occupation, of which the English forms a part. Returning to his hotel at midnight, a pistol was fired at his carriage. One of his aids was with him. Nobody was hurt. The report collected people, and some gendarmerie went in pursuit. The Duke made his coachman stop, got out, and looked around. Such is the account I hear. I learn that it was transmitted by a special messenger from the French King, to his ambassador at this court. The ambassador repaired to Carlton House, to express to the Prince Regent the concern felt by his sovereign; with assurances that all means would be used to discover the offender, and bring him to proper punishment. The ambassador afterwards went to Apsley House, the residence of the Duke of Wellington, to express to his family appropriate sentiments on the occasion.

February 21. Since my reception I have had calls from servants of official persons for '*favours.*' I became acquainted with the term at Portsmouth. They had no warrant from their masters; but came under ancient custom. There have also been to me, fraternities, more nearly allied to the Portsmouth bell-ringers; as the '*Palace drums and fifes,*' the '*Royal waits and music,*' and a third, the derivation of which I could not understand, and which no external signs that I saw bespoke, the '*King's marrow-bones and cleavers.*' Each presented me with a congratulatory address. Each had their '*book to show.*' They all have something to do with out-door arrangements when levees are held. These contributions upon the diplomatic stranger, awakened at first my surprise. I afterwards heard what, perhaps, may serve as explanatory. Ambassadors on leaving England, receive from the Government a present of a thousand pounds; and ministers plenipotentiary, five hundred. If then on their arrival, and afterwards, there are appeals to their bounty by those in menial and such-like situations about the Government, the latter, it seems, *pays back again!* I do not hint that it does so in the light of an indemnification; but the *customs harmonize.* True, the minister plenipotentiary of the United States never takes the five hundred pounds; the constitution of his country forbidding it. But this is a point which it may be presumed he does not stop to expound to the servants of the foreign secretary, or the '*Royal waits and music.*' It would doubtless be to them a novel plea in bar for not putting his hand in his pocket! Whenever he pays for music, he must consider himself as having an equivalent in its 'silver sounds.'

If I had calls like these, I am bound to mention others. A great number of persons of the court and other circles paid me visits. Their names I need not recount. Of the list, were those whose acquaintance any one might regard as a source of gratification. In me, the feeling was heightened, as it marked the estimation in which my country was held. Intercourse to which the door thus opened in my favour was afterwards extended, leading to hospitalities, that can neither pass from the memory nor grow cold upon the heart.

February 23. At a dinner at the Danish minister's we had half a dozen gentlemen; among them Sir Humphrey Davy. There were also ladies. One of the latter spoke of Benjamin Franklin; he was a captivating writer – so much nature – so much genius; Mr Jefferson had said that to see the junction of two of our rivers where one breaks through a mountain, was worth crossing the Atlantic; but she would think the voyage better undertaken to see Franklin's old china bowl and silver spoon his wife bought for him; she hoped both were kept; it would be sacrilege to let them perish. I was charmed at her manner of saying all this. Sir Humphrey took his share in the conversation. At the first words of this great chemist and philosopher, I was all attention. But he talked of neither chemistry nor philosophy. He agreed to what was said of Franklin. He spoke of the expedition preparing for the North Pole; it was fitted up, he said, with every thing but a philosopher; whether the sailors would have no such nondescript on board, or none would consent to go, he could not say; the ocean was a noble dominion for nations, but a bad place for landsmen; worst of all for philosophers. He spoke of the case about wager of battle, pending in the King's Bench; the very argument was so like a burlesque, that, he thought, the parties had better be allowed to fight it out at once, the '*fancy*' forming a ring, while parliament and the judges looked on. His elocution was remarkably prompt and smooth. In society he seems as pleasing, as in the lecture-room he is profound. He told me that the widow of Garrick was alive, at an advanced age, and lived not far from the house I had taken. Mr. Bourke, our kind host, had been much among the courts of Europe. Inclination and opportunity had improved his taste in the arts. In the drawing-rooms after dinner, pictures were talked of, his walls showing some fine ones. He said, that in distinguishing the various productions of the different masters, there was no more difficulty, where the eye had been practised among large collections, than in distinguishing the faces and handwriting of your living acquaintances.

February 25. Having brought from my Government a letter of credence to the Queen, I was this day presented to her. It was called a private presentation, and took place at Buckingham Palace.

I got to the palace before the hour fixed. Servants were at the door, and in the hall. Ascending an ample staircase, the master of ceremonies received me in one of the rooms of a suite, all open, but no one else in them. When five o'clock came, he conducted me to the audience-room, which I entered alone.

Immediately before me was the Queen. On her right was one of the Princesses, her daughter; on her left, another. Near them were two ladies in waiting. All were in full court-dresses; and all standing. In another part of the room were her Majesty's Chamberlain, and the Duke of Montrose. These made up the whole assemblage. All was silence. Approaching the Queen, I said; – 'Having been accredited by his Royal Highness, the Prince Regent, as Envoy Extraordinary and Minister Plenipotentiary from the United States, I have now the honour to present this letter to your Majesty. In executing the duties of my mission, I have it in charge from the President so to bear myself as to give hope of gaining your Majesty's esteem; and this I beg to assure your Majesty will be my constant ambition.' She received the letter. As she took it, she said, that the sentiments I expressed were very obliging, and entered into conversation. Learning I was from Philadelphia she asked questions about it, and others respecting the United States, generally; all put in a very kind spirit. The interview lasted about fifteen minutes.

The Queen was then seventy-six. Her birthday was the day following. As I entered the room, and during the whole interview, there was a benignity in her manner, which, in union with her age and rank, was both attractive and touching. The tones of her voice had a gentleness, the result, in part, of years; but full as much of intended suavity to a stranger. The scene as it first broke upon me; its novelty, its quiet yet impressive stateliness, became, almost immediately, by her manner, one of naturalness and ease. My immediate predecessor, Mr. Adams, when presented to her, made an allusion to qualities in her character, which, as I came to learn through a good source that it was advantageously remembered at the English Court, I will repeat. His mission commenced in 1815, directly after the war between the two countries. He said, that the political relations between them had been subject to the versatility that attended all human affairs; that dissensions had arisen, which however had been removed, and, he ardently hoped, permanently removed; but that the reverence commanded by her Majesty's private virtues had been subject to no such change; it had been invariably felt by his Government, and could utter no wish more propitious to the happiness of both countries, than that the future harmony between them might be equally unalterable. The allusion was happy, because it was just. Throughout a long life, she had been uniformly distinguished by her private virtues, and her efforts to imprint them upon the times. I saw her sinking below the horizon. But the serenity that I saw, betokened, that as the splendours of her day were setting, she had a consciousness that it was not for them alone she had lived.

February 27. Yesterday her Majesty held a drawing-room. It was in celebration of her birth-day. My wife was presented by Lady Castlereagh. Besides being a birth-day celebration, it was the first drawing-room of the season, and the first since the death of the Princess Charlotte. The weather was fine, with a brilliant sun. A permit had been sent from the Board of Green Cloth for my carriage to pass into St. James's Park, through the gate on Constitution Hill.

Going through Hyde Park, I found the whole way from Tyburn to Piccadilly (about a mile) filled with private carriages, standing still. Persons were in them who had adopted this mode of seeing those who went to court. Tenfold the number went by other approaches, and every approach, I was told, was thronged with double rows of equipages, filled with spectators. I was to be set down with the rest of the diplomatic corps, and others having the entrée, at a door assigned, within the court-yard of the palace. Arrived in its vicinity, my carriage was stopped by those before it. Here we saw, through the trees and avenues of the Park, other carriages rapidly coming up, in two regular lines from the Horse Guards and St. James's. Another line, that had been up, was turning slowly off, towards the Birdcage Walk. Foreigners agreed, that the united capitals of Europe could not match the sight. The horses were all in the highest condition; and, under heavy emblazoned harness, seemed, like war-horses, to move proudly. Trumpets were sounding, and the Park and Tower guns firing. There were ranks of cavalry in scarlet, with their bright helmets, and jet black horses; the same we were told, men and horses, that had been at Waterloo.

We were soon set down, and entered the great hall. What a contrast! The day before, I had gone up the staircase alone. Now, what did I see? We were not out of time, for, by appointment, my carriage reached the palace with Lord Castlereagh's; but whilst hundreds were still arriving, hundreds were endeavouring to come away. The staircase branched off at the first landing, into two arms. It was wide enough to admit a partition, which was let in. The company ascending, took one channel; those descending, the other; and both were full. The whole group stood motionless. The openings through the carved balusters, brought all under view at once, whilst the paintings on the walls heightened the effect. The hoop dresses of the ladies, sparkling with lama; their plumes; their lappets; the fanciful attitudes which the hoops occasioned, some getting out of position as when in Addison's time they were adjusted to shoot a door; the various costumes of the gentlemen as they stood pinioning their elbows, and holding in their swords; the common hilarity, from the common dilemma; the bland recognitions passing between those above and below, made up, altogether, an exhibition so picturesque, that a painter might give it as illustrative, so far, of the court of that aera. Without pausing to describe the incidents during our progress upwards, it may be sufficient to say, that the party to which I was attached, and of which Lady Castlereagh, towering in her bloom, was the pioneer, reached the summit of the staircase in about three quarters of an hour.

Four rooms were allotted to the ceremony. In the second was the Queen. She sat on a velvet chair and cushion, a little raised up. Near her were the Princesses, and ladies in waiting. The general company, as they reached the corridor by one arm of the staircase, passed on to the Queen. Bowing to her, they regained it, after passing through all the rooms, by an outlet that led to the other arm; which they descended. When my wife was presented, her Majesty addressed some conversation to her, as a stranger. This she could not do to all, time not permitting. The Regent was there, and the Royal Family; cabinet ministers and their ladies; foreign ambassadors and ministers with theirs. These, having the entrée remained, if they chose, in the room with the Queen. A numerous portion of the nobility were present, their wives and daughters; with others distinguished in life, though bearing neither title nor station. Conversation you got as you could, in so great and rich a throng.

If the scene in the hall was picturesque, the one upstairs transcended it. The doors of the rooms were all open. You saw in them a thousand ladies richly dressed. All the colours of nature were mingling their rays together. It was the first occasion of laying by mourning for the Princess Charlotte; so that it was like the bursting out of spring. No lady was without her plume. The whole was a waving field of feathers. Some were blue, like the sky; some tinged with red; here you saw violet and yellow; there, shades of green. But the most were like tufts of snow. The diamonds encircling them, caught the sun through the windows, and threw dazzling beams around. Then the hoops! I cannot describe these. They should be seen. To see one is nothing. But to see a thousand – and their thousand wearers! I afterwards sat in the Ambassadors' box at a coronation. That sight faded before this. Each lady seemed to rise out of a gilded little barricade; or one of silvery texture. This, topped by her plume, and the 'face divine' interposing, gave to the whole an effect so unique, so fraught with feminine grace and grandeur, that it seemed as if a curtain had risen to show a pageant in another sphere. It was brilliant and joyous. Those to whom it was not new, stood at gaze as I did. Canning for one. His fine eye took it all in. You saw admiration in the gravest statesmen; Lord Liverpool, Huskisson, the Lord Chancellor, everybody. I had already seen in England signs enough of opulence and power. Now I saw, radiating on all sides, British beauty. My own country I believed was destined to a just measure of the two first; and I had the inward assurance that my countrywomen were the inheritresses of the last. *Matre pulchrâ filia pulchrior.* So appeared the drawing-room of Queen Charlotte.

The ceremonies of the day being ended, as far as myself and suite were concerned, we sought the corridor to come away. In good time we reached the head of the descending channel. Will it be believed? both channels were full as ever of hoops and plumes. There was something in the spectacle from this position that presented a new image. Positively, it came over the eye like beautiful architecture; the hoops the base, the plume the pinnacle! The parts of this dress may have been incongruous; but the whole was harmony. Like Old English buildings, and Shakspeare, it carried the feelings with it. It triumphed over criticism. We got down stairs in about the same time it took to get up. As we waited in the hall for our carriage, military bands were playing in the court-yard, some mounted, some on foot; amidst the strains of which we drove off.

In the evening I dined at Lord Castlereagh's. It was a dinner in honour of the birth-day. All were in official costume. The foreign ambassadors and ministers, and several of the English ambassadors at European courts, at home on leave, were at it. Among the topics was the beautiful scene of the morning. All gave their voice to its attractiveness. I will say no more of the dinner. Lord Castlereagh, anxious for the pleasure of his guests, diffused his attentions in ways to promote it. We sat down at eight, and rose at ten. By eleven the company dispersed.

CHAPTER X

EMIGRATION – LITERARY INSTITUTIONS – CLUBS –
BOOKSELLERS' SHOPS – ST. JAMES'S PALACE – PARTY
AT THE DUCHESS OF CUMBERLAND'S – AT THE RUSSIAN
AMBASSADOR'S – AT THE MARCHIONESS OF
STAFFORD'S – AT LORD MELVILLE'S – THE DUKE OF
SUSSEX – DINNER AT THE MANSION HOUSE

March 1, 1818. I receive many letters from persons in
England, on emigrating to the United States. The writers seek
information and advice. I afford neither. The bad subjects of
Britain we do not want; the good, it is no part of my province
to be instrumental in drawing away. If the majority of the
applicants be what they profess, they would prove an acqui-
sition to any new country; where, land being abundant and
labour dear, men are the best imports. One, a farmer, represents himself to have six thousand pounds. Two of the same
class say, that they each would carry over about half as much. I
learn that another of the applicants, a manufacturer, is
reputed to be worth thirty thousand pounds. The naturalization laws of the United States give less encouragement to
emigrants than is generally supposed; less than some of their
citizens think wise. For one, I regard them as injudicious.
They do not confer citizenship upon terms at all as favourable
as Russia and Holland have formerly done, and are believed
to do still; as England did, for ages, when she even offered
bounties to certain classes of foreigners on coming to her
shores; and as France has done at periods when her population, in proportion to her soil, was far greater than that of the
United States. The latter require a full residence of five years,
with regulations that put further clogs upon the privilege.

I should fill many pages were I to detail applications of
another description; I mean from the authors of new projects.
One has an improved plan for making rockets; another thinks
he has discovered a mode of building ships that will all sail

alike; a third has a model of a gun-carriage, by which a 64-pounder can be worked like a swivel; a fourth a fire-machine to explode under water, with more destruction to every thing above than Fulton's torpedo. The projectors all desire patronage from the Government of the United States, and will go over, on proper encouragement from me. It will be inferred, that if I leave farmers and manufacturers to think and act for themselves, I abstain from all interference in the cases of these ingenious persons. In truth, we want them less. Most of their inventions are for destroying life; as if means enough were not known already.

March 2. Visited the Royal Institution in Albemarle Street. Its objects are scientific and literary. A lecture-room, with apparatus, is annexed, where Sir Humphrey Davy, and Professors Brande and Milligan, deliver lectures. It has a large library, and is furnished with the current periodical publications. I note it merely as one, though of much repute, among numerous establishments of the kind in London. Another was mentioned to me – the London Institution in Moorfields – founded a few years back, at an expense of upwards of fifty thousand guineas, obtained by subscription among private individuals in that range of the city. The Clubs also have libraries, and the periodical works. It is so at the Alfred, which is near the Royal Institution. The Club Houses appear to be among the largest in town, judging from those in St. James's Street. Let me here relate what I heard of one of them – White's – the great Tory Club, in St. James's. Somebody spoke of the lights kept burning there all night: 'Yes,' said a member, *they have not been out, I should think, since the reign of Charles II.* The London Clubs of the higher order are not associations for mere conviviality, but for intercourse upon a far broader scale; political, literary, scientific, dramatic, and objects more diversified. At a subsequent day I visited several, and had the freedom of some bestowed upon me. I was honoured with that of the United Service Club, the Travellers', and the Alfred. The first, for extent and completeness, I may almost add splendour, surpassed any that came under my observation, though all were more or less striking. None of its members are below the rank of field-officers in the army, or captains in the navy. Through the good offices of Sir

Humphrey Davy, I had the privilege of resorting to the library and reading-rooms of the Royal Institution. My gratitude is due for the facilities accorded to me at all times for reading and consulting books there, and attending lectures.

I have been to several of the great booksellers' shops; that of Payne and Foss in Pall Mall, whose collection is said to be very choice; some in Paternoster Row, and Lackington's, corner of Finsbury Square. A bird's-eye view of them shows the amount of capital employed in this great branch of business, the more imposing as it gives the idea of intellectual as well as moneyed capital. The mere external arrangement at Lackington's seemed the best, and I should have inferred, but perhaps erroneously, as I did not see the whole extent of some in Paternoster Row, that their collection was largest. One of the firm told me, that the number of volumes in two descriptions of books, Shakspeare and the periodical writers, amounted, as nearly as he could say, to about one hundred thousand. I should have conjectured that the entire collection could scarcely have fallen short of a million of volumes. Opening cursorily some of the catalogues, Lackington's appeared to contain the greatest number of works on America; especially on the early colonial history of the United States. The catalogues are made out with great care, and give the prices. They formed well-sized octavo volumes. Lackington's ran on to a thousand pages.

Of books, we expect catalogues. But it is much the habit of English shopkeepers generally to have printed lists of their articles. Stepping into a large hardware-shop, the proprietor handed me a stout pamphlet which presented his whole assortment in print, with the prices annexed to each item, no matter how minute. Haberdashers send out their inventories in print, and the dealers in a thousand other things theirs. Their packets come to my house in I know not what quantity; to the advantage of the paper-maker, job-printer, and other handicrafts in the system of subdivision.

March 4. Went the evening before last to a party at the Duchess of Cumberland's, St. James's Palace.

This is among the oldest buildings in London. It presents on the street a fortress-like appearance. To what order it belongs would be hard to say. The whole is an irregular pile.

But the very confusion in its plan, with its antiquity, and the sentinels pacing day and night about it, minister to the fancy, making amends for its want of good architecture. So says one, who, unaccustomed to the sight of edifices that go far back into time, finds this the ingredient which seizes most upon his first feelings.

We drove under a gatehouse leading to a paved court-yard. Here we were set down at the entrance to the Duke of Cumberland's apartments. Directed by servants who lined the way, we passed up to the rooms of entertainment. The company was not very large. In a rich arm-chair, sat the Prince Regent; on one side of him the Duchess of Cumberland, on the other the Marchioness of Hertford. The rest of the company stood. When we entered, all were listening to music. Members of the royal family, cabinet ministers, the foreign ambassadors, with their respective ladies, and others, formed the groups. I observed among them the Lord Chancellor, Sir William Scott, and Mr. Canning. On a pause in the music, there was conversation. The Duchess of Cumberland spoke kindly of my country, and individuals belonging to it; particularly Mr. and Mrs. Adams, whom she had known at the court of Berlin. The Duke talked to me of the United States, embracing in his inquiries, language; with a desire to learn how far, if at all, we fell into changes in idiom or pronunciation from the parent stock.

I had introductions to several persons. Whilst in conversation with the Earl of Hardwicke, a gentleman stood within a few paces. I did not know him. On separating from Lord Hardwicke, he advanced towards me, saying, 'I'm going to bring a bill into Parliament, making it indictable in any stranger, whether ambassador from a republic, kingdom, or popedom, ever to leave his card without his address upon it: how do you do, Mr. Rush, how do you do? I've been trying to find you everywhere – I'm Lord Erskine.' In this manner commenced my acquaintance with this gifted man. There was no one in England of whose fame I had oftener heard, or whom I more desired to know. He continued – 'I had a letter for you from my brother, the Earl of Buchan, but you made me carry it so long in my pocket that I lost it; it had no secrets; it was only to congratulate you on your arrival; he was long a correspondent and friend of your father's, and wants to transfer his feelings to you, that's all; so you can write to him as if you had received it.' I assured him of my gratification at meeting him, and made the due apologies for the omission on my card. He inquired for President Monroe, Mr. Pinkney, and others; said he had always loved the United States, and hoped to visit them yet, as he was an old sailor and cared nothing for storms. Such was his sprightly strain. He must have been seventy, or near it; but, as Sir Francis Burdett said, he illustrated the fable of youth peeping through the mask of age. It was a treat to see so much genius with so much playfulness; such a social flow from one whose powerful eloquence had been felt by the English nation, and helped to change, on some fundamental points, the English law. He sauntered about with me and looked at the paintings. There was a full-length likeness of George II, another of George III and one of Mary of Scots; a 'Royal jade,' he feared, 'but very pretty.' We ended in a room at the extremity of the suite, where was a table set out with golden urns for tea, and other light refreshments; to which those went who were inclined. At one o'clock we came away. The music was by professional performers. Not only are the first musical talents of England engaged for private entertainments at houses of distinction, but the best from Italy, France, and other parts of the Continent; the Fodors, the Pastas, the Ambrogettis, the Catalanis, who may always be seen in London.

March 10. Dined at the Russian Ambassador's. This distinguished diplomatist, Prince Lieven, is understood to enjoy in a high degree the good-will of his sovereign, and by all other titles is prominent in official and court circles. To the social assemblages of each, the Princess Lieven, his lady, brings dignity, intelligence, and grace. From the embassy, we experienced at all times the kindness in unison with the good relations subsisting between the United States and Russia. The guests consisted of the diplomatic corps, their wives, and some other foreigners. General conversation was kept up at table, and revived in smaller circles in the drawing-rooms afterwards.

I had some with the Minister Plenipotentiary from Naples. He directed it to the affairs of the United States. Of their com-

merce and marine he had been observant, particularly in the
Mediterranean. With the interests of the countries on this sea,
he seemed familiar. He had been minister at Constantinople;
his father had been in the same post before him, and now it
was filled by his son. He asked if my Government did not con-
template opening diplomatic intercourse with the Porte,
which led us to talk of the commerce of the Black Sea. He
doubted if we could derive benefit from it, unless as carriers,
should we even be admitted there. All that we desired, I said,
was the opportunity. The nations to whom it was open, were,
he said, Russia, Austria, England, and France. Naples enjoyed
it not; she was unwilling to pay what the court of Constantinople
asked.

Prince Lieven expressed to me his hope, that the late
appointment by the Emperor of Mr. Poletticca as Minister
Plenipotentiary to the United States, would improve the
friendship between our two countries. I joined in the hope;
the more, as Mr. Poletticca had been favourably known in the
United States since the days of Count Pahlen's mission. He
spoke of Mr. Adams, and the respect in which he was held
when minister in Russia. I said, that his titles to respect at
home had been increased by his correspondence whilst at St.
Petersburgh. Here I stated, that in 1811 and 1812 his
despatches relating to the great movements in Europe, were
frequent and full; that he proved himself master of them all,
anticipating the political combinations, and military results of
that era, with remarkable precision; above all, confidently predicting the failure of Napoleon's grand expedition to Moscow,
from the roused and warlike patriotism of Russia, and her
abundant resources. Such had been the uniform tenor of his
communications. They were on the archives of the American
government, as monuments of the writer's capacity to handle
public affairs of magnitude, with judgment and forecast. The
Ambassador heard with satisfaction my narrative.

March 12. Last night we were at the Marchioness of Stafford's.
The rooms were full. The Prince Regent, Royal family, many
of the nobility, and others thronged them. It was past eleven
when we arrived; yet fresh names were every moment

announced. All were in black under an order for a new Court mourning for the late King of Sweden, Charles XIII; who however did not die king, Bernadotte – the remnant of Napoleon's royal creations – occupying the Swedish throne. The rooms abounded in ornamental articles. The paintings commanded admiration. Under light judiciously disposed, they made a magnificent appearance. There is said to be no such private collection in Europe. It comprehends the productions of the first masters of the different schools. A considerable number are from the Orleans collection, procured in France by the late Duke of Bridgewater, from whom the estates of the Marquis of Stafford in part descend. These works of genius flowing from every part of the walls, formed of themselves a high attraction had the evening afforded no others.

It was the beginning of many hospitalities we had from this family. The Marquis is known to his country by the public character his peerage gives him, and the posts he has filled. The Marchioness is not less known by her rank; for she is of the oldest of the realm. But this is adventitious. She is known by her cultivated mind, her taste in the arts, her benevolence to her tenantry, by virtues unostentatious and refined, that commend her to the love of domestic and social circles, and endear her name to strangers.

March 17. Dined at Lord Melville's. Lord and Lady Melville, Lord and Lady Mulgrave, Lord Keith, the Ambassador of the Netherlands, the Danish Minister and Lady, Mr. Barrow, and a few more, made the party.

The Polar expedition was talked of. The prevailing opinion was against its success, but Mr. Barrow stood up for it. For every doubt, man of genius like, he had a solution, often in veins of pleasantry. I learned that he was the author of the article on this subject in the thirty-fifth number of the Quarterly Review, which every body had read with pleasure, at least. Lord Melville said, that nothing would be omitted by the Admiralty to ensure success to the expedition, as far as equipment was concerned; but I saw that he was not sanguine as to results.

I commended some delicious oranges on the table. His lordship asked if we had them in the United States. In the southern parts, I replied; in other parts we got them from the

West Indies. Copying Mr. Barrow's good vein I said, that those
from the English Islands would have a better relish if his
Majesty's Government would allow us to bring them in our
own ships! In the same spirit his lordship answered, that, for
one, he would be most happy to contribute to our enjoyments; but must hear what Lord Castlereagh had to say!

In the dining-room hung the original paintings of the places
seen by Cooke in his voyages. In the hall was one of Duncan's
victory over the Dutch off Camperdown. I asked if there was
no collection in England representing, in historical series, the
victories of the nation gained in fleet, beginning with those in
Cromwell's time. His lordship said, none.

In the drawing-room was a large vase of alabaster, about
eight feet high, and of the finest proportions. It stood before a
mirror. On the exterior surface, the whole story of Lucretia
was represented in figures of demirelievo. The work was
exquisite. The vase was illuminated inside, and cast softened
shades through the room. By the reflections of the mirror, all
the figures, though on a spherical surface, came under the eye
at once. This classic and beautiful ornament, which the size of
the room displayed to the best advantage, had been imported
from Florence. England, though carrying the manufacturing
arts to so high a pitch, is filled with the costly productions of
other parts of the world; the procelain, the silk damasks, the
or-molu, of France; the finest works in marble from Italy; the
table-linen of Holland and Saxony; the lace of Flanders; the
gems, the cashmeres of India. No amount of duty shuts out
such articles from her opulent classes. Their very costliness
brings them into demand.

March 18. The Duke of Sussex visited me. He had called
when I was out. Seeing the Secretary of Legation at Almacks's,*
he fixed to-day for calling again. I stayed at home to
receive him.

An ardour for constitutional liberty pervaded his conversation. It rose sometimes to an eloquent boldness. I had not
been prepared for quite as much in a prince of the blood, and
prized it the more.

Gibbon was mentioned. He thought highly of his historical

---

* A club of great exclusiveness, run dictatorially by a junta of great ladies.

research, but preferred Addison's style. The latter never tired. It was adapted to all subjects. He spoke of Mr. Adams, called him his friend, said he had known him on the Continent, where, as in England, he was esteemed by all to whom he was known. In paying a tribute to his talents, he mentioned his knowledge of languages.

The French was spoken of as the language of conversation in Europe. His Royal Highness said, that he would not perhaps object to this, as it was established but when used as the language of state papers and treaties, he was disposed to make a quaere. The French was acquired by foreigners with sufficient precision for conversation, and general purposes of literature; but in drawing up treaties, where the employment of words in their nicest shades of meaning was often of national moment, he who wrote in his native language had an advantage; and however slight, it was enough to lay the practice open to objection. He would suggest as a remedy, that treaties and other solemn state papers, to which two or more nations were parties, should be drawn up in Latin. This would put modern nations upon a par. Each would stand upon the scholarship of their public men. It was to this effect he spoke. I thought it in the natural feeling of an English prince.

The language of France has been diffused by her social manners, the merit of her writers, the exile of her protestants, and the power of her monarchy. Some of these influences are past. Others are shared by contemporary nations. Is it right that the monopoly of her language should last for ever? I would be much inclined to his Royal Highness's remedy, if there were no other, though open to difficulty, perhaps, from modern terms of art. But I venture upon the suggestion of another. Let the language most likely to be predominant throughout Christendom, be the common vehicle of Christendom. If a living language is to be adopted at all, this would be the fairest test. The European dominions of Britain have a population of upwards of twenty-two millions; the United States count more than twelve, to take no notice of the rapid increase of the latter, or numerous colonies of the former. Here is enough to authorize the belief, that, already, there are more persons to whom English is the vernacular tongue than French; and that it is destined to gain, not only upon the

French, but German, Spanish, and all others. There is another
fact more applicable. The foreign commerce of Britain and
that of the United States conjointly, exceed that of all Europe.
This serves, at the present day, to send forth the English
tongue more extensively to all parts of the globe, than the
French, or any of Christendom. Malherbe asserted the rights
of his native language so strenuously against all foreign usurp-
ation, that he gained at the French court the appellation of
'*tyrant of words and syllables.*' Very well, in a Frenchman! But if
treaties and all other international papers are always to be
written in French words and syllables, what becomes of the
equal independence of English words and syllables? The
French are too just to disparage the language of Milton, and
Newton, and Locke; and why should they insist upon the perpetual preference of their own? or rather why should
England acquiesce?

His Royal Highness, it must be added, is himself an
excellent linguist. To his knowledge of the classics, he adds
German, Italian, French, *Hebrew*, and it may be others, of
which I am not informed.

March 23. Dined at the Lord Mayor's. It was not *Lord Mayor's
Day*, but a city entertainment always given on Easter Monday,
at the Mansion-house. This edifice is sometimes called the
City palace. In size, it resembles one, and in some points of
architecture; but is badly situated, close by the Bank and Royal
Exchange. The streets are so narrow, you can see it but in part,
and it is with difficulty that carriages approach it at all.
Through the courtesy of the Lord Mayor, the diplomatic corps
are annually invited to this entertainment. It is a gratifying one
to them, for they see at it, the image of a powerful class in the
empire; the commercial class.

The Royal Dukes, some of the nobility, and persons in
station, were present. These, with the diplomatic corps,
occupied seats in a half circle at the upper extremity of the
room, on an elevation or dais. The tables in the area below
were filled with the opulent citizens of London. It was a fine
sight. They might be taken as a representative body from the
great ocean of mercantile wealth between Temple-bar and
London-bridge. The room was the Egyptian hall, of ample
dimensions and brilliantly lighted. A band played as we

entered. The Lord Mayor and Lady Mayoress were side by side in the centre of the half circle, at the top of the dais; the latter in a full court-dress. By her position she faced the whole company; a trying situation, which she bore with grace. After all the courses were over, toasts were given, the first I had heard in England. Music was kept up, the song rose, and every thing ministered to the festive feeling. On one side of me was Sir Benjamin Bloomfield. At intervals we conversed. It was principally of the United States. He spoke in a very friendly spirit; urging the benefit to both countries of mutual good-will and good offices. I listened the more, as he was Private Secretary to the Prince Regent.

The entertainment closed with a ball in another part of the building. Throughout the rooms, were insignia of the commerce and riches of London from an ancient day. The nation that commands the trade of the world, said Sir Walter Raleigh, commands its riches, and consequently the world itself. Whether the saying be true or not, the policy, the laws, the whole conduct of the English, attest that they never forget it.

CHAPTER XI

March 26, 1818. Visited Mr. West, President of the Royal Academy. I found him with his pencil in his hand.

The most curious piece in his collection, was one painted when he was eight years old. It was small, and very imperfect, he said; but added, that the primary colours, blue, red, and yellow, were so justly blended that he could not improve that part of the work. On asking if he had any previous instruction that enabled him to go right in so important a particular, he replied, no; he could no more say how his judgment had been formed to it, than how he learned his mother tongue.

The piece to which he pointed the most interest, was the 'Continence of Scipio.' It had been instrumental in bringing him into notice, forty years before. George III sent for it, and kept it for some time at his palace. At his Majesty's request, he had painted a series of historical pieces, from the New Testament. They were at Windsor – to be put up in a chapel the King contemplated building.

The number of pieces in his rooms was very great. He had been computing the dimensions of a gallery, to contain all he had ever painted. He found that it would require one four hundred feet long, fifty broad, and forty high. The piece from Lear, in the Academy of Arts at Philadelphia, was, he said, among those with the execution of which he had been best satisfied. I spoke of his 'Christ healing the sick,' in the hospital at Philadelphia, remarking how highly it was prized; all the town had flocked to see it. He spoke of a criticism upon it in Philadelphia, that had come under his notice; said it was written in a scholar-like manner, and with a perfect knowledge of the subject. He knew not the author, nor could I inform him.

This eminent and venerable artist was then near eighty. A native American, born near Philadelphia, he adverted to scenes of his early life. I was enabled to understand some of his local allusions. His patriarchal look and character gave me something of the filial feeling. What am I to do, I asked, as our conversation proceeded, to be able to judge of paintings? Wherever I go, I meet with them; in palaces, private houses, everywhere; engravings rest in portfolios; I see nothing but the works of your art, and all persons appear to have a knowledge of them; I the rather ask, as there is a growing taste for the arts in the United States; Republics have been celebrated for them; we cherish the hope that it may be our lot. He replied that he believed he could not do better, than name to me the discourses of Sir Joshua Reynolds. Those productions, I said, but increased my despair; we knew them in Philadelphia; they were ingenious, profound; but what a universe they opened! – wider than the poets in Rasselas; it was boundless; all kind of knowledge was necessary to the painter; and could we, with less, and without superadding the practice of the eye, become judges of painting? He agreed that the art was boundless; said that he every day saw something to learn in it; told the anecdote of the clergyman who preached one of Sir Joshua's discourses from the pulpit, omitting technical words, as a proof of its foundation in the principles of man's general nature, and admitted that it could only be successfully studied in conjunction with practice; in other words, that the eye could not gain a quick or sure perception of beauties and defects, but by familiarity with the best models. I said, it was this which gave to the English their facilities; foreign travel was so common with them, and then kept the eye in practice at home; the Vatican, the Louvre, the Museum at the Hague, the galleries of Sans Souci, the collections in the Low Countries and Spain, persons whom you met every day, had more or less seen. It was somewhat the same with books of travels. If you alluded to the latest in France, a gentleman by your side had been over the ground, and knew more than the book; if you spoke of the Coliseum or St. Peter's, half the company had been at Rome; and so of other places. He replied that it was true. Englishmen travelled a great deal; all did not bring back useful information in the arts, but so many went abroad, that the number was still great who did; hence there were more good judges of painting in England, than good painters; it was rare to meet with a person of leisure and fortune who had not visited Italy and France, if not more countries; England also contained more paintings than any other country, not in public depositories, for there were none worth speaking of, but in private houses; the rich bought up the best upon the Continent, wherever to be had; he would be glad to point out the private collections; those of Lord Stafford and Lord Grosvenor stood at the head, but there were others scattered about town, and all over the country. He invited me to call, whenever I had an hour to throw away, and saunter through his own collection, for all that it might be worth to me, saying that he would saunter with me, being always at home. It was thus that he received and talked to me. Once there was a tear, that the early recollections of his native land seemed to have drawn down. I felt in his fame the interest of a countryman. In his whole manner there was a cordiality which also inspired personal attachment even in a first interview. As often as I saw him afterwards, it was with renewed pleasure and advantage; but it was not long, before I was summoned to bear his pall.

March 27. We were entertained at dinner by Mr. and Lady Sarah Lyttelton. Mr. Lyttelton is in Parliament. Sir Humphrey Davy was at table. The newsmen had been blowing horns on a false rumour of Bonaparte's death. 'When that happens,' said Sir Humphrey, 'Europe will fly up, compression being off.' We had also Lady Davy, Miss Fanshawe, Earl Spencer, Lord Folkstone, and Mr. Luttrel. There was a flow of conversation that gives charm to a dinner-party; our reception having been as friendly as courteous by this accomplished pair.

March 29. Dined at Lord Holland's. His Lordship and Lady Holland, the Marquis of Landsdowne, Lord Morpeth, Lord Maitland, Sir James Macintosh, and Mr. Tierney, were of the company.

Lord Holland spoke of the institutions of the United States. Our system, he said, appeared suited to our circumstances; he hoped we would not put it to risk by a fondness for war; was there no fear that the excitements apt to arise under popular forms, and the courage that springs from freedom, might make us prone to war? I replied, that our reliance was in the checks which our constitution raised up, and chiefly, that the people, who must suffer from war, were the power who alone, by their representatives, could declare it. He bore testimony to the merit of President Monroe, whom he had known in personal and official relations, saying that in such hands our Republic, as far as depended on the chief magistrate, might always be considered safe.

I asked Sir James Macintosh, when we were to be favoured with the history the public had been led to hope he was preparing. He spoke doubtfully. Hume was mentioned. He could not always agree with him, he said, but commended the general spirit of his history; the whole, indeed, was masterly; the best portion, that which comprised the reigns of the Tudors, particularly Elizabeth's. He spoke of Robertson and Gibbon; both were careful inquirers into facts; Gibbon's research was profound, but he saw objections to his style. He spoke of Franklin's style with nothing but praise. It was more than pure; it was classic. It was neither the style of Addison nor Swift; it had the simplicity of theirs, but an original and graceful playfulness not carried too far, which neither of the others had in so great a degree.

Holland House, where we dined, four miles from London, is a venerable building. Among other associations that go with it, is the name of Addison. He lived here after his marriage to the Countess of Warwick. After dinner we went into the room that had been his library. It is now Lord Holland's. It is very long. Addison was not happy in his marriage; and the jocose tradition is, that he kept his bottle at each end of the room, so that in his walks backwards and forwards he might take a glass at each! It was in this room he wrote his despatches when Secretary of State. The Spectator being mentioned, Sir James said, that it had lost its value as a book of instruction, but as a standard of style would always last. I listened with interest to these and other remarks from him. His speeches and writings, read on the banks of the Delaware as those of the Thames, had taught me to regard his mind as kindred to Burke's; the same elementary power; the same application of the philosophy of politics and jurisprudence to practical occurrences; the same use of history, never heavily but always happily brought in; the same aptitude for embellishment, not so gorgeous, but always chaste; the same universal wisdom.

I resumed the topic of his history. I said, that when he got to the American revolution we should, on our side of the Atlantic, open his pages with peculiar interest. That we believed the full and proper account of it had not yet gone forth to the world; that among us were still left a few who were contemporary with it; their minds were the repositories of facts and reflections which, if not rescued in time, would perish. I instanced particularly, Mr. Jefferson and the elder Adams. The life of each hung by a thread; but their faculties were unimpaired. If he thought it worth while to embark in a correspondence with these fathers of our country, who, like himself, could have no object but truth, I would be happy to be the medium of its commencement. Some light he might hope to glean; and if, examining also for himself, he should find it the light of truth, would it not be worthy of both nations to establish this part of their common history, on a basis that both might approve? He caught at the suggestion, and followed it up with inquiries, saying he would avail himself of it. But it was not acted upon. I do not believe the omission arose from any diminished sense of the value of the aid he would probably have derived; but other causes. His parliamentary engagements took up much of his time; and shall I add, as another and natural hindrance, the claims of daily society upon him in the highest spheres, uniting as he did, the ease of the man of the world, to intellectual stores attractive and inexhaustible. Such men grow into favourites in these spheres in London. Chains are thrown round them, not easy to break.

The conversation from which I have minuted a small part, took place after we had risen from dinner, and were in the library. At table it was suited to the moment, and with the moment passing away. Of hospitality as dispensed by Lord Holland I had heard; of its kindness, its elegance. His standing as a peer is known. Not less, the many attainments which he makes subservient to the pleasures of society and friendship. In his house, opulence and refinement seem to lend their aids to invest letters with glory. The room in which we dined was richly ornamented. I understood that it had been painted and gilded as I saw, by one of Lord Holland's ancestors in the time of Charles I on the occasion of a fête given to Henrietta his Queen, when she came over from France.

I must mention an incident at one of the Holland House dinners, though I was not present. Scott's novels became a topic, a new one being out. One or two of the company expressed preferences among them. Before opinion had gone farther, Lady Holland proposed that each person should write down the name of the novel liked best. Paper and pencil were passed, and a slip torn off as each wrote. Nine were handed to her, and each had the name of a different novel! – a happy illustration of the various merit of this fascinating writer.

April 1. Went to Deptford with Sir Humphrey Davy. His carriage was at the door when I drove up at an early hour to his house. An accident happening to it, he took a seat in mine. Our conversation was chiefly about the United States, he leading it by his rapid, intelligent inquiries. One object of our excursion was, to see the ships fitting out for the Polar voyage. We went on board the Isabella. Outside she looked like any common merchant-vessel equipped for boisterous seas. There was double planking round her bow and sides to resist ice. The interior arrangements embraced whatever science could devise and mechanical skill effect to promote the objects of the expedition and comfort of the officers and men. Flues for diffusing heated air through the ship, nautical and philosophical instruments, with a library that seemed to contain the accounts of all former voyages of discovery, were to be seen. Parliament, to increase the zeal of the officers, had included them within the promise of reward to those who ascertained most nearly the longitude. After going through nearly all parts of the ship, we went into the Naval Dock-yard, and afterwards to Greenwich to see the Hospital.

Deptford is the smallest of the English dock-yards. We saw but few ships-of-war. Only one of the line, and three frigates were building. There were docks for repairing as well as building. We saw several royal yachts; among them, a very old one, the same that had conveyed Caroline Matilda, sister of George III to Denmark, on the occasion of her marriage to the King of that country. The Danes sent it back to England; refusing to keep it after the attack upon their capital, and capture of their fleet by Britain, in 1801. Although this is the smallest of the yards, it is not without importance, from being so near London. The business of supplying the navy with provisions is, or until lately was, carried on from a depôt adjoining it. Sir Humphrey spoke of their excellent quality, remarking how much the strength and courage of seamen depended upon food. They got, he said, bread and beef of the best quality, and in full quantity; an ample allowance of malt liquor, wine and cocoa, with all other things proper for the sea ration. In the timber piled up in the yard, I observed mahogany. The commissioner said, it was used, not merely for decks, as in the royal yachts, but with advantage, as knees and beams in heavy ships. The timber of all kinds on hand in the yard, generally amounted to a supply for three years. It consisted of English oak chiefly; but they also got supplies of foreign timber. A quantity was soon expected from the forests of Croatia and Dalmatia, under contracts with the Government of Vienna. They also obtained it from the Baltic. This they thought good when cut from the southern shores. From their North American possessions they did not get much, except for large masts. The attachments of George III to the navy were spoken of, his feelings as monarch being seconded, as was said, by a personal fondness for naval architecture and affairs of the sea. He had first evinced them in promoting the voyages of Byron and Cook, as soon as he got to the throne. It was added, that at Buckingham Palace, he was furnished with models of the dock-yards, and, occasionally, of the vessels building; which he took an interest in examining. These modes of exerting a superintendence over the navy, seem better in themselves, and, it must be owned, more befitted a sovereign, than if he had turned ship-carpenter, like Peter of Russia. The yard at Deptford was one of those in which that eccentric monarch worked.*

Commissioner Cunningham received us very kindly at his house within the yard. He would not allow us to depart without partaking of a collation.

We proceeded on towards Greenwich. Going through the streets, and stopping a moment, an incident arrested my

---

* In 1696 Peter the Great travelled incognito, and laboured with his hands in Dutch and British shipyards.

attention. A woman stood at the door of a house where cheap refreshments were sold. Some common people passing, she called to ask if they would take *tea*. It was about one o'clock. Houses of this kind, I understood, were not uncommon in London. I had myself observed tea sold in the streets near Charing Cross, by huckster women, who obtained the boiling water by means of coals in a pan, or lamp. In a country where the light wines are not produced, the first step into temperance is small beer; the next tea. The national schools in England have done much towards meliorating the condition of her people. The use of tea has co-operated, by doing more of late years, probably, than any other physical cause, towards lessening the appetite for ardent spirits. It acts not so much by reclaiming old drunkards, as diminishing the stock of new. What a sight to see this woman beckoning labouring men to tea instead of drams! The use of tea in England is universal. It is the breakfast of the wealthy, as of the poorer classes. On rising from the sumptuous dinner, coffee is first handed; but black tea comes afterwards. A general of the Duke of Wellington's army told me, that when worn down with fatigue, there was nothing for which the officers in the Peninsular war used to call so eagerly, as tea. Servants in London take it twice a day, sometimes oftener, and the occurrence at Greenwich shows the taste for it to be spreading among labouring classes at all hours.

We soon got near the Hospital. The day was fine. I saw, as we approached, men in uniform. They had a blue coat, full in front, flapped waistcoat, with breeches and stockings. All had three-cornered hats. Until we got near, a stranger might have taken them for an assemblage of old admirals. They were the pensioners – common seamen. Some were sunning themselves in seats. Others moved slowly about. I heard no talking from any. Altogether, they had a venerable appearance. Arrived within the high palisades of iron, I was struck with the extent and grandeur of the building. Domes; single and double rows of columns; flights of solid steps; Corinthian porticoes – met the eye on all sides. The whole was of Portland stone, and on a terrace fronting the Thames. I had heard that English hospitals were like palaces. The one before me far exceeded any palace I had beheld. The interior corresponded with the outside. There was space, neatness, universal order. The number of pensioners drawing the funds of the institution was more than thirty thousand. Those accommodated within the building, amounted to about three thousand. A Naval Asylum for minors is annexed, where are eight hundred boys, and two hundred girls, children of British seamen. These are educated and otherwise provided for. Some of the apartments of the Hospital, as the chapel and great hall, are superbly ornamented. In the first is the Shipwreck of St. Paul, a large painting by West. It fills the space over the altar, to which you ascend by a range of black marble steps. There are representations of Christ stilling the tempest and walking upon the waves, with various other costly emblems from the pencil and chisel, having relation to the sea. In the great hall, the ceiling exhibits paintings which years of labouring art had been necessary to perfect. They portray under appropriate allegories, astronomical and nautical science, intermingled with insignia of the naval glory of England. Probably no age or nation can show a charity more splendid; the first approach so imposing, the minute examination so calculated to augment admiration.

But there arose a reflection that I could not repress. Many of the veterans whom I saw, had, doubtless, fought under the compulsion of impressment. As I looked on their hoary locks and scarred faces, I thought that a country treating its seamen thus, was *bound* to lodge them like kings, when old or wounded; that in fact, it was only a payment back, and not adequate for, the previous infliction of such a wrong. It is to me an unaccountable anomaly, that a nation in which individual rights are guarded by barriers such as no other ever raised up, except the nation in the new world that springs from her; who would wade through blood sooner than part with her Habeas Corpus, or trial by jury, should yet sit calmly down under this unjust and tyrannical practice. It is said that her navy cannot otherwise be manned. Poor excuse! as if it were not universally true, that labour of any kind can be commanded by paying for it, and of course labour upon the ocean, with the risk of battle and death; and as if, supposing it to cost ten times over what would ever be asked, it ought not to be paid, sooner than such an outrage be committed! The statesmen, the philanthropists of England will at last awake from this dream of supposed necessity for the pressgang. It will cease, and the wonder be, that any arguments for sustaining it could have been made current so long. There have, it is true, been states ancient and modern, that have resorted to force for obtaining military service; but these precedents are to be shunned, not copied; especially by a nation whose fundamental code looks to the inviolability of personal liberty in a degree far above that of the civil law of Rome, or any of the codes of Continental Europe engrafted upon it. I did not volunteer my thoughts upon my English companion; but if I had, I scarcely think that dissent would have come from his liberal mind, accustomed as it was to analyze and reason.

We visited in the last place the Observatory at Greenwich. Mr. Pond, the astronomer-royal, received us in the same hospitable manner as Commissioner Cunningham. We ascended to the top of the edifice, seeing all the astronomical instruments in use. When chronometers were spoken of, it was stated, that the Government ordered twelve to be made every year by the best watch-makers in London. For the one which kept the most accurate time, a premium was given; for the next best, a diminished premium; and the remaining ten, if approved, were taken at fair prices. All were for the use of the public ships. In this way competition was kept up, no watchmaker suffered loss, and the navy got a supply of the best instruments for measuring time in all latitudes. The hour for our return pressing, we hastened back to town, after a day which, to me, had been one of great variety and interest. The Secretary of Legation, and Captain Thompson, of the party. Sir Humphrey's ardour of conversation did not abate going home. It related, in part, to what we had seen; he added anecdotes of eminent persons in England. We all regretted the moment of separation from him.

April 2. Dined at Prince Esterhazy's. Company – the diplomatic corps and their ladies. The dinner was one to have been expected from the munificence of the entertainer. Among a variety of wines, we had hock. By Austrian connoisseurs, this is not prized so much on account of its age, as original quality. When best, they think it does not improve after twelve or fifteen. Perhaps no wine does. The preference, at English as at foreign tables, in London, is for the light wines;

the strong, as Madeira and Sherry, are little used: Sherry most.
Generally, it is limited to a single glass after soup. With the latter
every dinner begins. Turbot follows, before the meats are
uncovered. We had French cookery, in its perfection. This I
find at English, as foreign tables. Mr. Morris, American Minister
in France at the time of the revolution, said, that if the French
had revolutionized the kitchens of Europe instead of its
courts, they would have rendered a service that no party
would have called in question. He was right. Food simply
roasted, or boiled, is thought temperance. The French know
better, and that to render it simple as well as savoury, a process
more artificial is required. Hence the made dishes, like the
light wines of France, promote health and cheerfulness.
Oppression seldom follows indulgence in them; gout as
rarely.

Talking with the Prince after coming out from dinner, we
spoke of the campaigns of Frederick. There is a pretty little fact
with which he was familiar on my allusion to it. After Berlin
was taken by the Austrians and Russians, the soldiers gave
themselves up to plunder. An officer high in rank was seen to
protect the palace at Potsdam. He would suffer nothing to be
touched; but asked as a favour to be allowed to take a small
picture of Frederick, and one of his flutes, that he might preserve them as memorials of so great a warrior and king. This
officer was Prince Esterhazy, a relative, as I learned, of our
accomplished host.

Although no political relations existed between the United
States and Austria, I received from this her ambassador in
London, invariable marks of esteem during my residence.

April 3. We dined at Earl Bathurst's. Earl and Countess
Bathurst, the Duke of York, the Duke of Gloucester, the Duke
of Montrose, Lord Lynedoch, Mr. and Mrs Villiers, Sir Henry
Torrens, General Maitland, Mr. Goulburn, and a few others,
were the company.

Conversation turned upon the United States; their climate,
government, productions, steamboats. On a question respecting the width of a river in one of the States, I was at fault. One
of the Royal Dukes put me right. Both of them spoke of our
Constitution. They asked how the Senate and Supreme Court
were modelled, not well perceiving the line between the

National and State authorities. I endeavoured in a few words to explain; which it was not easy to do, in a few words; and it was no place for dissertation. Inquiries were made as to the amount of our slave population, the ratio of increase, and others bearing on this subject. I answered with an admission of the general evil of slavery in the United States; but added that there were great mitigations in the good treatment of the slaves. To this the exceptions, I said, were rare, and scarcely known at all, among the better classes of our Southern planters. The effect of good treatment was, to diffuse in a large degree content and happiness among the slaves. Conciliatory sentiments towards the United States ran throughout all the conversation.

At eleven, we left the table. An hour passed in the drawing-rooms, where conversation was continued. All gave precedence to the Royal Dukes. From them there was urbanity to all.

April 8. The Princess Elizabeth was married last evening to the Prince of Hesse Homberg. The cabinet ministers, foreign ambassadors and ministers, officers of the royal household, persons in the suites of the Royal Dukes and Princesses, the Archbishops of Canterbury and York, the Bishop of London, the Lord Chancellor, the Lord Chief Justice, were present. The Prince Regent was not there, being ill. Our invitation was from the Queen, given through the Earl of Winchelsea, nearly three weeks before.

We got to the palace at seven o'clock. Pages were on the stairs to conduct us to the rooms. The ceremony took place in the throne-room. Before the throne was an altar covered with crimson velvet. A profusion of golden plate was upon it. There was a salver of great size on which was represented the Lord's Supper. The company being assembled, the bridegroom entered, with his attendants. Then came the Queen, with the bride and royal family. All approached the altar. Her Majesty sat; the rest stood. The marriage service was read by the Archbishop of Canterbury. The Duke of York gave the bride away. The whole was according to the forms of the Church, and performed with great solemnity. A record of the marriage was made. When all was finished, the bride knelt before the Queen to receive her blessing.

The consent of the King (or Regent) and Privy Council, is necessary to the validity of a royal marriage in England. There is another mode, where the party intending to marry, and being of the male branch, is of the age of twenty-six. In such case, a record of the intention on the books of the Privy Council will authorize the marriage at the expiration of a twelve-month, unless Parliament interpose an objection.

Soon after the service was performed, the bride and bridegroom set off for Windsor. The company remained. The evening passed in high ceremony, without excluding social ease. From the members of the royal family, the guests had every measure of courtesy. The conduct of the Queen was remarkable. This venerable personage, the head of a large family – her children then clustering about her; the female head of a great empire – in the seventy-sixth year of her age – went the rounds of the company, speaking to all. There was a kindliness in her manner from which time had struck away useless forms. No one did she omit. Around her neck hung a miniature portrait of the King. He was absent, scathed by the hand of Heaven; a marriage going on in one of his palaces; he, the lonely, suffering tenant of another. But the portrait was a token superior to a crown! It bespoke the natural glory of wife and mother, eclipsing the artificial glory of Queen. For more than fifty years this royal pair had lived together in affection. The scene would have been one of interest anywhere. May it not be noticed on a throne?

Tea was handed. The Queen continued to stand, or move about the rooms. In one was a table of refreshments. I went to it with Major-General Sir Henry Torrens, distinguished by service and wounds, whose acquaintance I had made at Lord Bathurst's. He was of the establishment of the Duke of York. On the table were urns and tea-kettles of fretted gold. Sir Henry recommended me to a glass of what I supposed wine, in a flagon near me; but he called it king's *cup*, given only at royal weddings.

Returning to the chief rooms, the Princess Sophia Matilda pointed out to Mrs Rush and myself the paintings, the representation of a bird from India formed of precious stones so as to resemble beautiful plumage, with other objects of curiosity or taste. She did more. She spoke of Washington. She paid a spontaneous tribute to his virtues. None but Americans can know how this would fall upon the heart. To hear his immortal name pronounced with praise in a palace of George III, had a high and touching value. Mentioning this Princess, I add, that myself and family afterwards experienced her obliging attentions in ways the remembrance of which is cherished with grateful pleasure.

At ten the company came away.

April 9. Dined at Lord Bagot's. We had the Earl of Mount-Edgecumbe, Lady Emma Edgecumbe, the Duchess of Leeds, the Countess of Dartmouth, Mr. Disbrow, Vice Chamberlain to the Queen, the Bishop of Oxford, and several Members of Parliament. The conversation had frequent allusions to the United States, their public institutions, and private society. The royal marriage was talked of. Lord Mount-Edgecumbe, who had been much an inmate of the palace, told anecdotes of the Queen illustrative of her domestic virtues. Another topic was, the attempt on the life of Lord Palmerston, Secretary-of-War. He was shot at and wounded, going into his office at the Horse-Guards, yesterday. The person who fired was supposed to be deranged. His acquittal was anticipated on this ground, as with Margaret Nicholson, and Hadfield, who attempted to assassinate the King. Whether the life of their King or the lowest subject be struck at, let the law have its course is the cry in England. Their code is sanguinary, but all are bound by it, all look up to it. One of the company considered the law too lenient upon these attempts to assassinate kings and their ministers; they recurred too often; he would punish the offender in the persons of his relations, as well as his own; as had been done with the Ravillacs and Damiens in France. This opinion found no countenance. It was canvassed with sprightliness.

After dinner an evening party followed. We had an invitation from Lord Bagot, to visit him at his country estate, Blithfield; and Lord Mount-Edgecumbe invited us to his, near Plymouth.

CHAPTER XII

INTERVIEW WITH LORD CASTLEREAGH – GENERAL
NEGOTIATION PROPOSED ON THE WEST INDIA TRADE,
MARITIME QUESTIONS AND IMPRESSMENT – NATURE
OF THE LAST QUESTION – THE SLAVE TRADE – OFFER
OF BRITISH MEDIATION IN THE AFFAIRS OF THE
UNITED STATES AND SPAIN – DINNER AT MR.
WILBERFORCE'S –AT THE EARL OF HARDWICKE'S –
ALMACK'S –LATE HOURS – COVENT-GARDEN THEATRE

April 11, 1818. Had an interview with Lord Castlereagh. I asked it, to apprize him of the desire of my Government to open negotiations for a general treaty of commerce, and arrange other matters of importance to both countries.

It was the wish of the President, I said, to see the commercial relations between the two countries placed upon a basis broader and more permanent than hitherto. The existing convention was not only limited as to time, but objects. The period not being remote when it would expire, it was desirable that the President should know the probable determination of his Majesty's Government as to forming one of a different character; one which, if not comprehending all the colonies of Great Britain, should at least include those in North America and the West Indies. I was aware of her past unwillingness to treat of this, and other subjects I should name; but had been instructed to present them anew, in the hope of other views prevailing. In this event, I was furnished with a full power to negotiate a treaty of the nature indicated.

His lordship was candid in reply. He said, that he could hold out no encouragement towards a treaty so comprehensive; too many interests hung upon their colonial dominion in the quarter mentioned. It would operate like a revolution in their commercial system. But I might be assured, that the determination of Great Britain not to bring the trade of those islands and colonies under such, or any arrangements by treaty, arose from no unfriendly feeling. It was only continuing a policy long established. Hence, no complaints would be made if the United States adopted countervailing measures; more especially if, not being vindictive, they were merely based upon fair competition. I replied, that the latter was the spirit alone in which they would be resorted to; that as Great Britain guarded her commercial interests very scrupulously, and in connexion with them those of her tonnage, the United States must do the same.

This subject being for the present disposed of, I passed to others. A time of general peace, as lately intimated by his lordship, seemed, I said, the proper time for settling points which, although of no immediate importance, were highly so in the future. The President was therefore desirous to take advantage of it, in the hope of being able to arrange the most important of this description; such as, trade with the colonies of enemies during war; that between colonies and the parent country; that from port to port of an enemy; the list of articles contraband; the doctrine of blockade, and the question of impressment. Past experience had shown the tendency of conflicting opinions on these points to embroil neutrals and belligerents; it had been unhappily too much the case as between Great Britain and the United States; the season when both parties were free from the excitements of momentary feeling or interest, was auspicious to attempts for adjusting them amicably, and I was empowered to enter upon negotiations on them all.

His lordship replied by concurring in the fitness of the time to the objects. He first spoke of blockade. Not much passed upon this, and scarcely any thing upon other points, both of us agreeing, that even if there could be an understanding upon them all, a treaty would be of little value that did not also comprehend that of impressment. To this question he therefore came, as of absorbing importance.

It is one prominent in the negotiations between the two Governments. I will therefore, before stating what was said on this first occasion of its being broached under my mission, offer some general account of it.

Great Britain, as a measure of state policy, impresses her seamen to serve on board her ships-of-war; in other words, takes them by force. The practice is one with which other nations have nothing to do, as long as it is confined to British seamen, the British dominions, and the decks of British vessels upon the seas. It may seem at variance with the high standard of personal rights upon which her laws are set in other respects; but that consideration is wholly for herself.

But she claims the right of searching the vessels of other nations upon the seas, for her seamen; and here begins the cause of complaint. For, how can the claim ever be enforced consistently with what is due to other nations?

Let the steps by which the enforcement proceeds be attended to. A British frigate, in time of war, meets an American merchant vessel at sea, boards her, and, under terror of her guns, takes out one of the crew. The boarding-lieutenant asserts, and, let it be admitted, believes, the man to be a Briton. By this proceeding, the rules observed in deciding upon any other fact where individuals or national rights are at stake, are overlooked. The lieutenant is accuser and judge. He decides upon his own view, instantly. The impressed man is forced into the frigate's boat, and the case ends. No appeal follows. There is no trial of any kind. More important still, there is no remedy, should it appear that a wrong has been committed.

Different is the mode of proceeding if an American merchant-vessel be stopped and examined at sea under circumstances subjecting her to suspicion as prize of war. In the latter case, the boarding-officer sends the vessel into port under accusation. Facts are inquired into judicially. Both parties are heard. Both have ample opportunities of bringing forward proofs. Should the tribunal decide that no lawful cause of seizure existed, the vessel is restored, the captors are answerable in damages, and there are adequate modes of making them pay. If, on the other hand, the *man* seized be in fact no Briton, the most he can ever hope for is, merely to be released. This can only take place after he has been kept an indefinite length of time on board the frigate, put to duty, and perhaps made to fight. He may be slain in battle. If this fate does not await him, his subsequent liberation, from the nature of the case, can only be effected at a distant day, and is not certain at last. He may not be able, whilst on board the frigate, to obtain documents to show that he is not a Briton. He may be transferred to some other vessel of war. Even to trace him through a navy scattered over all seas, must become to his country of friends a difficult, often a hopeless task. Should the chances, multiplied as they are against him, all turn out in his favour, and the order for his discharge be obtained, where is his action for damages? where his remedy for loss of liberty? – He has none!

A claim so *ex parte* in the whole enforcement, so intrinsically open to error, and the error so fatal, cannot, it should seem, rest upon public law. The United States say that it does not. They have never denied to Great Britain the *right of search*. They allege, however, that this means search for enemy's property, or articles contraband of war, not search for *men*. They say that no public code, or other adequate authority, has ever established the latter as an international right. If its exercise by any other State than Great Britain can be shown, the instances are averred to be too few, and too devoid of the evidences of general consent, to have made it part of the law of nations.

Great Britain places her claim on the ground of natural allegiance. She alleges that, by a principle of universal law, a man owes this kind of allegiance to the country of his birth. That he never can shake it off. That as his country protects him, so it may demand his services in return; especially in time of war.

The United States reply, that the principle of natural allegiance, however cherished by some states, is not universal. It may be held sacred by Britain; it may be of the highest practical importance under her own system; but the United States say, that its operation should be confined to her own territorial dominions, and decks of her own merchant-vessels. There is scarcely an important principle of public law that has not, at one time or other, had place in treaties among European States, the better to define or regulate it. This is especially the case with principles that belong to maritime affairs. Would a right of such concern to all nations using the sea, as a sovereign's, to enforce the allegiance of his own subjects in neutral vessels on its broad highway, have escaped notice in these solemn instruments between States? Yet no treaty contains any thing in relation to it.

The United States have been exposed to grievances from the exercise of the claim by Britain, heavier perhaps than ever fell to the lot of an independent nation. It springs from a cause rooted in nature, and irreversible; the resemblance of their seamen to those of England. Their language, dress, sea-phrases, every thing, are alike. To discriminate, is in most cases impossible. Of this, the proof is incontestable. It here follows.

Britain disavows, unequivocally, all claim to impress from American ships, any other seamen than her own. Her sense of justice would not allow her to set up any pretence of claim to take Americans; yet these she unavoidably does take, and in numbers sufficient to surprise those not informed upon the subject.

From a report made to Congress by the Secretary of State in April 1816, it appeared, that the impressed American seamen on board of British armed ships at the commencement of the war of 1812, a war occasioned chiefly by this cause, amounted to one thousand four hundred and twenty-two. Here is no exaggeration. The fact comes from the archives of Britain. It is taken from official lists, furnished by functionaries of the British Government to the American agent for prisoners of war in London. These men had been transferred from English ships to English prisons, on the breaking out of the war, or during its progress.

Furthermore. Britain, at a former period, liberated one thousand one hundred and thirty-two Americans who had been impressed prior to the month of September 1801. This fact also rests upon the authority of British archives, and was included in the same report to Congress. On the impressment of all these Americans, the British boarding-officers must have believed they were taking their own subjects; else they took them knowing them to be Americans. Hence the difficulty not to be surmounted, of distinguishing American from British seamen.

What then do we learn? more than TWO THOUSAND SIX HUNDRED AMERICAN CITIZENS, confessedly, the sufferers under this practice! and this by no means the whole list. All were native Americans. No British seaman, naturalized in the United States, was ever, if impressed, given back again. Can

Britain, whose pride and spirit have raised her to greatness, and who must know how to respect such qualities in other nations, – can she, for a moment, wonder, that a practice leading to such consequences should excite the deepest sensation in the United States?

She complains that she is aggrieved by the number of her seamen who get into the merchant-service of the United States, through our naturalization laws and other causes. This takes from her, she alleges, the right arm of her defence. Without her navy, her existence, no less than her glory, might be endangered. It is therefore vital to both, that, when war comes, she should reclaim her seamen from the vessles of a nation where they are so frequently found.

I have incidentally remarked in another place, that the naturalization laws of the United States are less favourable to foreigners than is generally supposed, and less than those of some of the principal states of Europe. England has statutes, unless recently repealed, under which foreigners serving only two years in her navy, become naturalized; which is going much beyond any facilities afforded by the United States. As to other causes that may bring her seamen to their vessels, the United States can only reply, that they do not entice them. Seamen are birds of passage; now under one flag, then another. Those of the United States often seek voluntarily the service of other nations, as those of other nations voluntarily seek theirs. The British navy, it is well known, is manned by a large proportion of foreign seamen. Some go there of their own accord. The decks of all nations show, more or less, an intermingling of the seamen of all. But no country is more desirous of employing their native seamen than the United States. They know the value of British seamen; nevertheless, they prefer their own. And why should it be thought that they have not enough of their own, as any other country whose interests and pursuits have long been maritime? New England alone is more populous than was Holland, when her sailors swarmed; and as maritime. 'Her farms are upon the ocean,' said one of her statesmen, 'and she gathers her harvests from every sea.' How numerous her sailors were as long ago as when she made part of the British empire, British statistics of that day may attest. This great nursery, passing by all other districts of a country with a vast sea coast, is perhaps sufficient to give to the United States as large a stock of seamen as they require. The supply, as in other fields, meets the demand. If ever interrupted by temporary causes, things soon return to this natural basis.

The United States not only desire to foster their own seamen, but have gone farther. In the hope of terminating the dissension about impressment, they have shown a willingness, as the progress of this work will make known, to exclude British seamen entirely from their service. They do not desire to hide the fact that they come, often in large numbers. It is a fact, however, which British records will also attest, that the number of *British* seamen regained by impressment out of the vessels of the United States, falls far behind the number of Americans taken in their stead. Under this view alone of the practice, apart from all others, the injury to the United States is greater than the benefit to Britain.

It is not immaterial to remark, that impressment, as a measure merely under the English laws and as exercised only in England, has a tendency to drive her seamen into the merchant-service of the United States on the breaking out of war. Obedient as the impressed British seaman may be to discipline when once on board a man-of-war of his country, it is not in human nature that he should like to be impressed. It is notorious that he does not. He dreads it. He tries to hide from the press-gang. His bold spirit would resist if he could; and sometimes he seeks foreign decks to get out of the way.

There is another heavy evil resulting to the United States. The voyages of their merchant-vessels are sometimes broken up by impressment. It is not to be supposed that they carry extra hands. Hence, when men are taken out of their vessels upon the high seas, it may happen, and has happened, that not enough are left for their safe navigation: and they have been compelled to make ports, other than of their first destination.

The foregoing is an outline of the question, in its main features. It may serve to give some idea of the manner in which it operates upon the United States. As between the two nations, it is a question *sui generis*. To both it is of the last importance. The diplomatic history of the United States will show how repeated and earnest have been their endeavours to settle it.

I return to my interview with Lord Castlereagh. He remarked, that intrinsic as were the difficulties respecting impressment, his desire was sincere to see them removed, and his efforts would be given with earnestness to remove them. I assured him, that, under all my instructions, my efforts would be equally sincere and earnest. The conversation proceeded. We adverted to the principles maintained by our respective countries. He said, that the abuse of the practice, for he freely admitted its abuse, had been the result of the peculiar state of the world, all Europe having been at war, and America neutral. He did not believe that the desire to enforce their right to the same extent, would exist in future; or that it would be drawn into exercise at all, if means could be devised to keep their men out of our vessels. I said, that the question never could be put to rest as long as a British naval officer was allowed to muster an American crew upon an American deck, to look for British seamen. Besides the indignity, so felt by all America, the inevitable consequences to which it must lead of subjecting Americans to seizure instead of Britons, would preclude for ever all hope of adjustment. The best mode we could devise of keeping British officers from our vessels on such errands, was that which he had hinted at; namely, to keep British seamen away altogether. This we were desirous to do, as far as in our power. I promised to furnish him with a proposal to this effect; and he, that it should have a liberal consideration.

His lordship next spoke of the Slave-trade. The Government of Great Britain felt, he said, an increasing desire, that the Government of the United States should lend itself to measures of regulation going forward in Europe for its extirpation. These were, mainly, a reciprocal submission to the right of search for slaves, and a limited number of the armed vessels of each of the maritime states to be empowered to search. It was contemplated to form out of an association of these, a species of international police in the African seas, from which the best effects were anticipated. No unusual structure of appearances in the vessel searched; no presence of irons or other presumptions of guilty intention; nothing but the actual finding of slaves on board, was to authorize a seizure and detention. Great Britain had lately urged France on this subject; but her consent could not, for obvious reasons, be made known, until the military occupation of her territory ceased. A recent vote, however, in both her chambers, on the principle of abolition, his lordship added, might safely be taken as a pledge of future co-operation. I replied, that I was destitute of instructions on the subject, but would transmit to my Government all that he said. The United States had long been awake to the evils of the Slave-trade. They had been the first nation to abolish it, unless Denmark led the way, and had directed against it the penalties of their own laws.

Before we separated, his lordship spoke of the late offer of Britain, through her minister at Washington, to mediate in our affairs with Spain. Although the offer had been refused, he desired to assure me that the refusal was taken in no unfriendly part; the less, from its conciliatory manner. Britain had in like manner refused the mediation of Russia, offered during the late war with the United States, without any unfriendly feeling towards Russia, or any question of her impartial dispositions. He was about to say something farther on the affairs of Spain, but, the hour being late, deferred it.

April 12. After my interview with Lord Castlereagh yesterday, I dined at Mr. Wilberforce's. Of the company, were Lord Teignmouth, Lord Rocksavage, Lord Gambier, Mr. Babington of the House of Commons, Mr. Neal, with others, ladies as well as gentlemen.

Many inquiries were made about the United States; their commerce, revenue, population, literature, and state of religion. A friendly spirit characterized the inquiries and remarks. Mr. Wilberforce's fame as a philanthropist and Christian has been known to me. His parliamentary labours, and those of his pen, had probably been more diffused over the United States than any country out of England. I expected to find him grave. He was full of animation. He led, without engrossing the conversation. His manner gave point to all that he said, and in his voice there were peculiarly eloquent intonations. He spoke of Mr Pitt. They had been at school together. He was remarkable, he said, for excelling in mathematics;

there was also this peculiarity in his constitution, that he required a great deal of sleep, seldom being able to do with less than ten or eleven hours; he would often drop asleep in the House of Commons; once he had known him do so at seven in the evening, and sleep until day-light. The ease with which some persons wrote, and the labour it cost others, were spoken of. Burke, Pitt, Windham, and Lord Ellenborough, were all great blotters, he said; Burke had begun a history of England, but gave it over.

One of the company mentioned the name of a gentleman who had large possessions in the West Indies. There is, said Mr. Wilberforce, in grammar, what they call a disjunctive conjunction; so there is in society. It is thus with that gentleman and me, he is so great a slave-holder; but we do very well when we meet; we pass by topics we should not agree upon, and exchange the small shot of conversation.

The income-tax being mentioned, he remarked, that having borne it once, they could bear it again; it yielded fifteen millions a-year, which would be good for a new loan of three hundred millions.

These things all flowed from him happily. Lord Teignmouth and others made their contributions. We were invited and arrived at an early hour. It was midnight when we got home, so agreeably had the time passed. Most of the company were public professors of religion; always the more attractive when in alliance with genius and accomplishments.

April 13. Dined at the Earl of Hardwicke's. Lord Somers was of the party. The English historical names as met in daily society, vividly arrest the attention of Americans. On this occasion I could not forget that I was with those of renown in the law; Lord Hardwicke being the grandson of the Lord Chancellor of that title, and Lord Somers a descendant of Lord Chief Justice Somers. The interest was heightened by portraits of the two ancestors hanging in view, the families having intermarried. We had also Lord and Lady Caledon, Lady Somers, Lady Catherine Halket, Admiral Sir Joseph Yorke, and Mr. Montagu.

The conversation turned upon France. Commendation was freely bestowed. Before coming to England, I had adopted an impression that the people were not prone to speak of the

merits of their neighbours on the other side of the Channel. I
remark the contrary in the circles I frequent. Another observation continues to force itself upon me; their taste for foreign
things. Among the embellishments of the table this evening,
were some beautiful ornaments in silver, from France.
Although the French take the lead in many of the finer
manufactures, I had supposed that English plate was preferred, from the more copious use of it in England leading to
superior excellence in its manufacture. The French use more
abundantly the sumptuous porcelain. The English import
that, in all its variety and costliness; but French plate, it seems,
is also imported. So it will always be with nations that are
opulent. Tired even of their own forms of superiority, they
seek novelty from abroad.

Sir Joseph York had been reading some of the official documents published by Congress, that treat of our navy. He made
its condition the subject of complimentary remarks.

It is not uncommon to hear, that at entertainments there
were all the luxuries of the season. In this metropolis, I witness
constantly those out of season; as, on this occasion, straw-
berries and pine apples, recalling the 'winter roses and summer
snows' of the Roman poet; *aestivae nives, hybernae rosae.* We had
also tokay that had been thirty years in his lordship's cellar;
and, better than all, respectful things said of our country, with
other attractive conversation.

April 16. We were at Almack's last night. The younger part
of the company danced. They were not the most numerous
part. Statesmen, cabinet ministers and their ladies, peers,
peeresses, and their daughters, foreign ambassadors, and
others, were present. In these circles, if all *classes* do not inter-
mingle, all *ages* do. Gibbon, writing to Lord Sheffield from
Paris, says, that Horace Walpole gave him a letter to Madame
du Deffand, '*an agreeable young lady of eighty-two,*' who had constant suppers at her house, and the best company. There may
be seen in society in London, and as part of its ornaments,
ladies whom I should set down as not much short of that
youthful age. It would be doing injustice to the stronger sex, to
suppose that they give up sooner.

We got to Almack's after having been at Covent Garden
theatre to see Miss O'Neil's Bianca. In like manner, it is after

the Opera, that we go to the weekly parties of Lady Castlereagh, the invitation specifying that time. Neither the Opera nor Covent Garden break up until twelve. Parties beginning at that hour, last until two and three. Most of those who have been at them, do not rise until towards noon next day. About two, commences the roll of carriages. At six in the evening, the *morning* ends. Then, scarcely sooner, the throngs of carriages, with gentlemen and ladies on horseback, disappear from the streets and parks, the hour of preparation for dinner being at hand. This is no overdrawn account, but the daily routine. It seems strange that health can be preserved, with such habits; yet the men look hale, the women blooming. Chiefly, they are of a class whose riches leave them at perfect leisure; but mixed in with them, are others, men of affairs, whose duties are arduous, and whose fame must be kept up by exertion – cabinet ministers, parliamentary orators, even chancellors and vice-chancellors – the last being seen on the bench next morning by nine. How these go through it all, seems more strange. This kind of life opens by degrees in February, gets to its crisis in May and June, and ends with July.

On the drop-curtain at Covent Garden, are seen the flags of nations with whom England has been at war. They are in a shattered state, and represented as in subjection to England. That of the United States is among them. The symbols are not historically true. If they were, they are misplaced at such an exhibition. Foreign nations do not take offence at such things now, and show good sense. The age is not remote when their sensibility was quicker. In the time of Charles II one of the reasons given by England for a rupture with Holland was, that a picture of the burning of the English ships at Chatham by the Dutch, was permitted to be hung up in the Town House at Amsterdam. England has fame enough, military and of all kinds, without straining in small ways after what does not belong to her.

CHAPTER XIII

WAGER OF BATTLE – INTERVIEW WITH LORD
CASTLEREAGH – IMPRESSMENT – COURSE OF GREAT
BRITAIN AND THE UNITED STATES, AS BETWEEN SPAIN
AND HER COLONIES – AFFAIRS BETWEEN THE UNITED
STATES AND SPAIN – SAFETY OF DIPLOMATIC
CORRESPONDENCE – THE DRAWING-ROOM –
BIRTHDAY DINNER AT LORD CASTLEREAGH'S

April 16, 1818. Went to the Court of King's Bench to hear the argument in the case of wager of battle. The parties were present. Through the courtesy of the Judges, I had a seat on the bench, next to Mr. Justice Bayley. On his left was Lord Chief Justice Ellenborough, and to the left of Lord Ellenborough were Mr. Justice Abbot and Mr. Justice Holroyd. If at Lord Hardwicke's I was awake to the associations which the great legal names of England call up, the feeling could not be less here. The room was extremely full. The case was so remarkable as to have become a topic in general society.

By the ancient law of England, when a person was murdered, the nearest relative of the deceased might bring what was called an appeal of death, against the party accused of the murder. Under this proceeding, the accuser and accused fought. The weapons were clubs. The battle began at sun-rise, and was in presence of the Judges; by whom also the dress of the combatants, and all other formalities were arranged. Part of the oath was, that neither combatant would resort to witchcraft. If the accused was slain, it was taken as a proof of his guilt; if the accuser, of his innocence. If the former held out until star-light, that also attested his innocence. If either yielded whilst able to fight, it worked his condemnation and disgrace.

It was a mode of trial for dark ages. Ashford the appellor, had accused Thornton the appellee, of the murder of one of his relations, and the latter desired to fight. In the highest tribunal of the most enlightened country in Europe, I was listening to a discussion whether or not this mode of trial was in force in the nineteenth century! It was difficult to persuade myself of the reality of the scene. Mr. Chitty, a lawyer of eminence, argued against the right of battle. Mr. Tindall had argued on the other side, on a former day. Fleta, Bracton, the Year-books, and other repositories of ancient law, were ransacked. Abundant ability was displayed on both sides. The greatest order prevailed; even gravity. The Judges were in their robes. About seventy lawyers sat in front of them; all in gowns and wigs. Finally, the Judges decided that trial by battle was in force. It had never, it seems been repealed.

To repeal laws, belongs to the legislature. Courts expound and apply them. Free government is complex, and works slowly; tyranny is simple, and does its work at once. An absurd law may sleep in a free code, because overlooked; but, whilst there, it is the law. It is so, I suppose, that we must reason; and generally the reasoning would be right. yet it might have been thought, that, in a case like this, long disuse added to obvious absurdity, would have worked the silent repeal of the law; according to the doctrine of *desuetude* under the Roman code.

In the end, no battle was fought. A technical flaw interposed to prevent it, and Parliament passed a repealing statute. But the case marks an incident in English jurisprudence, having come near to converting the Court of King's Bench into another Lyceum of Mendoza.

April 18. Had an interview with Lord Castlereagh. My object was, to submit a proposal for abolishing impressment. Its nature will be seen in the paper subjoined. It is not my general design to insert copies of official papers, meaning to content myself, when they come into view, with making known their substance and results. But there may be exceptions, and the subject of impressment is one. I therefore give the paper in its words, as follows:-

'Great Britain alleging a right to impress her seamen out of American vessels, upon the high seas, it follows, that whenever a mode can be devised for their previous exclusion from American vessels, the motive for the practice must be at an end. It is believed that this may be effected by each nation imposing restraints upon the naturalization of the seamen of the other, and reciprocally excluding from their service all seamen not naturalized. If Great Britain be allowed to naturalize American seamen, the United States must be allowed to naturalize British seamen. Each should be at liberty to afford the same facilities, or bound to interpose the same restraints. The greater the difficulty in acquiring the right of citizenship, the easier will it be to avoid imposition, and the more complete the desired exclusion. The law of Congress, of the third of March one thousand eight hundred and thirteen, of all the provisions of which Great Britain may command the benefit, will prove how sincerely the United States desire to settle this controversy on conditions satisfactory to Great Britain. By that law it is made indispensable for every British subject who may hereafter become a citizen, to reside five years in the United States without intermission, and so many guards are interposed to prevent frauds, that it seems scarcely possible they should be eluded. No British subject can be employed in a public or private ship of the United States, unless he produce to the commander in the one case, and to the collector of the port in the other, a certified copy of the act by which he became naturalized. A list of the crew, in the case of a private ship, must be taken, certified, and recorded by the collector; and the consuls or commercial agents of Great Britain may object to the employment of a seaman, and have the privilege of attending the investigation relative to his citizenship. The commander of a public ship receiving a person not duly qualified, is to forfeit a thousand dollars, and the commander or owner of a private ship, five hundred. It is also made a felony punishable by fine and imprisonment, for any person to forge or counterfeit, or to pass, or use, any forged or counterfeited certificate of citizenship, or to sell or dispose of one. The United States will also be willing to provide, that every British subject desiring to become a citizen, shall be bound to appear in person before the proper tribunal, once a year, for the term of five years, until his right shall be completed, or adopt any other more practical and satisfactory evidence that his residence within their territory was *bonâ fide* and uninterrupted, it being their sincere desire to employ their own seamen only, and exclude British. By requiring five years' uninterrupted residence as the condition of citizenship, it is confidently believed that, from considerations readily suggesting themselves, few if any British seamen would be found to take advantage of it. The nature of a seaman's life stands opposed to a different conclusion. If, in some instances, a residence should be commenced with a real intention, at the time, of submitting to this condition, the presumption is strong that, at the expiration of the term, such a change of habits and prospects would be superinduced, as to lead to the abandonment for ever of the sea as an occupation. If the proposal be accepted, the United States would farther agree, that none of the British seamen who might be within their territory when the stipulation to give it effect was entered into, without having already become citizens, should be admitted into either their public or private ships, until they had acquired the right, according to all the above regulations. In return for them, a clear and distinct provision to be made by Great Britain against impressment out of American vessels.'

I accompanied the delivery of the paper with renewed assurances to his lordship of the President's desire to see this cause of dissension for ever removed, and the expression of a hope that Great Britain would see in the proposal no surrender of any right or interest, whilst its acceptance would guard the United States against wrongs that were palpable. He replied, that he would lay the proposal before the cabinet; that it should have all the consideration due to its importance, and, I might be assured, in a conciliatory spirit.

Leaving this subject in his hands, I reminded him of his intention to speak on Spanish affairs. He resumed the thread. Great Britain, he said, lamented the long continuance of the contest between Spain and that country's colonies. She had done all in her power to heal it. She would not relinquish her efforts, always desiring that Spain should pursue a liberal course, not a narrow or exclusive one; he meant a course that would look largely to the commercial emancipation of the colonies. Great Britain, in particular, would not be instrumental to a settlement of the contest upon terms which, drawing to herself peculiar advantages, would exclude the United States, or any other nation, from a just participation in the trade of

South America. He hoped he might hear from me, that the United States would be governed by similar principles.

I replied, that they were the principles which had invariably governed the United States. They desired, as ardently as Great Britain, the termination of the contest. They considered it in the light of a civil war, injurious to other nations, and, from geographical and other causes, especially injurious to the United States. The latter lent aid to neither party, in men, money, nor ships. Spain made complaints; but they were unfounded. The United States maintained as strict a neutrality as was possible; they considered each party as having all the rights of war as between themselves, and as against other powers. If any of their seafaring or mercantile inhabitants gave illegal aid to either party, they did it at their peril; they were subject to belligerent capture by the party injured, and to prosecution under the laws of the United States; who, the better to enforce neutral conduct upon their citizens, had special statutes annexing penalties to a departure from it. If the colonies finally prevailed, the United States not only did not seek, but would not, by treaties or other compacts, accept, any exclusive advantages; these, they knew, would create jealousy in other nations; all that they desired was fair competition. Such were the maxims of the United States; they had been made known to the world, and there was no reason to think they would be departed from.

His lordship asked if I knew whether my Government had given notice to Spain of its intention to take possession of Amelia Island. I said that I did not; nor did I know that it would have been practicable. That island had been taken, not from Spain, but those who had previously wrested it from her. It adjoined territories of the Union; an expedition had been set on foot against it, ostensibly by the public enemies of Spain, viz. some of her colonies warring against her; but, in fact, by an irregular force from all countries, with such aid as could clandestinely be drawn from the United States in spite of prohibitory laws. This force took the island, and the Spanish authorities at the Havanna strove, but without success, to get it back. It became a rendezvous for freebooters, smugglers, and renegado slaves; and an entrepôt for fresh slaves from Africa. To put a stop to these and other enormities upon their border, the United States sent a small naval and military force to take possession of the island. They held it subject to a proper accountability, not doubting that the world would see in the measure nothing beyond a necessary precaution for the security of their commerce, and maintaining the authority of their laws. His lordship assented to the strength of these motives.

He inquired, lastly, if I was acquainted with the intentions of my Government as to the reception of deputies from the colonies of Spain.

I replied, that up to the time of my leaving Washington, no representatives of the colonies had been received in any official capacity. Informal agents had arrived, and been informally listened to. Spain complained of this, and had even demanded that the United States should exclude from their ports the flags of Mexico, Carthagena, Buenos Ayres, and other provinces in resistance. The demand was thought unreasonable, especially whilst the United States had, as they conceived, long and just causes of complaint against Spain. Some, I recapitulated. 1. Questions of territory, growing out of the purchase of Louisiana from France, by the United States, in regard to which Spain still failed to do them justice. 2. Her sudden and violent interruption of the trade of the United States descending the Mississippi, by cutting off the right of deposit at New Orleans, before Louisiana belonged to the United States. 3. Her neglect to award compensation to the citizens of the United States for spoliations during the wars of the French Revolution, although a treaty had attested their title to it; a treaty signed by her own minister at Madrid, but from which her Government withheld its ratification. These things I brought into view, that the forbearing policy of the United States towards Spain might be the better appreciated. His lordship expressed a hope that all our differences with that power might be satisfactorily accommodated. I joined in the hope, saying that the desire of my Government not to disturb the general peace, was steady and sincere, and that it would leave nothing undone in the way of further negotiations, earnest as had been its past endeavours.

April 21. Count ____ called on me. He had requested an

interview. After introductory words, he asked if I was aware that the English Government watched foreign ministers. I asked, how? He said, by having persons in its service. Watched then in what ways? In all ways; was I sure of my servants? did I lock up my manuscripts? did I send my letters through the post-office? I said, yes, as to the two last. As to my servants, I hired them, as others did, after learning their characters. Was I sure they were not in secret pay? Not sure, I said; did he know it? Not positively; he could bring no proof; it was a business that kept proof out of sight. Had he heard anything? I asked. No, but he had been long in London, and heard much on this subject; the Government with an outside of candour, knew how to work under ground; it thence became an adept in intrigue by lulling suspicion. But would he let me into the grounds of his suspicion in my case? what whispers were there? History enlightened us much, he said; – did not Walpole expend a million in secret service-money – had the English Government so changed since, as to be above all similar practices?

I replied that little would be gained by watching me. My Government was not one of mystery. Those in its service had to act and write under the responsibility of publication at home. Their secrets would thus come back to England, more fully than servants, or the post-office, could detail them. Nevertheless, he rejoined, the American and Russian legations were the two most watched; he believed so, and desired to render me a service by putting me on my guard. I thanked him, but said I was slow to believe. The English Government had its faults, but not of that kind. Why not? Because it was against the genius of the Government and people; they openly debated all that they did, and printed all that they said; twenty folios would scarcely hold the matter annually sent forth by Parliament about their finances, trade, foreign relations, army, navy every thing; into their public offices any one might go: into their barracks, arsenals, or any other depôt. Their press was everywhere, ferreting out every thing. But what did all that prove? Nothing, I said, if he had special facts to make good his suspicion; but, in the absence of them, it led me towards the conclusion, that a nation so devoid of conceal-ment in its own affairs, would be little inclined to bribe the servants of a foreign minister. What then had Walpole done with his million sterling? That was more than I could say; every Government, however open, had a secret fund; the Government of the United States had; some of Walpole's sent to pay newspapers, we were told, which would be foolish in these days, if not in his.

I do not know that I changed the opinions of my visitant. He spoke on other subjects and left me, after having stayed an hour.

April 23. Went to the Drawing-room. We had the hoops and plumes, the same spectacle in the hall, up-stairs, and going to the palace. It was one to bear repeating. The company was even more numerous.

The Queen was on her velvet elevation as before. I stood next to the Duke of Sussex. He named to me those who passed before her. The anxious countenances as the line slowly advanced; the dresses; the silence, increasing as the moment of presentation approached; the graceful timidity when at last the youthful fair curtsied before the Queen, gave to this real scene whatever imagination might picture. Close by me was the Duke of Bourbon; pale, silent, accustomed to Chantilly, to Versailles – even he stood gazing in admiration. It was the fine sensibility of a Condé, touched by the female beauty of England. Pensive though placid, it seemed, even at such a time, as if the remembrance of his son, the Duke d'Enghien, was stealing into his thoughts. Among the attractions of the day were Lady Elizabeth Leveson Gower, Miss Seymour, Lady Georgiana Fane, Lady Emily Bathurst. It was their first presentation at Court. The Queen cordially welcomed them, dispensing her accustomed kindness.

This drawing-room was in honour of the birth-day of the Prince Regent. It comes in August, but is not then celebrated. The conjecture ran that not fewer than two thousand persons were present. We got down stairs as we could, through *tulle*, gold net, hoops, and other glittering entanglements with which beauty obstructed the way.

In the evening, Lord Castlereagh gave a grand dinner. He was himself unwell, and not at table. His brother, Lord Stewart, did the honours. At the foot, were the Earl of Clanwilliam and Mr. Planta; the former, private secretary of Lord

Castlereagh, the latter, under secretary of state. Lord Stewart gave the Prince Regent as a toast. The company all rose. A few minutes afterwards, Prince Esterhazy gave Lord Castlereagh, which was received in like manner. In each case, the name alone was mentioned. Among the wines were dry champagne *non mousseux*, said to have been the favourite wine of Napoleon; and tokay, a present to Lord Castlereagh from one of the crowned heads.

***** said to me, that he believed the United States might obtain an island in the Mediterranean if desired. I said, that our interests were not European. Did we not keep a squadron there? he asked. I replied that we did; only, however, to guard our commerce from African pirates. How long would we continue that policy? Always, I remarked, rather than pay tribute. Had we no treaty with Algiers by which our commerce was to go free, without tribute? Yes, but the Dey gave us to understand, what might have been inferred, that he would abide by it no longer than he could help it; he had signed the treaty to save his fleet from attack; an enterprise resolved upon by the United States prior to Lord Exmouth's bombardment of his town; from that time we had kept a naval force in the Mediterranean strong enough as was believed, to check his. Then, would not this policy make it desirable to have a station for our ships, and for supplies? I replied, that our squadron readily obtained supplies from friendly ports, paying in specie which it took out, or bills on London; was not this safer than to run the risk of exciting jealousy, perhaps of exposing our purpose itself to frustration, by attempts to get footing in the Mediterranean? He said that he was under the belief that we might obtain Lampedosa in a manner to avoid objection; he meant the use and occupation of that island, Naples retaining the sovereignty. To such a transfer he did not see that Spain, England, France, or any power, could object. That might change, I said, some aspects of the question; still there might be stumbling-blocks. Here our conversation closed.

After we came out from dinner, Baron de Gerning, attached to the suite of the Prince of Hesse Homberg, spoke to me of the great and good Washington. So he called him. The United States were far removed, he said, from his part of Germany; but virtue was of all countries, and all revered it in the illustrious founder of mine. I had conversation with Admiral Van der Capellen, who commanded so ably the Dutch ships that fought with Lord Exmouth at Algiers. He had been on board the United States squadron in the Mediterranean, under Commodore Chauncey. There was, he said, throughout every part of it, a discipline that excited his admiration. It is always grateful to hear the things of one's country so spoken of abroad.

CHAPTER XIV

THE DAILY PRESS – ANNUAL EXHIBITION AT THE ROYAL ACADEMY – PUBLIC SOCIETIES – DINNER AT THE MARQUIS OF LANSDOWNE'S – EVENING ENTERTAINMENT AT CARLTON HOUSE – DINNER AT DR. PINCKARD'S

April 29, 1818. A country is not to be understood by a few months' residence in it. So many component parts go to make up the grand total, where civilization, and freedom, and power, are on a large scale, that the judgment gets perplexed. It pauses for re-examination. It must be slow in coming to conclusions, if it would be right. Often it must change them. A member of the diplomatic corps, an enlightened observer, said to me a few days ago, that, at the end of his first year, he thought he knew England very well. When the third had gone by, he began to have doubts; and that now, after a still longer time, his opinions were more unsettled than ever. Some he had changed entirely; others had undergone modification, and he knew not what fate was before the rest.

There was reason in his remark. If it be not contradictory, I would say, that he showed his judgment in appearing to have at present no judgment at all. The stranger sees in England, prosperity the most amazing, with what seems to strike at the roots of all prosperity. He sees the most profuse expenditure, not by the nobles alone, but large classes besides; and, throughout classes far larger, the most resolute industry supplying its demands and repairing its waste; taxation strained to the utmost, with an ability unparalleled to meet it; pauperism that is startling, with public and private charity unfailing, to feed, clothe, and house it; the boldest freedom, with submission to law; ignorance and crime so widely diffused as to appal, with genius and learning and virtue to reassure; intestine commotions predicted, and never happening; constant complaints of poverty and suffering, with constant increase in aggregate wealth and power. These are some of the anomalies which he sees. How is he at once to pass upon them all? he, a stranger, when the foremost of the natives after studying them a lifetime, do nothing but differ!

One of the things that strike me most, is their press. I live north of Portman Square, nearly three miles from the House of Commons. By nine in the morning, the newspapers are on my breakfast-table, containing the debate of the preceding night. This is the case, though it may have lasted until one, two, or three in the morning. There is no disappointment; hardly a typographical error. The speeches on both sides are given with like care; a mere rule of justice, to be sure, without which the paper would have no credit, but fit to be mentioned where party-feeling always runs as high as in England.

This promptitude is the result of what alone could produce it; an unlimited command of subdivided labour of the hand and mind. The proprietors of the great newspapers employ as many stenographers as they want. One stays until his sheet is full. He proceeds with it to the printing-office, where he is soon followed by another with his; and so on, until the last arrives. Thus the debate as it advances, is in progress of printing, and when finished, is all in type but the last part. Sometimes it will occupy twelve and fourteen broad closely-printed columns. The proprietors enlist the most able pens for editorial articles; and as correspondents, from different parts of Europe. Their ability to do so may be judged of from the fact, that the leading papers pay to the Government an annual tax in stamps, of from twenty to fifty thousand pounds sterling. I have been told that some of them yield a profit of fifteen thousand sterling a-year, after paying this tax, and all expenses. The profits of 'The Times,' are said to have exceeded eighteen thousand a-year. The cost of a daily paper to a regular subscriber is about ten pounds sterling a-year. But subdivision comes in to make them cheap. They are circulated by agents at a penny an hour in London. When a few days old, they are sent to the provincial towns, and through the country at reduced prices. In this manner, the parliamentary debates and proceedings, impartially and fully reported, go through the nation. The newspaper sheet is suited to all this service, being substantial, and the type good. Nothing can exceed the despatch with which the numerous impressions are worked off, the mechanical operations having reached a perfection calculated to astonish those who would examine them.

What is done in the courts of law, is disseminated in the same way. Every argument, trial, and decision, of whatever nature, or before whatever court, goes immediately into the newspapers. There is no delay. The following morning ushers it forth. I took the liberty of remarking to one of the Judges, upon the smallness of the rooms in which the Courts of King's Bench and Chancery sit, when the proceedings were so interesting that great numbers of the public would like to hear them. 'We sit,' said he, 'every day in the newspapers.' How much did that answer comprehend! What an increase of responsibility in the Judge! I understood from a source not less high, that the newspapers are to be as much relied upon, as the books of law reports in which the cases are afterwards published; that, in fact, the newspaper report is apt to be the best, being generally the most full, as well as quite accurate. If not accurate, the newspaper giving it, would soon fall before competitors. Hence, he who keeps his daily London paper, has, at the year's end, a volume of the annual law reports of the kingdom, besides all other matter.

In the discussions of the journals, editorial or otherwise, there is a remarkable fearlessness. Neither the Sovereign nor his Family are spared. Parliament sets the example, and the newspapers follow. Of this, the debates on the royal marriages in the course of the present month, give illustrations. There are countries in which the press is more free, by law, than with the English; for although they impose no previous restraints, their definition of libel is inherently vague. But perhaps nowhere has the press so much latitude.

Every thing goes into the newspapers. In other countries, matter of a public nature may be seen in them; here, in addition, you see perpetually even the concerns of individuals. Does a private gentleman come to town? you hear it in the newspapers; does he build a house, or buy an estate? they give the information; does he entertain his friends? you have all their names next day in type; is the drapery of a lady's drawing-room changed from red damask and gold to white satin and silver? the fact is publicly announced. So of a thousand other things. The first burst of it all upon Madame de Stael, led her to remark that the English had realized the fable of living with a window in their bosoms. It may be thought that this is confined to a class, who, surrounded by the allurements of wealth, seek emblazonment. If it were only so, the class is immense. But its influence affects other classes, giving each in their way the habit of allowing their personal inclinations and objects to be dealt with in print; so that, altogether, these are thrown upon the public in England to an extent without parallel in any country, ancient or modern. When the drama at Athens took cognizance of private life, what was said became known first to a few listeners; then to a small town; but in three days, a London newspaper reaches every part of the kingdom, and in three months, every part of the globe.

Some will suppose that the newspapers govern the country. Nothing would be more unfounded. There is a power not only in the Government, but in the country itself, far above them. It lies in the educated classes. True, the daily press is of the educated class. Its conductors hold the pens of scholars, often of statesmen. Hence you see no editorial personalities; which, moreover, the public would not bear. But what goes into the columns of newspapers, no matter from what sources, comes into contact with equals at least in mind among readers, and a thousand to one in number. The bulk of these are unmoved by what newspapers say, if opposite to their own opinions; which, passing quickly from one to another in a society where population is dense, make head against the daily press, after its first efforts are spent upon classes less enlightened. Half the people of England live in towns. This augments moral as physical power; the last, by strengthening rural parts through demand for their product – the first by sharpening intellect through opportunities of collision. The daily press could master opposing mental forces, if scattered; but not when they can combine. Then, the general literature of the country, reacts against newspapers. The permanent press, as distinct from the daily, teems with productions of a commanding character. There is a great class of authors always existent in England, whose sway exceeds that of the newspapers, as the main body the pioneers. Periodical literature is also effective. It is a match at least for the newspapers, when its time arrives. It is more elementary; less hasty. In a word, the daily press in England, with its floating capital in talents, zeal, and money, can do much at an onset. It is an organized corps, full of spirit and always ready; but there is a higher power of mind and influence behind, that can rally and defeat it. From the latter source it may also be presumed, that a more deliberate judgment will in the end be formed on difficult questions, than from the first impulses and more premature discussions of the daily journals. The latter move in their orbit by reflecting also, in the end, the higher judgment by which they have been controlled. Such are some of the considerations that strike the stranger, reading their daily newspapers. They make a wonderful part of the social system in England. Far more might be said by those having inclination and opportunity to pursue the subject.

May 3. Yesterday the Royal Academy gave their anniversary dinner at Somerset House. It was the fiftieth celebration. Froissart, when he found himself on the English coast said, that he was among a people who '*loved war better than peace*, and where *strangers were well received.*' If the latter were true in the time of Edward III, diplomatic strangers must say that it is, still. Invitations crowd upon them. If they did not decline more than they accept, there would be a poor account of their public business. The Royal Academy is an institution for the encouragement of the arts. Professorships of painting, sculpture, and anatomy, are annexed to it. The first President was Sir Joshua Reynolds. In that capacity he delivered his celebrated Discourses; a work invaluable to the student in painting, and to be read with scarcely less advantage by the student of any science or profession. The author, says Burke in his beautiful obituary notice of him, was the first Englishman who added the praise of the elegant arts, to the other glories of his country. Yesterday I had the satisfaction to see, as his successor in the chair, my venerable countryman Mr. West. There were present, the royal academicians, a large collection of the nobility, many of the cabinet ministers, the Lord Chancellor, the Bishops of London and Salisbury, artists and others, high in the walks of genius and taste; the foreign ambassadors, and an array of private gentlemen. Five of the rooms had their walls hung with paintings. There were more than four hundred. The rule being to receive none formerly exhibited, this number was therefore to be taken as the year's production of pieces deemed by the Academy worthy of exhibition. Additional rooms were open, containing architectural designs and specimens in sculpture.

The collection was rich in portraits. The English in this line do not perhaps fall behind any part of Europe. The productions of Lawrence, Beechey, Phillips, Davis, Newton, Jackson, and many others, were seen all around. The piece that excited most attention from the interest of the subject in British eyes, was a full-length likeness of the Duke of Wellington on the horse he rode, and in the dress he wore, at the battle of Waterloo. It was by Sir Thomas Lawrence. There was a fine piece by Mr. West, founded on an interview between the great Mogul and Lord Clive. But one was seen of surpassing charm; the family of Walter Scott, by Wilkie. The great author is seated on a bank, his wife and daughters near him in cottage dresses. If we had Shakspeare in a family scene on the Avon, by a distinguished artist of Elizabeth's time, how would it be prized now! In going through the rooms, it was not easy to avoid the reflection, that a day of fame in the arts awaits Britain. She is still in her youth in them. She has made hardly any efforts. Busy in climbing to the top of every thing else, she has not had time. The useful arts have occupied her. At the head of these in Europe, she is now at a point for embarking in the fine arts. And are not these *useful* too, when all ages pronounce that they enlarge the understanding, and improve the heart, as much as they refine the taste? To suppose the English climate not favourable to the fine arts, is strange. A climate where beautiful appearances of nature abound; that has been favourable to every kind of mental eminence, as mechanical skill; where the inferior animals are seen in full size and strength, and the human form in all its proportions and beauty, not a climate for painters and sculptors! But it is said there must be a certain delicacy of thought and feeling to appreciate the world of nature, and deck it with the glories of art! Is not then the country of Shakspeare and Scott, of Milton, and Byron, and Moore, one for painters? How came the Dutch with a school of painting of their own, and an eminent one? Is their sky more genial? And will not the English, with political institutions and social manners of their own, try new fields of art? An American adopts the anticipation the rather, because he clings to the belief that his own country, like republics of old, is by and by to take her stand in the arts. Her students even now go to Italy for instruction. They hold, that in the great world of art, there is still immeasurable room for originality, and this under the strictest rules of art.

We dined in the principal exhibition-room; a large one. Two tables ran down the sides, connected by another at the top. In the middle of the latter, sat the President; on one side of him, the Duke of Sussex, on the other, the Duke of Norfolk. The walls were so covered that every position commanded the paintings; and, through vistas, the eye could steal into the other rooms. The whole was extremely attractive. I enter into no criticism. I give general impressions. It is not, as I know, the habit of the English, fastidious from their familiarity with the exquisite models of the Continent, to value themselves much on this home exhibition; but for myself, bursting upon me as it did all at once, I thought it highly worthy to be extolled. I could have made bold to suggest a subject for a piece that I did not see in the collection; viz. *'The President and Royal Academy at the anniversary dinner with their guests.'*

The members of the diplomatic corps had seats near the head. After the Prince Regent and Royal family had been given as toasts, according to the custom at public festivals in England, the President gave the 'Foreign Ambassadors and Ministers,' who, as he was pleased to add, 'had done the Academy the honour to be present.' The toast was cheered with great courtesy. The corps looked to me as the organ of acknowledgment, English being my native tongue. Obeying their wishes, I returned thanks, adding that I was authorized to express the gratification we all derived in partaking British hospitality, surrounded by so many memorials of British art. Speeches were made by several of the nobility and gentlemen, but chiefly the Duke of Sussex and Lord Chancellor Eldon. They were in commendation of the arts, and on the usefulness of that institution towards their advancement in England. Dinner was served at six. Until past seven, we had the sun through sky-lights. Afterwards, there fell gradually from above, light from numerous shaded lamps in hanging circles.

They were burning, unobserved, when we sat down, and emerged from ambush only as night came on.

> ——— Dependent lychni laquearibus aureis
> Incensi: et noctem flammis funalia vincunt.

May 6. This is the season for public societies to hold their meetings. It would be next to impossible to ascertain the number, charitable, religious, literary, dramatic, philanthropic, and of all descriptions. I made some attempts, but ceased from their hopelessness. A public spirited individual, who is also a member of parliament, handed me a printed list containing the day and place of meeting of between fifty and sixty of those only with which he was connected. The Egyptian Hall, City of London Tavern, Crown and Anchor, or some other large building is chosen, and a round of dinners begins; this being most commonly the form of celebration. Persons who were together at the principal schools, as Eton and Harrow; and fellow graduates of the different colleges in the Universities, have also their annual dinners, to keep alive early friendships. Many of the associates come up to town from their homes at a distance in the country, on purpose to attend them.

The English are very remarkable for dinners. I do not allude to the kind last named, or those in private life; but to their habit of giving them in connexion with objects exclusively public. These, charitable ones among them, they constantly advance in this manner.

> 'The veins unfill'd, our blood is cold, and then
> We pout upon the morning, are unapt
> To give or to forgive; but when we have stuff'd
> These pipes and these conveyances of our blood
> With wine and feeding, we have suppler souls
> Than in our priest-like fasts.'

If the English meant to go by this doctrine of their great bard, they have done well, for their charities are stupendous. A newspaper can hardly be opened that does not hold up a long list of subscriptions, amounting to sums that are sometimes enormous. I have now reference to some for building churches and establishing schools, that within a few days have met my eye. So, in various parts of London, hospitals and other asylums for the distressed, arrest attention, bearing the inscription, 'FOUNDED BY VOLUNTARY CONTRIBUTION.' They would be less remarkable, were they not beheld in connexion with poor taxes to an amount such as no nation ever before paid. The buildings devoted to these charitable purposes, are often more spacious than the royal palaces, and show an exterior more imposing.

A grand annual dinner seems an indispensable adjunct to an English charity. Here is a 'Samaritan Society;' or an 'Infirmary for diseases of the Eye;' a society for the 'relief of decayed Artists;' another for relieving 'poor Authors;' a fifth for the 'indigent Blind;' a sixth for 'Foreigners in distress;' a seventh for the 'Deaf and Dumb;' a society for 'promoting Christian knowledge;' a 'Medical benevolent society,' and I know not how many more, for I merely take examples, all of which have their anniversary dinners. Whatever the demands upon the charitable fund, there seems always enough for a dinner fund. Eating and drinking are not the sole objects of this festivity. Business is transacted, reports on the state of the charity made, and speeches delivered, in the course of which the pocket is appealed to. Feeling rises as the inspiring glass passes, and the evening generally closes with an increase of the treasurer's store. Noblemen, including royal dukes, take part. They often preside at the dinners, and otherwise give their personal instrumentality, and freely their purses, towards the object of the societies. In France, before the Revolution, the noble families were computed at thirty thousand. In England, they may perhaps be computed at six or eight hundred. This hand-ful does more of the every-day business of the country, than the thirty thousand in France. In France, they did the work of chivalry; they fought in the army and navy. In England, besides this, you trace them not merely as patrons of the arts, but in road companies, canal companies, benevolent and public institutions of all kinds, to say nothing of their share in politics; in the latter, not simply as cabinet ministers, but speakers, committee-men, and hard-workers otherwise.

I have to-day been at a meeting of the British and Foreign Bible Society. Lord Teignmouth was in the chair. Lord Harrowby, President of the Council of cabinet ministers; Mr.

Vansittart, Chancellor of the Exchequer, the Bishops of Norwich and Gloucester, with several other bishops; Lords Gambier and Calthorpe, Mr. Wilberforce and others distinguished by character, title, or station, were present. A report was read, by which it appeared that the society had been the means of distributing two millions of bibles; had caused it to be translated into twenty-seven languages, and that since the last annual meeting, there had been collected in aid of the society's funds by private subscriptions in Britain, ninety-nine thousand pounds sterling. The report contained some complimentary allusions to Bible Societies in the United States. These passages were loudly cheered. Several speakers who addressed the meeting mentioned the United States in a similar spirit; amongst them, the Chancellor of the Exchequer, and Bishop of Gloucester. The former spoke of Great Britain and the United States, as the 'two greatest maritime nations of the world;' the Bishop of Gloucester called the latter 'a great and growing sister country.' I was requested, after entering the hall, to move a vote of thanks to the distinguished President, Lord Teignmouth. A resolution to this effect was put into my hands, which I moved accordingly. In fulfilling the duty, whilst joining in the tribute that all had rendered to the objects of the society, I was happy in the opportunity of responding as national courtesy demanded, to the notices taken of my country.

May 10. Dined at the Marquis of Lansdowne's. His name had been familiar to me with every prepossession. In the House of Lords I had already listened to his disciplined eloquence.

The company consisted of Lord and Lady Landsdowne, his Royal Highness the Duke of Gloucester, the Earl of Ilchester, the Earl of Rosslyn, Lord Holland, Lord Erskine, the Bishop of Sodor and Man, the Russian and Austrian ambassadors, the Vice-Chancellor, and the ladies of several of the guests.

In the dining-room were ancient statues. They were in ancient costumes, standing in niches. These time-honoured master-pieces of genius and art, had been obtained from Rome. As we walked in to dinner through a suite of apartments, the entire aspect was of classic beauty.

Conversation was various. The Floridas being mentioned in

connexion with the rumour of their intended transfer to the United States, Lord Erskine said, we ought to have them; that is, he added, 'if I belonged to the United States, I would maintain that doctrine.' There was the same vein about him as at the Duke of Cumberland's; a youthfulness of imagination that imparted its sprightliness to every thing.

The Duke of Gloucester spoke of General Washington. It was with the praise always annexed to his great name. He commended his farewell address. Lord Erskine called him an august and immortal man.

Architecture being a topic, Lord Holland said that it did not yet flourish in England. Italy, France, and other parts of the Continent, had better public edifices: specimens of domestic architecture were not wanting in England; but these were too often spoiled by putting the door in the middle; by this custom, good arrangement inside was sacrificed to external appearance, and he was not sure that a gain always followed in this respect; on the Continent, the entrance to the best private buildings, was generally at the side. The architecture of the ancients was spoken of, and other subjects touched as they arose.

After we came from table, I had more conversation with Lord Erskine. He spoke of the Emperor Alexander. He had seen La Harpe, his tutor, at Paris, who showed him letters from the Emperor, written soon after his accession to the throne. One of them ran thus: 'My dear friend: I feel the load of my responsibility; I feel how incompetent my youth and inexperience are, to wield the sceptre of such an empire; all that I can hope is, that I may be guided by the precepts you have taught me; I pray you, if ever you find me departing from them, to remind me of them. Do not wait for me to send for you; this I probably shall not do when I act in opposition to them; but write to me, *come to me*, to recall me from my errors.' All will agree, that such a letter was creditable to both pupil and preceptor. His lordship said that La Harpe told him the Emperor was fond of reading works on the institutions of the United States. Before separating, he said he intended to call on me soon, not by leaving a card, the common way, he believed, of visiting foreign ministers, but by coming in. I assured him he could in no way make me more happy.

May 19. Last evening we were at Carlton House. This seems the season for large routs by night, as the meeting of public societies by day. We have been to a number. I could give little description of them, unless to speak of their crowds, and the difficulty of getting to them and from them through phalanxes of carriages.

The entertainment last evening was different. The company found space in the ample rooms, although there was an array of all the principal persons of the court, a very full number of peers and peeresses, the foreign ambassadors and ministers, and many others. I caught conversation as I could. Lord Sidmouth, Home Secretary, assured me of the earnest desire of His Majesty's Government to strengthen the friendly relations between our two countries. He spoke of the United States with great cordiality. He inquired for Mr. King, saying that he had earned the lasting respect and good will of many persons in England. Nor did the Prince Regent conclude his salutations to me, without renewing his inquiries for him.

The scene was magnificent. The golden plate in display is said to be unrivalled in Europe. It includes some that belonged to Charles the First. One of the rooms led, through doors of reflecting glass, to a rich gothic conservatory, partially illuminated with coloured lamps. It was filled with flowers, than which there can be nothing more beautiful even in palaces. The effect was heightened by music from the Prince's band, which was stationed here, and played at intervals throughout the evening. It was not at an early hour that we got away from such a scene.

May 21. Dr. Pinckard, an eminent physician of Bloomsbury Square, entertained us at dinner. He was formerly attached to the British army, and on service in the West Indies. Thence he visited Philadelphia, where I made his acquaintance; listening, at my father's table, to his various and intelligent conversation.

We had a pleasant party. Of the guests, were Lieutenant-general Sir Charles Green. Advanced in life, he was still a fine-looking man, with little of age in his manner. He had been distinguished by his services in the wars of the French Revolution. I found that his military career took an earlier date. He was a captain in Burgoyne's army, had been captured at

Saratoga in 1778, with that army, and marched as a prisoner from Albany to Boston. He related anecdotes of the campaign, and of his march; it need scarcely be added, with urbanity and good humour.

I mention the incident, because although the first, it was not the only instance in which I met in England those who had shared in the war of the American Revolution, and who spoke of its events in the same spirit. Belonging to an age gone by, it seems no longer to be recalled in any other spirit than that of history.

CHAPTER XV

THE UNITED STATES AND IONIAN ISLANDS – AFFAIRS BETWEEN THE UNITED STATES AND SPAIN – MONUMENT TO BURNS – BRITISH INSTITUTION – PALL MALL – DINNER AT MR. CANNING'S – LORD ERSKINE

May 24, 1818. * * * * from the Ionian Islands called upon me. He had a communication to make of interest, as he said, to his country, and he hoped I would think it so to mine. By a treaty concluded at Paris in 1815, the seven Ionian Islands had been formed into an independent state, denominated 'The United States of the Ionian Islands,' and placed under the protection of Great Britain. It was a protection the Islands did not like. Did the constitution of my country prohibit our acquiring foreign possessions? I said, no. He asked if it would accord with our policy, to have a connexion with the seven Islands; such a measure, he believed, would be practicable, if the United States would consent. In short, he thought that the islands, particularly Corfu, Zante, and Cephalonia, would be willing to place themselves under the protection of the United States, if the terms could be arranged.

I asked what England would say, and Russia, and Europe generally? He replied, that he did not see what ground of objection there could be, if the Islands desired it; remarking that he had perceived by the newspapers that *my Government had protested against Great Britain exercising sovereignty over them any longer.*

I was little prepared for his communication. I cannot say that I was an entire stranger to the publication he alluded to, for I had seen it. I had considered it in the light of a burlesque upon a previous newspaper paragraph, stating that Great Britain had protested against the United States acquiring the Floridas. But what is penned in mirth, it seems, may pass for earnest. I assured * * * * that there was no foundation for the account. He appeared to have believed it fully, until this interview. He did not urge the less that my Government should take into consideration the expediency of assuming the protectorship of the Islands. He enlarged on the prospects of commercial advantage it would open to us by an intercourse with the Morea, Albania, Constantinople, and the Ottoman dominions generally. I replied, that it was no part of the system of the United States to get into European politics, and least of all, to interfere in the relationship between Great Britain and these Islands. This was the amount of the interview. He was attended by two other persons from the Islands.

As the English newspapers have lately abounded in vituperative articles against the United States in connexion with their affairs with Spain, without understanding them, or exhibiting only the Spanish side, I will here insert a letter I addressed to the President. It bears upon the foregoing interview. My regular weekly despatches, and oftener when necessary, were addressed to Mr. Secretary Adams. These went on the public files of the Department of State. I wrote to him, also on public matters, in a way not designed for those files, it being my good fortune to enjoy his confidence; and, not unfrequently, I wrote to the Presidend in the same manner. The communication in question was dated the 20th of this month. Its material parts are as follow:

'Since my last, no steps that were practicable have been omitted to ascertain from what source the letter, a copy of which I transmitted, proceeded; or how far the information which it disclosed, is to be relied upon. The writer states himself to be in connexion with a person high in station, but declines an interview. Since the tenth instant, he has addressed several letters to the Legation. I would send copies, but that all are to the same effect, and the one already sent, will be to you a sufficient sample of his style and manner. Keeping to points that are essential, I will condense the information they purport to convey, thus saving your valuable time.

'He continues to assert, that Great Britain has secretly determined to support Spain in a contest with the United States; that the cabinet of the former has resolved that our territory shall not be extended, and more than all that the Floridas shall not be added to it, as bringing us too near to Cuba. That Spain is to begin the contest, not by a formal declaration, but by letting loose her privateers; that she will take the step as soon as the armament now preparing at Cadiz to go against South America, shall have sailed, and that this is the opinion of the Spanish Ambassador at this court, founded on communications from Madrid. That the manifesto of Spain will soon appear, calling upon all other powers who have colonies to assist her in her struggle; that an officer high in the Spanish embassy, was sent off express to Paris on these objects last week, and that a Spanish secretary lately sailed from the Thames with definitive instructions to the Spanish minister at Washington, Mr. Onis, under the crisis that is approaching. That Spain is to have no quarrel with Portugal, such a measure not falling in with the views of England. That five of the daily newspapers of London have their columns open to the Spanish embassy, and that the Spanish Government is actively employed in buying up vessels to be fitted out and manned in England, to cruise under the Spanish flag against our trade. That Spain has her agents at work in several of the ports of equipment in this kingdom; also in France, Holland, and the Netherlands, expecting, under cover of her own flag, to enlist the privateering means of half Europe against the commerce of the United States whilst everywhere exposed, and that the vessels will be fitted out under pretence of acting against South America. That a person lately arrived here from Madrid, with full powers from the King to the Spanish Ambassador to act at his discretion in procuring the instruments and means of striking at our commerce; that the ambassador, who is represented as having large private resources, which he spends liberally in addition to his public allowances, has the unbounded confidence of his King, who will confirm that he does. Finally, that the ambassador has caused a pamphlet to be written against the United States, dilating upon their alleged injustice and rapacity towards Spain, which, by raising odium against them, is intended to aid the hostile views of Spain; and that many thousand copies of it are to be circulated in French, Spanish, and English, in quarters where it will be likely to be most effective.

'The question is, how far do the above allegations, or any of them, appear to be sustained by facts. The most material are, the asserted purchase and equipment of vessels in the ports of Great Britain. This, if true, cannot easily be hidden. As yet I have obtained no information that would authorize me in saying that it has been done. I have made, and will continue to make, every inquiry. Persons connected with the American trade are the proper sources to resort to. Their sagacity will be sure to make the first discoveries; nor will our vigilant consul, Colonel Aspinwall, be asleep.

'As to the newspapers being open to the Spanish embassy, this is not improbable. Most of the violent articles against the United States touching their affairs with Spain, that have lately appeared in the London papers, have proceeded, I have little doubt, from Spaniards, or pens they enlist. They bear marks of this origin. There was, I believe, an officer of the Spanish embassy despatched to Paris ten days or a fortnight ago. I have been able to procure no evidence of the nature of his errand, beyond the assertions of the letter-writer. Upon these alone, reiterated indeed with great confidence, rests for the present, the credit due to all his other communications. The pamphlet of which he speaks, has been written; at least in part. He sent to the Legation some of the printed sheets, which I enclose. It is said that the writer – an Englishman – has received, or is to receive, sixty guineas from the Spanish embassy. I should pronounce it more than the pamphlet is worth. The Spanish ambassador is the Duke of San Carlos. He formerly represented Spain at the court of Vienna, where his household was on a munificent scale; as here. We exchange visits, and reciprocate other civilities.

'In addition to the communications of the letter-writer, I have been waited upon by a member of the Congress of Venezuela, now in London. He regards a rupture between the United States and Spain as so near, that, on the ground of his acquaintance with the condition and resources of Spanish America, he came to tender me all his information in aid of our cause. I said the United States meditated no hostile steps. He replied, that Spain did. I suggested the objections, unless she expected co-operation from England; and that I could not think the latter meant to go to war with us without cause. He met the objections by saying that England had promised no co-operation; but that the condition of Spain was desperate:

she must lose her colonies if things continued on the present footing; the only hope of saving them, rested upon her being able to bring England by some means or other to her assistance. That she counted upon the jealousy between England and the United States on the ocean, and by going to war herself with the latter, the course of events would soon draw the former into it, whatever she might say at first. At any rate, that this was a game of chances Spain had resolved to play, as, at the worst, it could only accelerate a catastrophe otherwise inevitable, viz. the total loss of her dominion in America. This Venezuelan, although liable to be warped by his political wishes, is intelligent and cool-minded, and full of activity in seeking information. I therefore report what he said, although he referred to no specific facts. However plausible his way of reasoning, it is not sufficient with me to overcome weightier reasons opposed to it. Hence, that either Spain or England design to strike a hostile blow at us, I am not able at present to believe. Still I have not felt at liberty to be altogether passive under my own incredulity. I am taking steps of precaution from which, be the issue what it may, no evil can arise. I have written to our ministers at Paris and Madrid, and to the commander of our squadron in the Mediterranean. I have not expressed myself in a way to excite alarm, but watchfulness. I shall continue attentive to what passes, and should any new or more distinctive grounds be laid before me, adopt such other measures as prudence may dictate, hoping those already taken may have your approbation. It is proper I should add, that there has been no open departure whatever in the English cabinet or court from a frank or conciliatory course towards us. If any thing is going on, it is profoundly in the dark.'

The matter of the above letter points to occurrences which belong to the history of a public mission. Light is shed by them on incidents otherwise not so well understood. It was easy to believe that Spain desired a rupture between the United States and England, and that those in her service would labour in all ways to that end. But it was not to be believed, that she would go to war with the United States, on a mere speculation that the force of circumstances might draw England into it. The navy of the United States was efficient, and the certainty of its immediate co-operation with the Spanish colonies, for which their proximity afforded advantages, could not have failed to set before Spain the risks, on the ground alone, of seeking such a war. That England would rather the Floridas belonged to Spain, than the United States, was no more than natural to suppose. She remembered that the treaty of Utrecht had prohibited Spain from transferring any of her colonial possessions to other powers. But the Congress of Vienna had been silent on such a policy. England, a party to that congress, knew as well as other powers, that the day for its revival was at an end.

May 27. A few persons desiring to see a monument erected to Burns, put an off-hand notice in the Morning Chronicle, that the admirers of his genius would dine to-day at the City of London Tavern. About two hundred assembled. The stewards invited me as a guest. The Duke of York was in the chair.

The leading person was Mr. Boswell, son of the biographer of Johnson, and a member of parliament. He made a speech on the genius of Burns, and urged the propriety of erecting a monument on the site of the cottage where he was born. A son of the poet was present. On 'Success to the family of Burns' being given as a toast, he thanked the company in a modest, feeling manner. The punch-bowl that belonged to Burns, and of which it is known he was too fond, was handed round the table, as a relic. A full band was in the orchestra. We had a great deal of fine old Scotch music, with several of Burns's songs, and a good one written for the occasion by Mr. Boswell. The Duke of York was toasted, with a complimentary allusion to the share which, as commander-in-chief of the British army, he had taken in improving its condition. He returned thanks, adding that it was his highest pride to merit the approbation of his sovereign, and good-will of his fellow-subjects. 'The admirers of Burns in the United States' came next; on which I made my acknowledgments, saying that my countrymen were alive to the charms of his poetry, as he wrote for the heart, which was of all nations. The Duke asked if we made speeches at our public dinners, as they were forced to do in England. I said, not hitherto; but it was a custom which tended, I thought, to improve the character of public dinners, by introducing excitements beyond those merely jovial. He assented. We had other speeches – short ones. They would otherwise, all must agree, lose a chief merit for such occasions.

Several hundred pounds were collected towards the monument. Three or four of my countrymen, accidentally in London, were present, and marked their admiration of the genius of the bard by being contributors. It may serve as an instance to show how the pocket is opened at public dinners in London.

May 28. Visited the British Gallery in Pall Mall. The collection of paintings is very choice. It is made up exclusively of pieces from the Italian, French, Dutch, Spanish, and Flemish masters. They belong to persons in England, who annually send specimens from their private collections to this exhibition for the gratification of the public, and to aid in fostering taste in this branch of the arts. You wander through rooms where hang productions on which the public taste of different ages and nations had put the seal of approbation.

It has been said that painters can flourish only in Roman Catholic countries. That the Scriptures have afforded the grandest subjects for the pencil, is true. In Catholic countries, the Church influences largely secular feeling. This is a sufficient reason why their painters so frequently take subjects from Scripture. But they have not confined themselves to these; and are not the same subjects open to the pencil in Protestant countries? The very variety of religions, as of character, in England, will tend to advance her in the arts when she takes her stand in them. She has an established church with every species of dissent; a powerful aristocracy with popular forms and practices, that in some respects Athens never equalled; a King venerated and lampooned; more than all, an amount of riches, not hereditary merely, but self-acquired, in the hands of individuals in every part of the kingdom, making a greater number independent in their circumstances, and giving them consequently more command over time and inclination, than has probably ever before been known among the same number of people, existing as one nation. All these are materials for the arts. A school founded in such a soil, could neither be formal, nor limited. Mannerism belongs to feelings and pursuits more circumscribed. It would be a soil too for patronage; not by a few nobles or the hand of an amateur Prince; but diffused, as through rich republics, all over the land.

The annual exhibition of the works of the masters is not the only way in which this Institution aims at advancing the Fine Arts. Its governors and patrons purchase the productions of British artists, where merit is high. It was so that Mr. West's picture of 'Christ healing the Sick,' was purchased for three thousand guineas. This is the picture, the fellow to which was presented to the Hospital at Philadelphia. There needs no other proof of the interest the venerable artist felt in the land of his birth. It was a munificent donation. He contemplated with delight the growth of the arts in the United States. He had studied painting as carefully, and understood its rules with as just a discrimination as any artist living. He had opportunities of knowing that the study was pursued with both zeal and judgment in the country always dear to him. He had seen in her infancy every presage of future eminence; and to aid in stimulating tendencies so noble, was one of the motives to his generous gift.

June 5. We were at another brilliant entertainment at Carlton House on Tuesday evening. To-day I attended the levee. Lord Castlereagh said to me that his constant engagements in parliament had prevented his asking an interview with me during the past fortnight, as he had wished. Its dissolution was at hand, immediately after which he would fix a time for our meeting.

June 6. Dined at Mr. Canning's. His residence is at Gloucester-lodge, two miles from town. We had exchanged visits by cards. The latter periods of my mission, during which he was Secretary for foreign affairs, brought me into much intercourse with him, personal and official; but this was the first time I had met him except at levees and drawing-rooms. To the space he filled in public estimation, I could be no stranger. He received his guests cordially. The grounds about his house were not extensive, but shut in by trees. All was seclusion the moment the gates closed; a common beauty in villas near London. The drawing-rooms opened on a portico, from which you walked out upon one of those smoothly-shaven lawns which Johnson, speaking of Pope's poetry, likens to velvet. We had the soft twilight, which at this season lasts so long in England, and sets off verdure to such advantage. 'You see,' said Mr. Canning, 'how we prize your plants,' pointing to some Rhododendrons; 'you must be fond of horticulture in the United States, from the specimens we have of your flowers.' I said it was a growing taste with us, but that we had much to do before we should equal England. And we in England, he said, are behind Holland, and I believe France, in flowers. Dinner was soon announced. Mr. and Mrs Canning, the Marquis and Marchioness of Stafford, Lady Elizabeth Leveson Gower, the Spanish Ambassador and his Duchess, the Neapolitan minister and his Countess, my wife, Mr. Chinnery, and some members of the family, made the party. Mr. Canning sat at the head. His quick eye was all round the table; his aim to draw out others. Occasionally, he had touches of pleasantry. He asked for Mr. Pinkney of Maryland. 'I once,' said he, 'had a skirmish with him about language, but he worsted me; I said there was no such word as *influential*, except in America, but he convinced me that it was originally carried over from England.' Lord Stafford remarked, that it was so good a one, they ought to bring it back. 'Yes,' said Mr. Canning, 'it is a very good *word*, and I know no reason why it should have remained in America, but that we lost the *thing*.'

A library was attached to the suite of rooms. When we came from dinner, some of the company found pastime in turning over the leaves of caricatures, bound in large volumes. They went back to the French revolutionary period. Kings, princes, cabinet minister, members of parliament, everybody, figured in them. It was a kind of history of England in caricature for five-and-twenty years. Need I add, that our accomplished host was on many a page. He stood by. Now and then he threw in a word giving new point to the scenes. It is among the contradictions of the English, that, shy and sensitive as the higher classes in many respects are, perhaps beyond any other people, they are utterly indifferent to these kind of attacks. Their public men also, exclude politics from private life. You see persons of opposite parties, mingling together.

He asked, who were our favourite authors in the United States. The English, I said. But among the English? Johnson, Dryden, Addison, or Swift? Opinions varied, I said; Johnson had his admirers; but I thought that after five-and-twenty, our readers for the most part came round to the others. They were his favourites, he said. Next he asked, is not Junius* liked? Generally, I said. I had heard of a young gentleman in Philadelphia, who transcribed all his letters in the hope of catching his style. He made no comment; but I thought I saw that *he* would not recommend a young friend to that trouble. From the Spanish ambassador I had every civility, notwithstanding the *pamphlet*.

So, briefly, was my first dinner at Mr. Canning's. Many and agreeable ones followed. Sir James Macintosh said of him in debate, that he had incorporated in his mind all the elegance and wisdom of ancient literature. It was a high tribute from a political opponent and competent judge. Both were first-rate men, as well by native endowments, as the most careful cultivation; and both disciplined by an advantageous intermixture in great political and social scenes; Macintosh, universal and profound; Canning, making every thing bend to parliamentary supremacy; the one, delivering speeches in the House of Commons for the philosopher and statesman to reflect upon; the other winning, in that arena, daily victories. Both had equal power to charm in society; the one various and instructive; the other intuitive and brilliant. Let me add, that both were self-made men; enjoying, by this title, the highest political consideration and social esteem, in the most powerful hereditary and other circles of the British empire.

June 7. Lord Erskine called upon me according to promise. He touched on many topics. I pass by all to come to what he said of Burke (his long-time political opponent). My boys being in the room, he asked if I had found a good school for them. I said they were at present with Mr. Foothead, in my neighbourhood. 'You are lucky,' he said, 'if Burke's recommendation goes for anything, for he thought well of him as a teacher of the classics. What a prodigy Burke was!' he exclaimed. 'He came to see me not long before he died. I then lived on Hampstead hill. "Come, Erskine," said he, holding

* Anonymous political journalist (probably Sir Philip Francis) notorious for his attacks, from the Whig standpoint, on prominent public figures, including George III.

out his hand, "let us forget all; I shall soon quit this stage, and wish to die in peace with everybody, especially you." I reciprocated the sentiment, and we took a turn round the grounds. Suddenly, he stopped. An extensive prospect broke upon him. He stood, rapt in thought. Gazing in the sky, as the sun was setting, "Ah! Erskine," he said, pointing towards it, "you cannot spoil *that* because you cannot *reach* it; it would otherwise go; yes, the firmament itself – you and your reformers would tear it all down." I was pleased with his friendly familiarity, and we went into the house, where kind feelings between us were further improved. A short time afterwards he wrote that attack upon the Duke of Devonshire, Fox, and myself, which flew all over England, and perhaps the United States.' All this his lordship told in the best manner. In my form of repeating it, I cannot do him justice.

Desiring to hear something of Burke's delivery from so high a source, I asked him about it. 'It was execrable,' said he. 'I was in the House of Commons when he made his great speech on American conciliation, the greatest he ever made. He drove everybody away. I wanted to go out with the rest, but was near him and afraid to get up; so I squeezed myself down, and crawled under the benches like a dog, until I got to the door without his seeing me, rejoicing in my escape. Next day I went to the Isle of Wight. When the speech followed me there, I read it over and over again; I could hardly think of anything else; I carried it about me, thumbed it, until it got like wadding for my gun.' He said that he was in the House when Burke threw a dagger on the floor, in his speech on the French Revolution, and it '*had liked to have hit my foot*.' 'It was a sad failure,' he added, 'but Burke could bear it.'

He sat upwards of an hour, leaving me to regret his departure.

CHAPTER XVI

DISSOLUTION OF PARLIAMENT – REVENUE AND
RESOURCES OF ENGLAND – INTERVIEW WITH LORD
CASTLEREAGH – IMPRESSMENT – THE SLAVE-TRADE –
COMMERCIAL CONVENTION OF 1815 – DINNER AT
THE MARQUIS OF STAFFORD'S – FURTHER INTERVIEW
WITH LORD CASTLEREAGH ON IMPRESSMENT AND
THE SLAVE-TRADE – THE HUSTINGS AT CONVENT-
GARDEN – DINNER AT THE CHANCELLOR OF THE
EXCHEQUER'S

June 10. Parliament was dissolved by the Prince Regent in person. This is regarded as one of the most imposing public
ceremonies in England. It derives this character, in part, from
the manner in which the Sovereign goes to Parliament.

In all ages, the horse has helped to swell the pomp of public
processions. Dryden renders Virgil's 'bellator equus,' led in
the train of Pallas's funeral, '*The steed of State*.' On this occasion
the carriage of the Prince Regent was drawn by eight horses
used only for this ceremony. They were of beautiful form, and
richly caparisoned;

'With golden bits adorn'd, and purple reins.'

There sat with the Prince, the Duke of Montrose, Master of the
Horse, and Lord Amherst, as Lord in Waiting. Even in the
insignia of a state carriage England does not forget the field of
her power. Conspicuously upon this, was a figure of Neptune,
in massive gilding. Next in the procession came four carriages
and six, all in rich decorations. These made the royal train. It
moved from St. James's palace through the Park. Thence it
came out, under the arch-way of the Horse Guards. My carriage got to that point, and stopped with others, as the whole
slowly turned into the street. The sight was gorgeous. Windows, balconies, house-tops, were lined. It was the spot,
where like crowds had witnessed the execution of Charles the

First. When the train reached the end of Parliament Street, the number of equipages in the direction of Westminster Abbey was immense. All were in rows, and glittered in the sun. The universal beauty of the horses, for which the English are so celebrated, the completeness of every equipage, the turrets of the ancient Abbey, the vast multitude, presented a scene of great animation and brilliancy. The state carriage drew up before the entrance to the House of Lords. A groom held each bridle, the horses champing the 'foaming gold.' The Prince Regent on alighting, was greeted with long shouts.

The ceremony of the dissolution took place in the House of Lords. Close in front of the throne a space was set apart for the Foreign Ambassadors and Ministers. All attended in their national costumes. The chamber, when I arrived, was filled with Peers and Peeresses, the former wearing robes of scarlet and ermine. In a little while the Prince Regent entered. A salute of cannon was at that moment heard. A procession formed by a portion of his cabinet ministers, preceded him, the Premier, Lord Liverpool, going first, and carrying the sword of state. The Prince took his seat upon the throne. In a few minutes, doors opened at the extremity of the chamber, and the Commons entered, the Speaker at their head. They stopped at a barrier, from which the Speaker commenced his address to the Throne. It recapitulated the important business of the Session, gave a prominent place to the subject of income and expenditure, saying that, although a heavy pressure continued upon the finances, the revenue was increasing, and concluded with praying the royal assent to a bill of Supply which the House brought up, the last of a series that had been passed. The title of the bill was read, on which a Clerk of Parliament exclaimed, '*Le Roi remercie ses loyal subjects, accepte leur benevolence, et aussi le veut.*' The titles of other bills were successively read, and the royal assent given by the same officer pronouncing the words, '*Le Roi le veut.*'

The Prince, who had not yet spoken, now addressed both Houses. He said that there had been no alteration in the state of the King's health; that he continued to receive from Foreign Powers assurances of friendly dispositions, on which he turned with a manner appropriate towards the diplomatic corps; he thanked the House of Commons for the supplies

they had granted; he informed both Houses of his intention to
dissolve the present and call a new Parliament, in making which
communication he could not, he said, refrain from adverting
to the great changes that had occurred since he first met them
in that chamber. Then, the dominion of Bonaparte, whom he
spoke of as the 'common enemy,' had been so widely extended,
that longer resistance to his power was by many deemed hopeless; but that by the unexampled exertions of Britain in co-
operation with other countries, Europe had been delivered
from his oppression, and a contest the most eventful and
sanguinary known for centuries, terminated with unparalleled
success and glory. These were the main points of the speech.
When it was ended, the Lord Chancellor rose from the
woolsack and said, that it was the will and pleasure of the
Prince Regent acting in the name of the King, that the Parliament be dissolved; and he pronounced it to be dissolved
accordingly.

The Prince remained seated whilst delivering his speech,
and wore a hat. The Peers and Commons stood, and were
uncovered. Mr. Canning in a speech to his constituents described the British constitution as a monarchy, intended to be
checked by two assemblies, one hereditary, independent alike
of crown and people; the other elective, springing from the
people; but, said he, there are those who argue as if it were
originally a democracy, merely inlaid with a peerage, and
topped with a crown. This gives, in a word, the opposite
theories of antiquarians on the origin of the British constitution. The passing remark may be made, that its external
ceremonies point to a regal, rather than popular root. They
are strikingly so at a coronation, as at the dissolution of Parliament. Take another incident at the latter, in addition to the
wearing of the hat. The Clerk, before reading the title to each
bill, made a reverence to the Throne; and another, on laying
the bill down upon the table. On receiving the nod of royal
assent, he turned towards the Commons, gave them a look,
and barely said, without any reverence, *Le Roi le veut.*

The scene would have been more imposing had the chamber been better. It is not merely deficient in architectural
form, but in space. The Commons stood in a confused heap,
pressing one upon another. Their own room below, is even

inferior in appearance, and alike inconveniently small. Both may have answered their original uses centuries ago; one as a banqueting-room, the other as a chapel to a palace; but are unsuited to the accommodation of Parliament. The mode of giving the royal assent to bills, I had read in books; yet it sounded strangely to me as a fact. It has been remarked by a great English writer, that these old words serve as a memento that the liberties of England were once destroyed by foreign force, and may be again but for vigilance. The remark is a strained one in this connexion. England balanced the account of warlike exploits with France, in the days of her Edwards and Henrys. Her own sovereign at last gave up his titular claim to be King of France. Hence it would seem that this little badge of the Norman conquest might now be allowed to drop off. It was discontinued under the Protectorate of Cromwell, the form in his time being 'The lord Protector doth consent.' When the Commonwealth ended, the foreign jargon revived.

The Speaker in his address stated that the revenue was increasing. I cannot pass this subject by. The income for the year was fifty-one millions of pounds sterling. The largest item was from the Excise, which yielded upwards of twenty-one millions. The Customs stood next. They gave upwards of eleven millions. The Assessed and Lane taxes third, from which eight millions were obtained. The Stamps fourth, which produced seven millions. The remainder was from the Post-office, and miscellaneous sources. Large as this sum may appear for the produce of one year's taxes, it is less by more than twenty millions than was raised two years ago, the Property-tax and certain war duties being then in force. It may safely be affirmed that no nation, antient or modern, of the same population, has ever before paid so much under the regular operation of tax-laws. Besides the fifty-one millions, which made up the national taxes proper for Great Britain and Ireland, the sums levied on account of Poor-rates for England during the year, have amounted to nine millions.

The exports from the kingdom for the same time, amounted, in value, to fifty-three millions of pounds sterling. The manufactures of the United Kingdom constituted four-fifths of this sum. The imports amounted to thirty-four millions;

considerably less, therefore, than the value of manufactured articles exported.

Expenditure for the year has been about the same as income. In its great branches, it may be classed thus: For interest on the public debt, twenty-nine millions. For the Army, nine millions; the military force on the present peace establishment, amounting to about a hundred thousand men. For the Navy, seven millions; the peace establishment of that arm being one hundred and thirty ships, twenty thousand seamen, and six thousand marines. For the Ordnance, one million. The Civil list, and miscellaneous items absorb the residue. In statements whether of British income or expenditure, I observe that fractions of a million or two seem to be unconsidered. They are scarcely understood but by those who will be at the pains of tracing them amidst the rubbish of accounts, and not always then.

As to the debt, what shall I say? To find out precisely what it is, seems to baffle inquiry. Dr. Hamilton in his work on this subject states a curious fact. He says, that in an account of the public debt presented to the House of Commons in 1799, it was found impossible to ascertain the sums raised at different periods which created the funds existing prior to the thirty-third year of George the Third. This candid avowal of ignorance, where all official means of information were at command, may well excuse a private inquirer if his statements be imperfect. But I will set the debt down at EIGHT HUNDRED MILLIONS. This as an absolute sum, strikes the world at enormous. It loses this character when viewed in connexion with the resources of Great Britain, the latter having increased in a ratio greater than her debt; a position susceptible of demonstration, though I do not here design to enter upon it. It may be proof enough, that in the face of this debt, her Government could, at any moment, borrow from British capitalists fresh sums larger than were ever borrowed before; and than could be raised by the united exertions of all the Governments of Europe. Credit so unbounded, can rest only upon the known extent and solidity of her resources; upon her agricultural, manufacturing, and commercial riches; the first coming from her highly cultivated soil and its exhaustless mines, not of gold and silver, but iron and coal, for ever profitably worked; the second, from the various and universal labour bestowed on raw materials, which brings into play all the industry of her people, suffering none to be lost for want of objects; the third, from a system of navigation and trade, followed up for ages, which enables her to send to every part of the globe the products of this vast and diversified industry, after supplying all her own wants. This system of navigation and trade is greatly sustained by a colonial empire of gigantic size, that perpetually increases the demand for her manufactures, and favours the monopoly of her tonnage.

These are the visible foundations of her incalculable riches; consequently of her credit. Both seem incessantly augmenting. It is remarkable that she extends them in the midst of wars. What cripples the resources of other nations, multiplies her's. Not long ago I went to Guildhall, to witness the sittings of the King's Bench, after term-time. The court-room was so full, that I could hear or see little, and soon left it. I was compensated by loitering among the monuments in the hall close by. The inscription on Lord Chatham's drew my attention most, because Americans always hang with reverence on his name, and because of the inscription itself. It dwells upon the services he rendered his country, BY 'UNITING COMMERCE WITH, AND MAKING IT FLOURISH DURING, WAR.' Such was his title to fame, recorded on the marble. Other nations should look at it. War, by creating new markets, gives a stimulus to industry, calls out capital, and may increase the positive wealth of the country carrying it on, *where the country is powerful and not the seat of war.* Moscow may be burned; Vienna, Berlin, Paris sacked; but it is always, said Franklin, peace in London. The British moralist may be slow to think, that it is during war the riches and power of Britain are most advanced; but it is the law of her insular situation and maritime ascendency. The Prince Regent pronounced the contest with Bonaparte the most eventful and sanguinary known for centuries. Yet, at its termination, the Speaker of the House of Commons declared, whilst the representatives of nations stood listening, that the revenues of Britain were increasing. What a fact!

It was also in 1815, at the close of the same contest, that the world beheld her naval power more than doubled; whilst that of other states of Europe was, in a proportion still greater, diminished. Hitherto, at the commencement of wars, the fleets of France, of Spain, of Holland, if not a match for those of England, could make a show of resistance. Their concerted movements were able to hold her in temporary check. Where are the navies of those powers now? or those of the Baltic? France is anxious to revive her navy. She builds good ships; has brave and scientific officers. So, Russia. But where are the essential sources of naval power in either? where their sailors trained in a great mercantile marine? Both together have not as many, of this description, as the United States. England, then, in her next war, as against Europe, will start, instead of ending with her supremacy completely established. I will not speak of a new agent in navigation, 'that walks,' as Mr. Canning said, 'like a giant on the water, controlling winds and waves – steam.' This great gift to mankind, in its first efficient power upon the ocean, was from the United States; but all Europe will feel its effects in the hands of Britain. . . .

June 11. Had an interview with Lord Castlereagh, on his invitation. He informed me, that he had brought before the cabinet my proposal on impressment, and that it had been considered with the care due to its importance.

He went into some of the arguments to which the subject always leads. . . . His lordship was forced, he said, to add, that on a full consideration of my proposal, the cabinet had not found it practicable to forego under any arrangement, the right of Great Britain to look for her subjects upon the high seas, into whatever service they might wander.

The proposal thus rejected, I asked his lordship what difference it would make if the United States would agree to exclude from their ships of war and merchant-vessels, *all natural born subjects of Great Britain?*

He replied, that this indeed would be going a step further, but that it would still leave the proposal within the principle of their objection.

I said, that I heard this determination with regret. I had been ready, otherwise, to submit a proposal to the effect last mentioned. My regret was the stronger, as it would exhaust all the offers the United States could make. I requested him, in fact, to consider such an offer as actually made, under full authority from my Government.

I now inquired if any proposals would be submitted on the part of Great Britain. His lordship was prepared with none which did not assume, as a basis, the right of entering our vessels. For the exercise of this right in a manner not to injure the United States, Great Britain was willing, he said, to come into the most effective regulations; such as restricting the boarding officers to those of rank not below lieutenants; giving responsible receipts for the men taken out, or any other safeguards that the Government of the United States might propose as better adapted to the end; that she would receive, and in the most friendly manner discuss such proposals, in the hope of some satisfactory arrangement. I said that the United States never could admit the right to enter their vessels for such a purpose. Besides the objection to it in principle, the practice must be liable to perpetual and fatal abuse. This had been shown by past experience, and it was impossible to remain blind to it. His lordship again admitted these evils, expressing his hope that they might never recur.

He next spoke of the Slave-trade. Great Britain, he said, had concluded treaties with three of the powers of Europe on this subject, Portugal, Spain, and the Netherlands. To Spain and Portugal Britain had paid, from first to last, 700,000*l.* as inducements to the treaties, the money to be as compensation to Spanish and Portuguese subjects, for the loss of the trade. The Netherlands had agreed to abolish, immediately and totally, without pecuniary inducement. . . . The period had arrived, his lordship continued, when it was the wish of Great Britain to invite the United States to join in these measures, and it was his design to submit, through me, proposals to that effect. It had occurred to him to send me, with an official note, authentic copies of the treaties themselves; they would best unfold in all their details, the grounds on which a concert of action had been settled with other powers, and it was on similar grounds he meant to ask the accession of the United States, anticipating large benefits from their maritime co-operation in this great work of humanity.

I replied, that I was altogether devoid of instructions on the subject, but would transmit the treaties for the consideration of the President. The United States, from an early day, had regarded this traffick with uniform disapprobation. For many years it had been altogether prohibited by their statutes. The existence of slavery in several of the states of the American Union, had nothing to do, I remarked, with the slave-trade. The former grew up with the policy of the parent country anterior to the independence of the United States, and remained incorporated with the domestic laws of the particular states where it had been so introduced, and always existed. Yet, those who could not allow their laws in this respect to be touched, went hand and heart with the rest of their fellow-citizens in desiring the abolition of the slave-trade.

June 12. Dined at the Marquis of Stafford's. I am no votary of the *rout*. The private dinner-party shows society differently. The diplomatic stranger can hardly command other opportunities of seeing it at all. Evening visits he cannot make; the late hour of dining is an obstacle. Morning calls are a mere ceremony performed by his card. Midnight crowds are not society. It is only at dinners that he finds it.

These seem the chosen scenes of English hospitality. They are seldom large. Mr. Jefferson's rule was, not fewer than the Graces, nor more than the Muses. At the London dinners, from twelve to sixteen seem a favourite number. Sometimes they are smaller. Individual character and accomplishments, reserved at first in these classes, here begin to open. All obey forms, with which all are familiar. Conversation moves along under common contributions and restraints. There is no ambition of victory. To give pleasure, not try strength, is the aim. You remark nothing so much as a certain simplicity, the last attainment of high education and practised intercourse. Such are some of the characteristics of these private dinners. Beginning with such, I must proceed a little farther. The servants are so trained, as to leave to the master and mistress no care but of looking to the guests. The arrangements of the table are orderly and beautiful. The services of silver strike me as among the evidences of a boundless opulence. Foreigners from whatever part of Europe, are in like manner struck with this profusion of solid and sumptuous plate upon English tables, as unknown in any other capital to an extent at all approaching to comparison. The possessors, long accustomed to it, seem unconscious of its presence; but the foreigner sees in it all, national and individual riches. Whence proceed, he asks himself, the incomes, so large, so increasing, that retain, and acquire in fresh accumulation, luxuries so costly, but from the land? and what would be the land with all the works upon it, what the crops on its surface, the mines underneath, but for the manufactures and trade which bring all into value by a vast and ever increasing demand; increasing at home as abroad, increasing in war as in peace?

Our dinner to-day illustrated, as one instance might, the characteristics alluded to. It was not large. Lord and Lady Stafford, the Earl and Countess of Surrey, Lady Elizabeth Leveson Gower, Lord Francis Gower, and a few more, made the party. The country life in England was much spoken of; also the literary publications of the day, this family being distinguished by the literary accomplishments of its members. The paintings of the masters were all around us. Our hospitable entertainers invited Mrs Rush and myself to visit them at their seat, Trentham, in Staffordshire, than which we could not have known a higher gratification. Another topic, always grateful, was not passed by; our country. Cordial things were said of it, and enlightened wishes expressed that two nations so connected as England and the United States, might long see their way to mutual good-will. Leaving the table, we were an hour in the drawing-rooms, always an agreeable close to English dinners. Ladies make part of them, and rise first, the gentlemen soon following and rising all together. We had music from St. James's Park, into which the windows of Stafford-house look. Its notes were the softer from the stillness of that scene, and the breezes of a charming summer night.

June 20. Had an interview with Lord Castlereagh. He read the first draft of a note to me, inviting the United States to co-operate in putting down the Slave-trade, asking my suggestions as to any modifications. I had none to offer. It was accordingly sent as prepared. I drew up an answer, promising to refer the whole subject to my government.

I renewed the topic of impressment. Although in our conference of the 11th I had made known the willingness of the

United States to exclude from their naval and merchant service all British seamen, native as well as naturalized, I did not
think proper to let the proposition rest on the footing of a verbal offer. I reduced it to writing . . . and handed the paper to
his lordship. The proposal had, as I knew, been rejected; but I
knew the President's desire to settle this great question, and
believed that I should be more truly the organ of his will, by
putting the proposal in a shape in which it might go upon the
archives of his Majesty's Government. I even cherished the
hope, that other views might yet be taken of it. . . . Nothing
farther passed at this interview.

The general election for a new House of Commons being in
progress, and the hustings at Covent Garden open, I said,
when about to come away, that I intended to go there to see
what was doing. 'If you can wait a few minutes,' said his
lordship, 'I will go with you; I want to vote.' I replied that I
should be happy to go under such auspices. 'You might have
better,' he remarked.' At that moment Sir William Scott* was
announced, and I took my leave, finding my own way to the
hustings. They gave a repulsive picture of an English election.
Sir Murray Maxwell was the ministerial candidate; Sir Francis
Burdett, Sir Samuel Romilly, and Mr. Hunt, on the other side.
The first was not only hissed and hooted by the populace, but
on a former day had been wounded by missiles. He appeared
with his arm tied up, and a bandage over his eye. I was glad to
get away from the scene of tumult. In a little while Lord
Castlereagh came. His remark was prophetic; he was mobbed.
Having given his vote for Sir Murray Maxwell, he was
recognized, and four or five hundred of the populace under
the opposite banners, pursued him. He took refuge in a shop
in Leicester Square, whence he was obliged to escape by a
back-way, until finally he found shelter in the Admiralty. If the
ministerial candidate and his supporters were thus roughly
treated, they bore it with good-humour. The former on re-
appearing after his wounds, again mounted the hustings to
make a speech. Being told that pains would be taken to discover and punish the authors of the outrage, he forbad all
inquiry, saying he had no doubt they acted thoughtlessly

---

* Celebrated Judge of the English Court of Admiralty.

without any intention of hurting him; a stroke of policy that brought fresh votes. As to Lord Castlereagh, I was informed that, on reaching the Admiralty, he turned round and with much complaisance thanked his pursuers, then close upon him, for their escort, saying that he would not trouble them to accompany him farther; which drew huzzas in his favour.

July 1. Dined at the Chancellor of the Exchequer's. His residence is in Downing Street, I may add, historical. His dining-room was once Mr. Pitt's. Here he lived while Prime Minister; still earlier, Sir Robert Walpole. A portrait of the latter, was on the wall. There were at table Mr. and Miss Vansittart, Mr. and Mrs East, Lord Harrowby, the Ambassador from the Netherlands, the Prussian Ambassador, Mr. Arbuthnot, Secretary of the Treasury, and Mr. MacKensie.

Mr. Pitt was spoken of. Lord Harrowby said that he was a fine Greek scholar; also that he had retained with singular accuracy his mathematics acquired at school. Lord Harrowby himself has high reputation in modern languages as well as the classics, both being at his command in great purity. He spoke of words that had obtained a sanction in the United States, in the condemnation of which he could not join; for example, *lengthy*, which imported what was tedious as well as long, an idea that no other English word seemed to convey as well. I remarked, that we were unfortunate in my country, for that if persons, no matter how illiterate, used wrong words, they were brought to light as *Americanisms*, whereas in other countries such things were passed by as merely vulgarisms; thanking his lordship however for throwing his shield over *lengthy*, which I also thought a very expressive word.

Mr. Vansittart had been reading some of the official documents of our Government. He said that our appropriations for the military service for the year exceeded those of Great Britain, in proportion to the size of the armies; remarking that the British army was the most expensive in Europe. The Dutch was next, he said; the Russian cheapest. The last cost but a seventh part as much, man for man, as the British. I said that the expense of an army in the United States arose from the ease with which subsistence was otherwise obtainable; moreover, that the service was not popular in peace. He assigned a further reason – our large proportion of artillery;

we had three thousand to an army of ten thousand; whilst the British artillery, to an army of an hundred thousand, amounted to not more than seven thousand. This I explained by saying, that one of the chief uses of a small standing army in the United States was to keep fortifications in order, adding, that we also made large expenditures upon them, under our military appropriations.

July 15. Went to an entertainment at Carlton-house. It was in honour of the marriages of the Duke of Clarence, and Duke of Kent, who, with their royal brides, were present. These marriages, with those of the Princess Elizabeth and Duke of Cambridge, all within a few months, have led to a succession of entertainments in which the diplomatic corps have participated.

CHAPTER XVII

INTERVIEW WITH LORD CASTLEREAGH – GENERAL
NEGOTIATION PROPOSED – COMMERCIAL
CONVENTION OF 1815 – EUROPEAN MEDIATION
BETWEEN SPAIN AND HER COLONIES – DINNER AT
MR. VILLIERS'S – THE QUARTERLY REVIEW – INTERVIEW
WITH LORD CASTLEREAGH – PROPOSAL FOR A GENERAL
NEGOTIATION ACCEPTED – MR. GALLATIN TO JOIN
IN IT – MR. ROBINSON AND MR. GOULBURN, THE
BRITISH NEGOTIATORS – COMMERCIAL CONVENTION
OF 1815 – DINNER AT SIR JOHN SINCLAIR'S – AT MR.
BENTHAM'S – AT THE FRENCH AMBASSADOR'S –
INTERVIEW WITH LORD CASTLEREAGH – COURSE OF
GREAT BRITAIN AND THE UNITED STATES AS BETWEEN
SPAIN AND HER COLONIES – AFFAIR OF PENSACOLA

July 16. Lord Castlereagh returned from Ireland on the 14th.
To-day I had an interview with him, on my application.

I entered upon the subject of the commercial relations between the two countries. I remarked, that it was with reluctance the President had given his consent to the act of
Congress to exclude from ports of the United States, British
vessels coming from the West Indies or other British colonies,
from whose ports vessels of the United States were excluded.
The act indeed was founded on equal justice, and could lay no
ground of complaint. Still, the President could not but know,
that its practical operation might be irritating to individual
interests affected in both countries, it was therefore that I was
once more instructed to propose to His Majesty's Government the negotiation of a general treaty of commerce. The
President desired also, that the negotiation should include
other matters. I recapitulated the four following. 1. The question respecting slaves carried off from the United States, in

contravention as we alleged of the treaty of Ghent. 2. The question of title to Columbia River. 3. That of the north-western boundary line, from the Lake of the Woods. 4. The question, of such immediate importance, relating to the fisheries.

... His Lordship asked what was to be understood by a general treaty of commerce. I replied, a treaty that would open not a temporary or precarious, but permanent intercourse with the British West Indies and their colonies in North America to the shipping of the United States; a subject which I admitted it might seem unnecessary to bring forward after the recently expressed opinions of his Majesty's Government, were it not that others of interest to both nations were now coupled with it in a way to give the proposition in some measure a new character.

He said that the British Government would be willing to enter upon a negotiation on the commercial relations of the two countries; but he had no authority to say that the colonial system would be essentially altered. Broken down, it could not be. Nevertheless, he was not prepared to answer definitively upon any of the subjects, but would lay them before the cabinet. He professed it to be the earnest desire of the British Government to see the commercial intercourse between the two countries placed upon the best footing at all points; the stake to each being alike important.

I next passed to South American affairs. I said that my Government was desirous of ascertaining the intentions of the European Alliance in regard to the contest in that hemisphere, and especially of learning those of Great Britain.

His lordship made the following replies. He said that the British Government was not only willing, but desired, to communicate to the United States, every thing in relation to the question; but that, in fact, no plan had been matured. Difficulties had arisen with Spain, on points the most essential; they were increased by obstacles to a quick intercourse of counsels among parties so remote from each other, as London, St. Petersburgh, Vienna, and Madrid. The Allied sovereigns when assembled at Aix la Chapelle in the autumn as planned, would probably take up the subject, although meeting primarily for the consideration of others; and as soon as a basis of pacification had been laid down, he would not fail to apprise me of it.

Before parting, he gave me the following piece of information: that in consequence of the depredations committed by cruisers ostensibly sailing under commissions from the Spanish colonies, the British Government had issued instructions to some of its armed vessels to arrest and bring in cruisers of this description, for the purpose of putting a stop to the vexations and losses they inflicted upon British commerce.

July 20. Dined at Mr. Villiers's, North Audley Street; to whom I owe obligation for kindness on many occasions; and not less for his invariable expressions of good-will towards my country. Field-marshal Lord Beresford, Lord Fitzroy Somerset and Lady Fitzroy, the Duchess of Wellington, Mrs Pole, Lord Maynard, Mr. Ponsonby, Mrs Villiers, and my wife, were the party. Conversation turned chiefly on France. It was in the spirit of commendation I remark to be so usual.

After dinner, Lord Beresford in conversation with me, spoke of the United States. He was under the impression that the Union would not last. Our Government, he said, had worked extremely well, so far; but must give way, he thought, when the country grew to be highly populous as well as powerful. I inculcated other doctrine, mentioning, as among our safe-guards, the federative and national principle interwoven in our constitution, and referring to shocks the Union had already withstood in peace and in war. He complimented our navy; it had taken England by surprise, high praise, had it earned no other, he said; but, from its nature, not likely to happen again. I expressed the hope that all such occasions might be far off; in which he cordially joined.

July 21. Mr * * * called upon me. He said that there would appear in the next Quarterly Review, an article on the life and character of Benjamin Franklin. It was to be the medium of an attack upon the United States. It would disparage the people, and underrate the resources of the nation. It would particularly examine the claims of the United States as a naval power, and strip them of importance. It would state their tonnage at less than nine hundred thousand, and as decreasing. The object of the publication was to lower the reputation of

the United States in Europe. To this end, it would be translated into French, republished in Paris, and thence widely circulated. Finally, that the article was already known to persons
who stood high in England, and countenanced by them.

The last part of what my informant communicated, may, or
may not, be true. The whole is of small concern. Cromwell
said, that a *government* was weak that could not stand paper
shot. Who then shall write down a *nation?* If the United States
have long been exposed to these assaults, so has England.
They come upon her from abroad, but more at home. Any-
body who will spend six months in London and look at only a
portion of the publications daily thrown from the press, will
be surprised at the number of denunciations he will surely
find of England. The crimes and other enormities committed
by her people; the profligacy of the lower orders, the vices of
the higher; the corruptions of the Government, its partiality,
injustice, tyranny; the abuses of law; the abuses in the Church;
the appalling debt, the grinding taxation, the starving poor,
the pampered rich – these and like topics, on which are based
assertions of wide-spread depravity and suffering unparalleled, are urged in every form, and run out into all details.
Sometimes France is fiercely attacked, sometimes Russia,
sometimes the United States; but England always. The
battering-ram against her never stops. What English writers
thus say of their own country, and the picture is commonly
summed up with predictions of national ruin, crosses the
Channel next day, is translated into French, and, as foretold of
the forthcoming article in the Quarterly Review, circulated
over Europe. In a month it has crossed the Atlantic, and is cir-
culating in America. Millions read, millions believe it. In the
midst of it all, England goes on in prosperity and power.
Europe and the world see both, in proofs irresistible. The
enlightened portions of the world perceive, also, alongside of
the picture of moral deformity, no matter how much may be
true, or how much over-coloured, counteracting fields of
excellence, public and private, that exalt the English nation to
a high pitch of sober renown.

It is in this manner I content myself as a citizen of the
United States. The last forty years have witnessed their steady
advance, in prosperity and power. . . . They will continue to

widen, until Britain herself, encompassed as she is with glory, will in time count it her chiefest, to have been the original stock of such a people. Of the frame of our Government, so often denounced and little understood, a British Statesman, wanting neither in sagacity nor knowledge of history – Mr. Fox – remarks, that it was precisely that constitution which the wisest men of the world would give to the people of the present age, supposing that they had to begin on a clear foundation, and not to destroy any thing existing at the cost of anarchy and civil war. Concluding, in the additional words of Mr. Fox, that it is the 'British Constitution with the improvements of the experience of ten centuries.'

July 23. A note from Lord Castlereagh requested I would meet him at the Foreign Office to-day. I found Mr. Robinson with him. The latter is President of the Board of Trade, and recently been called to a seat in the cabinet.

His lordship informed me that he had made known my proposals to the cabinet, and that a general negotiation would be agreed to, on all the points I had stated. With regard to the commercial question, the British Government did not pledge itself to a departure from the colonial system in any degree greater than hitherto, but would bring the whole subject under review; willing to hope, though abstaining from promises, that some modification of the system, mutually beneficial, might be the result of frank discussions.

I replied, that my Government would hear this determination with great satisfaction, and joined in the hope that the new effort might be productive of advantage to both countries.

I now informed his lordship, that Mr. Gallatin, minister of the United States at Paris, would take part in the negotiation, and come to London as soon as it might suit the convenience of his Majesty's Government to appoint plenipotentiaries on the side of the Great Britain.

He replied, the sooner the better, saying that Mr. Robinson and Mr. Goulburn would be appointed. He added that he himself would be obliged to set out for the Continent, in August, to attend the congress at Aix-la-Chapelle, and that the negotiation would have to proceed in his absence; but expressed a wish that it might open before he left town.

In the early part of the present month, by information transmitted to me, more of our vessels were in the port of Liverpool, than those of any foreign power, or even English vessels, coasters excepted. The latter fact surprised me. It may be taken as an indication that in the trade between the two countries, the United States are likely to have their equal share as carriers, as long as the charges upon the vessels of each continue equal. This is all that the United States ask. It is the offer they make to all nations. They hold it out in a permanent statute, as the basis of their code of navigation.

July 24. Dined yesterday at Sir John Sinclair's, Ormly Lodge, in the neighbourhood of Richmond. He had invited us to spend the day for the sake of an excursion upon the Thames. Hampton Court, Pope's Villa at Twickenham, Strawberry Hill, with other places to call up historical or classic recollections, would have been within our range; but we were, for this occasion, disappointed. My interview with Lord Castlereagh had been fixed for an hour that prevented our leaving town in season, so that the pleasure of dining and passing the evening at Ormly Lodge, was all we could command.

It was the first time I had been so far into the country, since our arrival. Gardens, hedgerows, village churches, houses and walls with ivy growing about them, met the eye in all directions. Here, were evergreens cut into shapes as in Queen Anne's time; there, the modern villa, where art was exerted to avoid all appearances of it; so that, even in this short distance, the taste of different ages might be seen. Looking on the whole, I could not avoid the thought, that the lawns so neat and fields so fertile, were the soil that the plough had gone through when the Romans were here. The more did this thought come over me, as in the United States we have what we call '*old fields*,' worn out by too much use, as we think, and abandoned on that account. They are abandoned, I must remark, for new ones, more fertile; but when these in turn become '*old fields*,' it seems we need be in no despair of making the former '*old fields*' fertile again, any more than the latter! We drove through Richmond Park, which completed the beauty of the scene.

Arrived at Ormly Lodge, we were courteously received at the door, and soon went to dinner. Sir John and Lady Sinclair with several members of their family, Mr. and Mrs Basil Cochrane, of Portman Square, Sir Benjamin and Lady Hobhouse, with a few others, made the party. Sentiments the most liberal were expressed towards the United States. Sir Benjamin Hobhouse, President of the Agricultural Society at Bath, spoke of the agriculture of the United States. It had long been his desire, he said, that the agriculturists of the two countries should correspond, exchanging observations, and the results of their experiments. I said that those of my country could scarcely object, seeing how much they would be likely to gain. He replied, that agriculturists in England would gain too, and spoke of the advantage he had himself derived from a correspondence with Mr. Peters, of Belmont, President of the Agricultural Society at Philadelphia; to whose knowledge he bore testimony, and his happy manner of imparting it. He spoke of Mr. Coke's farm at Holkham, in Norfolk; it was in the highest order in which it seemed possible for ground to be; he did not know that a weed could be found upon it. He called it horticulture upon a great scale. This celebrated farm consists of several thousand acres. Having had the gratification at a subsequent day, of visiting Mr. Coke at his Holkham estate, I am here reminded of what he told me was jocosely said when he first took possession of it; that there was but one blade of grass on the whole, for which two half-starved rabbits were fighting! All accounts agree that it was sterile. Skilful farming, aided by capital, had brought it in the course of a single life, into the state Sir Benjamin Hobhouse described, and repaid, as was added, the large expenditures upon it.

Sir John Sinclair's conversation was instructive and entertaining. He had the double fund of a large mixture with the world and books, to draw from. Early rising was a topic; he thought it less conducive to health than was generally supposed, owing to the morning exhalations; we had heard of the robustness of the old Saxons, but he doubted if they were as powerful a race, physically, as the English of the present day; and as to their going to bed at dark and getting up with the dawn, that, he pleasantly said, was natural among a people ignorant of the art of making candles! In the evening, further company arrived from neighbouring country seats. Of the number were the Miss Penns, descendants of the founder of Pennsylvania. Pastimes followed.

July 27. Dined at Mr. Jeremy Bentham's. If Mr. Bentham's character be peculiar, so is his place of residence.

From my house north of Portman Square, I was driven nearly three miles through streets for the most part long and wide, until I passed Westminster Abbey. Thereabouts, things changed. The streets grew narrow. Houses seemed falling down with age. The crowds were as thick, but not as good-looking, as about Cornhill and the Poultry. In a little while I reached the purlieus of Queen Square Place. The farther I advanced, the more confined was the space. At length turning through a gateway, the passage was so narrow that I thought the wheels would have grazed. It was kind of blind-alley, the end of which widened into a small, neat, court-yard. There, by itself, stood Mr. Bentham's house. Shrubbery graced its area, and flowers its window-sills. It was like an oasis in the desert. Its name is the Hermitage.

Entering, he received me with the simplicity of a philosopher. I should have taken him for seventy or upwards. * Every thing inside of the house was orderly. The furniture seemed to have been unmoved since the days of his fathers; for I learned that it was a patrimony. A parlour, library, and dining-room, made up the suite of apartments. In each was a piano, the eccentric master of the whole being fond of music as the recreation of his literary hours. It was a unique, romantic little homestead. Walking with him into his garden, I found it dark with the shade of ancient trees. They formed a barrier against all intrusion. In one part was a high dead wall, the back of a neighbour's house. It was dark and almost mouldering with time. In that house, he informed me, Milton had lived. Perceiving that I took an interest in hearing it, he soon afterwards obtained a relic, and sent it to me. It was an old carved baluster, from the staircase, which there was reason to think the hand of the great bard had often grasped – so said the note that accompanied the relic.

The company was small, but choice. Mr. Brougham, Sir

---

* Jeremy Bentham was born in 1748.

Samuel Romilly, Mr. Mill, author of the well-known work on India, M. Dumont, the learned Genevan, once the associate of Mirabeau, were all who sat down to table. Mr. Bentham did not talk much. He had a benevolence of manner, suited to the philanthropy of his mind. He seemed to be thinking only of the convenience and pleasure of his guests, not as a rule of artificial breeding, but from innate feeling. Bold as are his opinions in his works, here he was wholly unobtrusive of theories that might not have commanded the assent of all present. Something else was remarkable. When he did converse, it was in simple language, a contrast to his later writings, where an involved style, and the use of new or unusual words, are drawbacks upon the speculations of a genius original and profound, but with the faults of solitude. Yet some of his earlier productions are distinguished by classical terseness.

Mr. Brougham talked with rapidity and energy. There was a quickness in his bodily movements indicative of the quickness of his thoughts. He showed in conversation the universality and discipline that he exhibits in Parliament and the Courts of Law. The affairs of South America, English authors, Johnson, Pope, Swift, Milton, Dryden, Addison, (the criticisms of the last on Paradise Lost, he thought poor things); anecdotes of the living Judges of England; the Universities of Oxford and Cambridge; the Constitution of the United States – these were topics that he touched with the promptitude and power of a master. He quoted from the ancient classics, and poets of modern Italy, (the latter in the original also,) not with the ostentation of scholarship, which he is above, but as if they came out whether he would or no amidst the multitude of his ideas and illustrations. He handled nothing at length, but with a happy brevity; the rarest art in conversation, when loaded with matter like his. Sometimes he despatched a subject in a parenthesis; sometimes by a word, that told like a blow. Not long after this my first meeting with him, one of his friends informed me that a gentleman whose son was about to study law, asked him what books he ought to read. 'Tell him to begin with Demosthenes and Dante.' – 'What, to make a lawyer?' said the father. – 'Yes,' he replied, and 'if you don't take, we won't argue about it.' Mr. Mill, M. Dumont, and Sir Samuel Romilly, did their parts in keeping up the ball of conversation.

Sheridan being spoken of, Sir Samuel Romilly, who had often heard him in the House of Commons, said, that 'nothing could be more marked than the difference between the parts of his speeches previously written out, and the extemporaneous parts. The audience could discover in a moment when he fell into the latter. It was well known,' he added, 'that all the highly wrought passages in his speeches on Hastings' impeachment, were prepared beforehand and committed to memory.'

After we rose from table, Mr. Bentham sought conversation with me about the United States. 'Keep your salaries low,' said he; 'it is one of the secrets of the success of your Government. – But what is this,' he inquired, 'called a Board of Navy Commissioners that you have lately set up? I don't understand it.' I explained it to him. 'I can't say that I like it,' he replied; 'the simplicity of your public departments has heretofore been one of their recommendations, but *boards* make *skreens*: if any thing goes wrong, you don't know where to find the offender; it was the board that did it, not one of the members; always the *board*, the *board*!' I got home at a late hour, having witnessed a degree of intellectual point and strength throughout the whole evening, not easily to have been exceeded.

July 30. The French Ambassador gave a dinner to the Prince Regent. There were present all the foreign ambassadors and ministers, Lord Castlereagh, Lord Melville, Lord Stewart, Lord Binning, the Vice-Chancellor, and other official characters, the company being large. The arrangements were on the models of France; for wines, we had Burgundy, Tokay, St. Julien, Sillery Champagne, and others in esteem at such tables. The fruit course displayed the mingled fruits of France and England; from the gardens of the former, and hot-houses of the latter. In England it is only by heat so obtained, that fruit can have its full flavour; yet so numerous all over the island are these receptacles of artificial heat, that they become as another sun to the English climate.

Beautiful as was the appearance of the table, the chief attraction did not lie there; but in the distinguished entertainers, the Marquis and Marchioness D'Osmond. French society has always been celebrated; the Sevignés, the du Deffands, the de

Leviss, and a thousand others, have told us of it. The manners of the French of those days, in spite of the alloy mixed with them, command admiration. They are embalmed in the literature of the nation. Their influence survives in France; for even those who discard totally the politics of the same ages, cherish the example of personal accomplishments that gave grace and ornament to social life. The memory of them was recalled on this occasion.

But among personages of the class assembled, exterior attractions are not all that engage the thoughts. In the drawing-rooms of London as the saloons of Paris, intervals are found for other topics. 'What is it?' whispered to me in the course of the evening an ambassador from one of the great powers – 'what is it we hear about Pensacola? are you going to have difficulty with Spain?' I replied that I hoped not. 'May I hear from you the circumstances – I should be glad to inform my court what they are.' I said they were simply these: The United States were at war with the Seminole Indians, a tribe dwelling partly in Florida; Spain was bound by treaty to restrain their hostilities from within her own line; nevertheless, they crossed the line, attacked our people, and fell back into Florida; there, they recruited for new attacks, and when pursued, found shelter, it was hoped without the knowledge of Spain, in the Spanish posts of St. Mark's and Pensacola. Such were the facts on which General Jackson, commander of the United States troops, had acted. He had accordingly taken possession of those fortresses; not as an act of hostility to Spain, but in necessary prosecution of the war against the Indians, and defence of our own frontier. The ambassador said, that Europe would look with interest upon the progress of the affair. I gave the same information to one of the ministers plenipotentiary. The latter remarked, that the diplomatic corps were full of the news; for, said he, 'we have had nothing of late so exciting – it smacks of war.' I said that I had no belief the United States would detain the posts an hour after the necessity that led to their being taken, ceased.

Mr. Poleticca, appointed minister from Russia to the United States, was of the company. He spoke of the friendly dispositions he should carry with him to my country, by command of his sovereign. So strongly, he said, were his instructions imbued with this spirit, that he would not scruple to read them to Mr. Adams, when he got to Washington. I learned, not from Mr. Poleticca, but otherwise, that they related in part to the United States joining the Holy Alliance. This may seem strange. It may be explained by the remark, that there was nothing objectionable in the ends proposed on the face of this alliance. Religion, peace and justice among nations, were its professed objects. It was, however, a sufficient objection to any free Government becoming party to it, that it sprang from the wills of irresponsible sovereigns, was perfected by their autograph signatures, and susceptible, from its very nature, of being interpreted and enforced to their own ends. The Emperors of Russia and Austria, and the King of Prussia, first signed it. England declined; on the ground that by the forms of her constitution, no treaty or league of any kind was ever signed by the monarch in person, but by ministers responsible to the nation. A representative of one of the second-rate powers of Europe remarked to me on the mortification which such powers felt at having all their movements brought under the inspection and control of this alliance. He told in this connexion the anecdote of the Dutch ambassador who was sent to make peace with Louis XIV, after his first successes against Holland; but who, on hearing the extravagant terms demanded by Louis, swooned away, as being of a nature never to be yielded, and which he knew not how to resist.

The Prince Regent sat on the right of the French Ambassador. The whole entertainment was sumptuous. The company remained until a late hour in the drawing-rooms, under the spell of French affability and taste.

July 31. Had an interview with Lord Castlereagh, by appointment at the French Ambassador's yesterday. He informed me that the Court of Madrid had made propositions to Great Britain to mediate between Spain and her colonies, and invited the European Alliance to join. The invitation was given in a note from the Spanish Ambassador in London. He could not better unfold the subject than by putting into my hands the notes that had passed.

I read each note. The introductory matter of the Spanish Ambassador's, spoke of the rebellious nature of the war in the colonies, of the past clemency of Spain, and her continued willingness to terminate the quarrel. It then laid down the following as the basis on which a mediation was asked. 1. An amnesty to the colonies on their being *reduced*. Lord Castlereagh explained this word, which was a translation from the Spanish, by saying that Spain did not mean *conquered*, but only that her colonies must desist from hostility. 2. The King of Spain to employ in his public service in America, *qualified* Americans as well as European Spaniards. 3. The King to grant the colonies privileges of trade *adapted to the existing posture of things*. 4. The King to acquiesce in all measures the mediating powers might suggest to effect the above objects.

The British answer approved the propositions, as general ones, but called for explanations by which the meaning of some of them might be rendered more definite. It expressed an opinion that the dispute ought to be healed without taking away the political supremacy of the parent state. It declared that the trade of the colonies ought to be free to the rest of the world, the mother-country being placed upon a footing of reasonable preference. Lastly, it made known, that Great Britain would do no more than interpose friendly offices, using no compulsion should they fail. . . .

When I had finished reading, his lordship asked if I was in possession of the views of my own Government as to a basis of settlement.

I replied in the affirmative; informing him that the desire of my Government was, that the colonies should be completely emancipated from the parent state. It was also of opinion, that the contest never would, or could, be settled otherwise.

I added, that the United States would decline taking part, if they took part at all, in any plan of pacification, except on the basis of the independence of the colonies.

This was the determination to which my Government had come on much deliberation, and I was bound to communicate it in full candour. It had hoped that the views of Great Britain would have been coincident.

His lordship appeared to receive the communication with regret. He admitted that the United States stood in different relations to the contest, from those which Great Britain held. The fundamental point of difference was farther discussed between us; but I gave his lordship no reason to suppose that the determination of the United States would undergo a change. The conversation was conducted and terminated in a spirit altogether conciliatory.

The policy of the United States on the great question of Spanish American independence, could not have been different. They owed it to the actual position of the colonies; to their future destinies; to the cause of human liberty in the new hemisphere. The determination of the United States to act upon the policy, was accelerated by the exertions of a distinguished patriot and statesman of the Republic, Mr. Clay; whose ardent, commanding eloquence, never tiring in this cause, made its impression on the legislative counsels and public opinion of the nation. It was a noble spectacle to see the United States stretch out their powerful hand to these infant communities, anticipating the freest government of Europe in accouncing the decree of their independence.

When we had done with this subject, his lordship asked if I had any accounts from my Government of the capture of Pensacola. I said, none that were official. I improved the opportunity, as in other cases at the French Ambassador's, of giving him an outline of the transaction. He expressed a hope that it would not lead to a breach of our peaceful relations with Spain, adding that nothing had yet been received on the subject from the British Minister at Washington.

CHAPTER XVIII

INTERVIEW WITH LORD CASTLEREAGH – IMPRESSMENT – CASES OF ARBUTHNOT AND AMBRISTER – MR. GALLATIN ARRIVES IN LONDON – PREPARATORY CONFERENCE AT NORTH CRAY, THE SEAT OF LORD CASTLEREAGH, IN KENT, WHERE THE NEGOTIATORS DINE AND PASS THE NIGHT – APPEARANCES OF THE COUNTRY – OPENING OF THE NEGOTIATION – THE POINTS RECAPITULATED – LAST INTERVIEW WITH LORD CASTLEREAGH ON IMPRESSMENT, PRIOR TO HIS DEPARTURE FOR AIX LA CHAPELLE

August 14, 1818. Called on Lord Castlereagh by his invitation.

He informed me that causes had occurred to prevent the Congress of Sovereigns assembling at Aix la Chapelle as soon as had been expected. The time was now fixed for the 20th of September; he was the better pleased, as it ensured him the opportunity of being present at the commencement of the negotiation. I expressed my satisfaction at the communication, and in turn informed him, that the full powers and instructions to Mr. Gallatin and myself had arrived, and that I expected the former from Paris in a day or two.

He next surprised me agreeably by reviving the subject of impressment. I feared that it had been expunged from our conferences. He premised, that what he was going to say, was, for the present, without the knowledge of his colleagues in the administration. He had reflected upon my late proposals; they had, it was true, been rejected, as they stood; but feeling the great importance of this subject, and willing to avoid, if possible, shutting it out from the general negotiation, it had occurred to him to offer some suggestions to me.

1. That any treaty or convention founded on my proposals, should be limited to eight, ten, or twelve years, with liberty to

each party to be absolved from its stipulations on a notice of three or six months.

2. That the British boarding-officer entering American ships at sea for a purpose agreed by both nations to be justifiable under the laws of nations, should be entitled to call for a list of the crew; and if he saw a seaman known to him, or on good grounds suspected, to be a British seaman, should have the further privilege of making a record, or *procès verbal*, of the fact, in such manner as to bring the case under the notice of the Government of the United States, but not to take the man out of the ship.

The latter regulation, his lordship observed, would operate as a further incentive to the faithful execution of our home prohibitions for excluding British subjects from our vessels; the former, guard against any irrevocable relinquishment by Great Britain of what she believed to be her right of impressment – a relinquishment which the feelings of the country might not on trial be found to bear.

To the first modification I saw no insurmountable objection. The second I viewed very differently. But as, in the progress of the negotiation, a hope might reasonably be entertained of getting rid of the second if the first were adopted, I said to his lordship, that although I would express no opinion on the proposed modifications, I saw enough of the suggestion of them to bring the subject again within the pale of our discussions.

His lordship passed to a new subject, his manner showing the interest he felt in it. It was the execution, by order of General Jackson, of two British subjects, Arbuthnot and Ambrister. This transaction grew out of the war against the Seminole Indians. Ambrister was taken in the field, fighting on their side against the forces of the United States. Arbuthnot was made prisoner in the Spanish fort of St. Mark's, and charged with instigating the Indians to war against our troops and people. His lordship said that he could have no complaint to make at present, the case not being officially before the British Government; but assuming the rumours to have any foundation, the execution of these men under the mere authority of the commanding general, without any reference to the Government of the United States, seemed an extreme measure. He asked if I could account for it. I replied, that I could only account for it by supposing the offences to have been extreme. This, combined with the distance of the commanding general from Washington, had probably presented the whole case to his mind, as one for his own discretion; the Indians, when waging war, destroyed their prisoners, sparing neither age nor sex, which necessarily exposed those who took side with them to their own rules of warfare, if captured; a momentary humanity might regret this kind of retaliation; but perhaps the permanent interests of humanity would be promoted, as its tendency would be to deter others from instigating the Indians to attack our people. It was so that I spoke. His lordship made no other commentary than to express a hope that every thing would be well explained, the occurrence being of a nature to excite unusual sensibility in England. I remarked that I saw with concern the inflammatory comments of the public journals, before the occurrence could be rightly understood in England; not that the press in either country should be left to any other influence than its own will, but from the fear that it might forerun, in this instance, the real nature of the case, and raise up difficulties not intrinsic to it. He replied by disavowing all connexion on this as on other occasions, between the Government and such of the public prints.

August 16. Mr. Gallatin arrives in London.

August 17. Address a note to Lord Castlereagh, informing him of Mr. Gallatin's arrival, and that we were ready to open the negotiation.

August 19. Receive an answer. His lordship being out of town, says that he will be happy to see us at dinner at his country residence, on the 22nd. We are asked to come early, to give time for a conference before dinner, and remain all night.

August 20. Employed to-day and yesterday in going with Mr. Gallatin to leave our cards at the houses of the members of the cabinet and diplomatic corps.

August 23. We arrived at Lord Castlereagh's country seat, North Cray, Kent, sixteen miles from town, yesterday at three o'clock.

We found there, Mr. Robinson and Mr. Goulburn, the two

British plenipotentiaries. After a courteous welcome, we all withdrew to his lordship's cabinet. An informal beginning was made in the negotiation. His lordship said, that this first meeting was one in which he took much interest, though its principal design was to bring the plenipotentiaries together, and fix the subjects, rather than discuss them. The negotiation was important to both countries; he sincerely felt it so to Great Britain; his Majesty's Government earnestly desired that every question which had led to past misunderstandings, might be amicably adjusted at this season of peace, so as to lay a foundation of stable harmony for the future. In short, let us strive, said he, so to regulate our intercourse in all respects, as that each nation may be able to do its utmost towards making the other rich and happy.

Next, he spoke of impressment. The modifications suggested to the proposals I had submitted for excluding British seamen from our service, he would, he said, repeat, for the information of Mr. Gallatin. We expressed at once our decided objection to the second; but agreed, that the general subject should come into the negotiation. With impressment, it was also agreed that we should let in other subjects of a maritime nature; such as, the doctrine of blockade; the right of a neutral to trade with the colonies of an enemy in time of war; the right of search, and list of contraband. General conversation was had under each head. The conference closed with an understanding that the plenipotentiaries should re-assemble on the 27th, the negotiation then to open in form.

Business being over, we took a turn through the grounds. The day was fine. We walked on lawns and along shady paths by the Cray side. The Cray is a narrow river, whose waters here flow through grassy banks. Close by, were hedges of sweetbriar. Such, and other rural appearances, might naturally have been anticipated at such a spot. But they were not all that we saw. There was something I had not anticipated. It was a *ménagerie*. Taste, in England, appears to take every form. In this receptacle were lions, ostriches, kangaroos, and I know not what other strange animals. Those who collect rare books and pictures, are too numerous to be computed; so, those who gather relics and curiosities from different parts of the world. Some persons have the shells of all coasts arranged under scientific classification, like plants in botany. Some collect *pipes*. I hear of an individual who has laid out several thousand pounds sterling upon this taste. And now, amidst lawns and gardens; amidst all that denoted cultivation and art, I beheld wild beasts and outlandish birds – the tenants of uncivilized forests and skies – set down as if for contrast!

Getting back we were shown into our rooms to prepare for dinner. At dinner, we were joined by Lady Castlereagh and Lady Sandwich. Lord Clanwilliam, and the two Mr. Stewarts, nephews of Lord Castlereagh, were also of the guests, with Mr. Robinson and Mr. Goulburn. Every thing was talked of but the negotiation. The four-footed and feathered *exotics* seen in our walk, were not forgotten. We rose from table at an early hour. The remainder of the evening went by in conversation and conversation-games. My colleague and myself felt ourselves at home. Invited for the purpose of fulfilling public duties to the house of an English minister of state, entrenched in confidence and power, we found ourselves of his domestic circle, the partakers of a hospitality as easy as delightful. At twelve we separated for our bed-rooms.

We were under the necessity of leaving this agreeable mansion after breakfast this morning. It was Sunday. Lord and Lady Castlereagh walked to the village church not far off. They were followed by their servants, by whom they are said to be beloved for their kind treatment of them. Those who oppose his lordship in politics, accord to him every merit in the relations of private life.

The country between London and North Cray was undulating. Crossing the Thames at Westminster Bridge, we left Shooter's Hill to the north. The whole way presented one universal face of cultivation. The hop is extensively grown in the county of Kent. It is relied upon as a principal crop by the *Kentish yeomen*, who are said to illustrate finely the comforts and character of the middle class of rural population in England. I was told that but for the heavy duty on the importation of foreign hops, amounting to prohibition except when the home crop fails, not a hop vine would be planted in Kent, or any part of England. The hops from several other countries, including the United States, would be preferred, as of superior strength, and far cheaper.

The same policy, it seems, extends to eggs, apples, cherries, chesnuts. Watch is thus kept upon the orchards and barn-yards of France!

The old custom of *gavel-kind* still prevails in Kent. This made me look with an eye of curiosity upon the country. By this cus-tom, on the death of a parent, his land is divided equally among all his sons, instead of going to the eldest, as in other parts of England. The latter mode of descent the English defend, as necessary to their prosperity and power. It is doubt-less necessary to their form of government. Nothing else could give stability to their aristocracy, without which the throne would not long be stable. But they say that it is necessary to their agriculture, the root of all their riches. They allege, that without the capital which it places in the hands of great landholders, farming could not be carried on to full advan-tage; the soil could not be improved to its utmost capability, small farmers not being able to command the means for experimental agriculture, especially in connexion with expen-sive and constantly improving machinery. They also say, that, in the national aggregate, agriculture is cheaper when farms are large, than when too much subdivided. The same enclosures last through ages; and stocks, implements, and labour of all kinds, are more economically applied when kept together and applied under one system.

It is so, that they reason. I could not see the proof of it, in the portion of this county that fell under my observation. The farms, to a rapid glance, showed thrift, neatness, and fertility. Nor did I learn from those better informed, that there was any inferiority in the modes of farming; or in general productive-ness, as compared with other counties in the kingdom. The gross product of agriculture in all England, is, indeed, amazing, when it is considered what extensive tracts of her territory are still in downs and heath; and how much of the fertile part is in pleasure-grounds. The wonder augments when we see how much large classes of her population, and of the domestic animals, consume without working. The horses in England, kept for luxury, are reckoned as fifteen to one to those in France. The very *pheasants* are consumers; grain being raised for feeding them as they fly about the domains of the opulent.

Gavel-kind creates subdivided inheritances only when the owner of an estate dies intestate. He may, by will, prefer the eldest son; and the general feeling in England, which is so strong in favour of keeping estates together that even younger sons acquiesce in it, exerts an influence in Kent. It is said that Surrenden House in this county, the present residence of Sir Edward Dering, was rebuilt, upon its old foundations, in the time of Edward III; the linege of the proprietor being traceable by family records to a period earlier than the Norman conquest. In gazing upon these ancient, massive structures, we forget the tyranny under which they were first reared, and rude customs and superstititions of their age. These are gone. The romance of their history remains, stealing into the feelings when they are approached as seats of modern hospitality.

The interest of the whole excursion was increased to me by the companionship of Mr. Gallatin. His station as Minister Plenipotentiary at Paris has added to all his other information, much insight into the courts and cabinets of Europe. A keen observer of men, and possessing a knowledge of books, his stores of conversation are abundant and ever at command. He did me the favour to take a seat in my carriage, and in his flow of anecdote and reflections I had an intellectual repast.

August 27. The Plenipotentiaries assembled at the office of the Board of Trade, Whitehall. The full powers on each side were exhibited, and inspected by the other. A copy of ours was handed to the British plenipotentiaries, and a copy of theirs promised at the next meeting.

We presented a paper containing a recapitulation of the subjects which, by our understanding, were to be treated of. They were as follow: 1. The Slave question under the treaty of Ghent. 2. The Fisheries. 3. The North-western boundary line. 4. Columbia river question. 5. Renewal of the commercial convention of 1815. 6. Intercourse between the United States and British West India islands. 7. Intercourse by sea between the United States and British North American colonies. 8. Inland intercourse between same and same. 9. Impressment. 10. Blockades. 11. Colonial trade in time of war. 12. List of contraband. 13. Miscellaneous, minor, questions.

The British plenipotentiaries agreed to this recapitulation.

Referring to the fifth head, they asked whether we intended to discuss the provisions of the existing convention. That instrument might not, they remarked, contain for either party all that was wished; but if opened, each would have alterations to propose, which would throw the whole at large. Under ths reasoning, it was determined not to open it for discussion. We expressed a desire not to proceed immediately to the formal act of renewal, but wait a reasonable time to ascertain the progress made on other points. The desire was acceded to. After some conversation on other points, the meeting adjourned to the 29th.

Whitehall is one of the ancient palaces of London. The room in which we assembled, had been the chamber of the Duke of Monmouth. It was also mentioned that Gibbon had often written at the table before us, when a member of the Board of Trade.

August 29. The Plenipotentiaries met. The protocol of the last conference, as drawn up by the British plenipotentiaries, was read, and adopted. They gave us a copy of their full powers.

Regular discussions now commenced. The question about the slaves first presented itself. During the war of 1812, great numbers of this description of population belonging to the landed proprietors of the southern states, had found their way to British ships in the Chesapeake, or other waters of the Union. A large portion had gone on board of them, under proclamations from the British naval commanders; some without these incentives. Others had been captured during the progress of the war. Their loss was heavily felt by the owners. By the first article of the treaty of Ghent it was provided, that '*all territory, places, and possessions, taken by either party from the other during the way. . . ., shall be restored without delay, or any of the artillery, or other public property, originally captured in the said forts or places,* OR ANY SLAVES, OR OTHER PRIVATE PROPERTY.'

Slaves came under the denomination of private property, by the highest sanction of our laws. The United States held it to be the true meaning of the foregoing clause, that the British were to carry off no slaves within our limits, whether such slaves were on board their ships, or in forts, or other places on shore.

Great Britain contended for a more restricted construction. She said that those slaves only were not to be carried off who were in forts and such places. This was the question at issue between the two nations.

Of the slaves of whom the proprietors had, by one means or other, been despoiled, very few had been in forts; so that, in effect, the British construction of the clause would have rended it nearly inoperative as to any benefit to the owners of the slaves.

We unfolded the views of our Government on this subject. The British plenipotentiaries replied and stated theirs. . . .

No definite proposals resulted from this day's discussions. It was agreed that we should adjourn to Friday the 4th of September. The British plenipotentiaries hoped to be ready by that day to submit proposals on impressment, we promising to hand in, immediately afterwards, ours on other maritime questions. We made known our intention not to discuss any maritime question, unless that of impressment was brought forward by Great Britain.

September 1. Called on Lord Castlereagh. He had sent a note requesting to see me. His travelling-carriages were at the door, preparatory to his departure for Dover on his journey to the Continent. He had delayed this interview, he remarked, as his last act of business; but not one least in his thoughts. It was to make a communication to me on impressment. He had reported to the Cabinet all that passed at the meeting at North Cray, making known especially our objections to the condition which went to authorize a British boarding-officer to call for a list of the crew. The British Government felt an anxious desire to accommodate this difficult subject, and had determined upon going all practicable lengths. He had therefore to inform me, that this condition would be waved. Such had been the determination of the Cabinet. He took great pleasure in apprising me of this determination, hoping I would see in it proof of the friendly feeling which prevailed in the councils of the Cabinet towards the United States.

I replied in suitable terms to his communication. Continuing his remarks he said, that the course which the Cabinet had resolved upon, would probably give a shock to public feeling in England when known; but its members would be prepared to meet it. He concluded by observing, that the great principle being at last settled, viz. that on our engaging not to employ British seamen, the practice of impressment from our vessels would cease, he hoped all details would be easily arranged; their proposals, put into form, would be ready as soon as we were prepared with ours on the fisheries and West India trade. . . .

Our conversation dropped. His lordship was on the eve of departure and could not prolong it. He requested I would impart to Mr. Gallatin what had passed on impressment, and gave me his adieu. A few minutes after I left him, he set off.

The affairs of the Foreign Office were confided, during his absence, to Earl Bathurst. He received, and corresponded with, the foreign ministers. The chief purpose of the Congress of Aix la Chapelle was, to determine whether the armies of the allied powers should be withdrawn from France this autumn, or remain two years longer. Besides other considerations galling to France in the occupation, the expense, which she was made to bear, pressed upon her. Other European topics were to engage the attention of the Congress; and the business of Spanish America was not to be passed by, as Lord Castlereagh had, on a former occasion, intimated to me.

CHAPTER XIX

PROGRESS OF THE NEGOTIATION – A CONVENTION
CONCLUDED – QUESTIONS ARRANGED BY IT, VIZ.: THAT
OF THE FISHERIES – NORTH-WESTERN BOUNDARY LINE
– COLUMBIA RIVER AND TERRITORY WEST OF THE
ROCKY MOUNTAINS – COMMERCIAL CONVENTION –
SLAVES CARRIED OFF CONTRARY TO THE TREATY OF
GHENT

The Plenipotentiaries assembled again at Whitehall, according to appointment.

Having given an account of the first stages of the negotiation in the order of dates, it is no longer my design to proceed in that way. It has been seen that the subjects were multifarious. All demanded attention; some, copious discussions. These, with the documents at large, the protocols, the projets and counter-projets, debated and modified by the scrutiny of each side, would present a mass of matter through which the diplomatist or politician might perhaps wade; but be little attractive to any one else. My endeavour will be to present an intelligible history of the negotiation by giving results rather than details. Some of these results are important to both nations. To record them with impartiality, is the aim I propose to myself.

Throughout September and October, meetings were as constant as was compatible with maturing in a proper manner the various subjects. By the 20th of October all appeared to have been fully discussed. The points were ascertained on which there could be agreement, as well as those on which it was hopeless in the existing disposition of the two Governments, to continue the negotiation longer. Accordingly, on that day, a convention was signed which comprehended the following subjects:

I. That of the FISHERIES. This, although not first in the order of discussion, came first in the convention. The points of misunderstanding had not risen to much height practically; but it is scarcely going too far to say, that they menaced the peace of the two countries. . . .

Neither side yielded its convictions to the reasoning of the other. This being exhausted, there was no resource left with nations disposed to peace, but a compromise. Great Britain grew willing to give up something. The United States consented to take less than the whole. After various proposals by the former which the latter rejected as inadequate, we at length, as their Plenipotentiaries, acceded to the following: viz.

That the United States should have, for ever, in common with British subjects the liberty to fish on the southern coast of Newfoundland from Cape Ray to the Rameau Islands; and from that cape to the Quirpon Islands on the western and northern coasts; and on the shores of the Magdalen Islands; and on the coasts, bays, harbours, and creeks from Mount Joly, on the southern coast of Labrador, through the Straits of Belleisle, and thence indefinitely along the coast, northwardly; but without prejudice to any exclusive rights of the Hudson's Bay Company. Also the liberty, for ever, to dry and cure fish in any of the unsettled bays, harbours, and creeks of the southern coast of Newfoundland, as above described; and of the coast of Labrador; subject, after settlement, to agreement with the proprietors of the soil. In consequence of the above stipulations, the United States renounced for ever the liberty of fishing within three miles of any other part of the British coasts in America, or of curing or drying on them. But American fishermen were to be permitted to enter bays or harbours on the prohibited coasts for shelter, repairing damages, and obtaining wood and water, subject to restrictions necessary to prevent abuses.

Such was the article finally agreed upon. The most difficult part of our task, was on the question of permanence. Britain would not consent to an express clause that a future war was not to abrogate the rights secured to us. We inserted the words *for ever*, and drew up a paper to be of record in the negotiation, purporting that if the convention should from any cause be vacated, all anterior rights were to revive. The insertion of any words of perpetuity, was strenuously resisted by the British plenipotentiaries. We replied, that we could agree to no article on the subject, unless the words *for ever* were retained; or if any counter record was made on the protocol impairing its effect. . . .

To the saving of the exclusive rights of the Hudson's Bay Company, we did not object. The charter of that Company had been granted in 1670, and the people of the United States had never enjoyed rights in that bay that could trench upon those of the Company. Finally, it is to be remarked, that the liberty of drying and curing on certain parts of the coast of Newfoundland, as secured in the article, had not been allotted to the United States even under the old treaty of 1783.

When the convention was made public, it underwent criticism in Britain as too favourable, throughout, to the United States. But this article on the fisheries was assailed with peculiar force. The leading presses of London opened upon it. The claims of the United States were described as of alarming magnitude; the concessions, as of a character corresponding. Important maritime interests of the British empire were said to have been sacrificed. Complaints poured in from the colonies. The legislative assembly and council of Nova Scotia sent forward remonstrances, with which were mixed up, not unsparingly, denunciations of American ambition and encroachment.

British statesmen, more calm, thought and acted otherwise. They had not been deterred by the anticipation of clamour from entering into the article. They felt that, if they had a duty to fulfil by guarding British interests, they were not released from the obligation of looking to the just rights of an independent nation. It was in this spirit that a formidable cause of collision was removed, without impairing the honour, or, as is believed, the essential interests of either country.

II. The second article related to the Boundary line, from the Lake of the Woods*. This line had been originally laid down in the treaty of 1783. It proved defective. The cession of Louisiana by France in 1803, gave to the United States new and extensive territory west of the Mississippi. This altered the relative position of Great Britain and the United States in this

---

* On today's US/Canadian border between North Minnesota, and Manitoba, Ontario.

quarter, and the hitherto unsettled boundary was now arranged. It was provided, that a line drawn from the most north-western point of the Lake of the Woods along the forty-ninth degree of latitude, due west, should be the line of demarcation, forming the southern boundary of the British territories and the northern boundary of the United States, from the Lake of the Woods to the Rocky Mountains. In case such a line would not run along the forty-ninth degree, but fall above or below it, then the line was to be traced by first drawing one from the same point, north or south as the case might be, until it struck forty-nine; from which point of intersection the western line was to begin. Thus it was definitively settled.

An attempt was made by the British plenipotentiaries to connect with this article, a clause securing to Great Britain access to the Mississippi, and right to its navigation. We said that we could consent to no clause of that nature. Its omission having, in the end, been agreed to, that subject was also put at rest. Hence all opportunity for Britain to claim the right of navigating a river which touched no part of her dominions, ceased. The United States have claimed in a subsequent negotiation, the right of navigating the St. Lawrence, from its sources to it mouth. The essential difference in the two cases, is, that the upper waters of the St. Lawrence flow through territory belonging to both countries, and form a natural outlet to the ocean for the inhabitants of several states of the American Union.

III. The third article effected a temporary arrangement of claims beyond the Rocky Mountains and to Columbia river. The treaty of Utrecht had fixed the forty-ninth degree of latitude as the line between the possessions of Britain and France, including Louisiana since ceded to the United States. If, therefore, the United States and Britain arranged their claims westward, the same line, carried on to the Pacific, seemed the natural one. We contended that, as far as prior discovery could give the right to territory, ours was complete to the whole, on the waters of the Columbia. It derived its name from the American ship that first entered its mouth. It was first explored from its inland sources under the express authority of the Government of the United States. The British traveller,

Mackensie, had mistaken another river for a branch of the Columbia; the American travellers, Lewis and Clarke, as was now fully ascertained, having been the first to trace the Columbia from the interior to the ocean.

The British plenipotentiaries asserted that earlier voyages of English navigators, amongst them Cook's, gave to Britain the rights of prior discovery on this coast. They spoke also of purchases of territory from the natives south of this river, before the American revolution. They made no formal proposal of a boundary in these regions, but intimated that the river itself was the most convenient, and said they could agree to none that did not give them the harbour as its mouth, in common with the United States. To this we could not assent, but were willing to leave things west of the mountains, at large for future settlement. To this they objected, and made in turn propositions objectionable in our eyes. Finally it was agreed, that the country on the north-west coast of America westward of the Rocky Mountains, claimed by either nation, should be open to the inhabitants of both, for ten years, for purposes of trade; with the equal right of navigating all its rivers.

Under this branch of the discussion, might be seen power seeking its own augmentation. How strong the case for this reflection! A nation whose dominions in Europe, established her in the front rank of power; whose fleats predominated on the ocean; who had subjects in Asia too numerous to be counted; whose flag was planted at the Cape of Good Hope and other posts in Africa; who had Gibraltar, and Malta, and Heligoland, enabling her to watch the Mediterranean and Baltic; who had an empire in the West Indies as the East; and, added to all, vast continental colonies in America—this nation was anxiously contending for territorial rights in deep forests beyond the Rocky Mountains and on the solitary shores of the northern Pacific! In the time of Queen Mary, when the communication with Muscovy was first opened by the discovery of a passage to Archangel, the English ventured farther into those countries than any Europeans had done before. They transported their goods along the Dwina in boats made of one entire tree, which they towed up the stream to Wologda. Thence they carried their commodities a long journey over-land, and down the Volga to Astracan. Here they built ships, crossed the Caspian sea, and introduced their manufactures into Persia. It makes a parallel passage in their history, to see them at the present day pressing forward to supply with rifles and blankets savage hordes who roam through the woods and paddle their canoes over the waters of this farthest and wildest portion of the American continent.

IV. The fourth article prolonged for ten years the existing commercial convention. . . . It was originally negotiated in the summer of 1815, by three of the public men of the United States long signalized in the home and foreign service, Mr. Adams, Mr. Clay, Mr. Gallatin. Between the time of its signature in London and exchange of ratifications at Washington, an event occurred to modify one of its provisions. It was determined by the Allied Powers, that Napoleon, whose reign and dynasty closed at Waterloo, should end his days at St. Helena. As a consequence, the ratifications were exchanged with an exception of the right of touching there, the sentence against the deposed Emperor containing a clause that neither British nor any other vessels, should stop at that island, whilst his prison.

The parts of this convention which establish an equality of duties, are liberal and wise. That the interest of nations is best promoted by discarding jealousies, is a truth which, in the abstract, few will question. But they should be discarded reciprocally, without any of the reservations for which favourite interests will always plead. The doctrine hitherto has been known but little in the practice of the world. The United States, as one of the family of nations, did their part, at the commencement of their history, towards giving it currency; not always however with the success that attended this convention. Its provisions seemed to serve as a model. Within short periods after it went into operation, Denmark, Prussia, the Netherlands, Hanover, Sweden, and the Hanseatic cities of Hamburg, Lubec, and Bremen, formed treaties with Britain, adopting wholly, or in part, its regulations. In some of the instances, I have reason to know that it was specially consulted as the guide. France too, always slow to enter into compacts of this nature with Britain, at last consented to a similar arrangement. Such appears to have been the influence of its example. The United States have long desired to place their intercourse with the colonies of Britain, on the basis which this convention establishes with her dominions in Europe; but as yet ineffectually.

V. The fifth article related to the Slaves. I stated in the last chapter, the nature of this question. All attempts to settle it by discussions proved fruitless. It was no question of international law, but of sheer grammar. In the end, we came to an agreement which this article embodied, to refer it to the umpirage of a friendly sovereign.

The Emperor Alexander was chosen. It will be proper to state the issue. The case was submitted to him in full form. His decision was:-

That the United States were entitled to claim from Great Britain a just indemnification for all slaves that the British forces had carried away from places and territories of which the treaty stipulated and restitution; and that the United States were entitled to consider as having been so carried away, all slaves who had been transported from the above-mentioned territories to British ships within their waters, and who for that reason might not have been restored.

This was the construction for which the United States had contended. The broad principle of right was thus settled in our favour; but much remained to be done. The number of slaves carried away, their value, and the rightful claimants in every case, were to be ascertained. To effect these objects a convention was entered into at St. Petersburgh between the United States and Great Britain, Russia lending her meditation. By this instrument various provisions were adopted for settling, thro' commissioners and other fit tribunals, the above and all other matters necessary to be adjudged. The tribunals were organized at Washington, and proceeded to the execution of their duties. Difficulties and delays arose. To get rid of all, another convention was concluded at London between the United States and Great Britain, by which the latter agreed to pay twelve hundred thousand dollars in lieu of all further demands. This sum was accordingly paid into the Treasury of the United States, thence to be distributed among the claimants; Great Britain being absolved from all further responsibility. In this manner the dispute was finally and satisfactorily closed.

VI. The sixth and last article was merely one of form, with the usual stipulations for the exchange of ratifications.

Looking at the convention as a whole, it must be judged by the nature, rather than number, of its articles. In settling the controversy about the fisheries, the calamity of a war was probably warded off. In fixing a boundary line long uncertain, the seed of future disputes was extinguished at that point. In the temporary arrangement of conflicting claims beyond the Rocky Mountains, something was gained. In the renewal for ten years of the commercial convention, limited at first to four, a further and more encouraging example was set of liberal terms of navigation between the two greatest navigating powers of the world. It may be hoped that it will ripen into permanence as between themselves, and continue to shed its influence more and more upon other states. Lastly, in the article about the slaves, a foundation was laid for the indemnification awarded to the citizens of our southern states for heavy losses they had suffered.

CHAPTER XX

SUBJECTS WHICH THE NEGOTIATION LEFT UNADJUSTED, PARTICULARLY THE WEST INDIA TRADE AND IMPRESSMENT

1818. Having given the subjects which the negotiation arranged, the task, scarcely secondary, remains to state those that were not.

I. FIRST, AS TO THE WEST INDIA TRADE. Ample discussions were had on this head. It was a cardinal purpose under our instructions, that entire reciprocity should be the basis of any regulations by treaty, for opening this trade. We offered the following proposals as essential to the groundwork of our plan:- That the vessels of the United States be permitted to import into the principal ports of the British West Indies, which we enumerated, into the colonies of Britain in North America, and into British ports on the continent of South America, naval stores, live stock, provision of all kinds, tobacco, lumber, and other productions of the United States, the importation of which was allowed from other places. And also that they be permitted to bring back cargoes of sugar, coffee, molasses, rum, salt, and other productions of the foregoing ports or islands, the exportation of which was allowed to other places. The vessels of Great Britain to be confined to the same articles of trade, duties of import and export to be the same on all cargoes, so that they might have no advantage over those of the United States.

The British plenipotentiaries, on receiving these proposals, declared them to be inadmissible. They amounted, they said, to a much greater departure from the colonial system of Britain, than she was prepared to sanction. . . . In the end they remarked, that one of our proposals went the length of re-straining Great Britain from laying higher duties upon articles imported into her Islands from the United States, than on similar articles coming from her own possessions in North

America. To this they decidedly objected. They spoke of the natural right of Great Britain to resort to discriminating duties for the purpose of favouring the productions, agricultural or otherwise, of any part of her own dominions.

We did not pretend to deny this last principle; but remarked, that truth in abstract propositions did not always bear enforcement internationally. We contended that the application of this principle to the trade in question, would prove altogether unjust to the United States. . . .

It was so that we reasoned. Nevertheless, it was our duty to pay a just regard to the considerations which Great Britain had presented. We expressed a desire to listen to any specific proposals she would make. We asked for a scale of duties that would exhibit the maximum of those intended for the protection of the produce of her own dominions; but no such document was prepared for our consideration. In further reply to this British doctrine about duties, we naturally remarked, that, if enforced against the United States, the latter ought certainly to retain the option of laying higher duties on the productions of the British Islands.

After these and other particulars had been fully canvassed, it became evident that the parties were too wide asunder to give hope of meeting on ground that would satisfy both. The British plenipotentiaries candidly expressed themselves to this effect. But as we invited proposals, they gave them. Their proposals adhered to the principle of protecting the productions of their North American colonies, by levying higher duties on similar productions from the United States. They also claimed the right for British vessels from her European dominions, to touch at ports of the United States to take in cargoes for the West Indies.

Britain would agree to no arrangement of the intercourse by land, or inland navigation, with her possessions bordering on the United States, different from the one rejected with the four articles submitted by Lord Castlereagh. Nor would she let us take our produce down the St. Lawrence as far as Montreal, or down the Chambly as far as the St. Lawrence.

On referring her proposals to our Government with all the views elicited from her Plenipotentiaries, they were rejected. In progress of time renewed negotiations were held between the two Governments, some whilst I remained at the British court, some afterwards. Each Government gave up some of the ground taken in this negotiation; but no arrangement by treaty has ever yet been made upon the subject. The trade stands upon regulations adopted by the statutes of each nation, which each is at liberty to modify or recall.

II. I come, secondly, to IMPRESSMENT. Faithful as were our labours on this subject, disappointment was their portion.

It will be remembered that I delivered to Lord Castlereagh two propositions, which, taken together, embodied an offer by the United States to exclude, by all the means in their power, British seamen, native born, as naturalized, from their service. As an equivalent, they demanded that impressment from their vessels should be totally relinquished.

Our offer of exclusion, it will also be remembered, was at first rejected. It was afterwards agreed that it should be considered. Two conditions were annexed to it by Lord Castlereagh. One, that any treaty containing the mutual stipulations, should be revocable on short notice by either party. This would serve, he thought, to pacify persons in England who would otherwise be disposed to think the arrangement derogatory to the rights of England; whilst the treaty, as he hoped, would be sliding into permanence. The other condition was, that the British boarding-officer entering American vessels at sea for purposes agreed to be lawful in time of war, and finding British seamen, or men suspected to be such, should be allowed to make a *procès verbal* of the fact, to be presented to the notice of the American Government; but the officer to be prohibited taking away the men.

This latter condition seemed to imply distrust of America. It breathed suspicion, that the regulations for excluding British seamen would not be fully executed. If objectionable on this ground, it was more so on others. It did not ask, in terms, that the boarding-officer calling for a list of the crew, should have the power of mustering them; but the mere view of the paper would be useless without that power. The men must have been inspected for the purpose of comparison with the list. Such inspections had been found among the most insupportable aggravations of impressment. Their tendency, in every instance, was to produce altercation between the foreign officer and the master of the American vessel. If the officer made a record of his suspicions, the master, and seaman, must have the privilege of making a counter record. Where then would be the end, or what the good, of these tribunals of the deck? We did not desire the first condition, but were willing to come into it. To the second, we declared our utter repugnance and unequivocal dissent. It will be farther remembered, that Lord Castlereagh withdrew the second; which brings me to the footing on which the subject was taken up in the negotiation.

Repeated advances having been made by the United States, the understanding was, that Britain should now bring the subject forward in a shape matured for discussion. The leading principles seemed to have been settled. It remained, as we thought, only to settle details. At the third conference, the British plenipotentiaries submitted a projet of six articles designed for the regulation, by a separate treaty, of the whole subject.

It received from us a deliberate and anxious attention. We brought to the task an unaffected desire to smooth down every obstacle. It was not to be supposed that a subject that had divided the two nations for five-and-twenty years, and been the principal cause of a war, could be definitively arranged by the first projet of a treaty drawn up by one of the parties. But we hailed the entire plan as the harbinger of adjustment, believing that we saw in its spirit and outline the sure hope of success. Taking an interval for advisement we said, that the proposals heretofore made by the United States could leave no doubt of their constant desire to settle this question, and declared our readiness to agree, with some amendments, to the plan submitted. It becomes unnecessary, however, to dwell on these and other points as to which the parties did not agree at first, since they might have agreed ultimately, had it not been for two that proved fatal to the plan. To the explanation of these I confine myself.

The second article, with a view to ascertain the persons who were to be excepted from those intended to be excluded from the sea-service of either nation, provides, that each shall furnish the other with a list of their names. This list was to specify the place of their birth, and dates of their naturalization; and none but persons whose names were upon it, were to fall within the exception. To this provision we were obliged to object, our laws not enabling us to meet all that it required. Anterior to 1789, aliens were naturalized according to the laws of the several states composing the Union. Under this system, the forms varied and were often very loose. The latter was especially the case when they were drawn up by justices of the peace, as sometimes happened.

It must be added, that, for several years, no discrimination as to the birth-place of aliens was recorded. If attempts were made to procure the lists required, a further objection might have been, that the courts of the several States were not bound to obey, in this respect, a call from the general Government.

From this summary it is manifest, that a compliance with the British article would have been impracticable.

All these obstacles we presented to the British plenipotentiaries. They were plainly such as we could not remove, whatever our desire.

But we could not prevail upon the British plenipotentiaries to recede from their ground. They appeared to have taken up an impression, which we were unable to expel, that the great numbers of their seamen intended by the treaty to be excluded, would, but for the condition annexed, find their way into our service.

An error insensibly prevailing in Britain, seems to lie at the root of the evil. It consists in supposing that the United States cannot obtain seamen of their own, but must depend upon Britain. Why, any more than on Britons to till their farms, seems strange! I will give an instance of this error. When the Franklin anchored off Cowes, visitors came on board. Her decks were filled with her seamen. To be sure, they looked like English seamen, and spoke the same language. Soon the rumour went, that many were English. All rumours grow; so this. In a fortnight I read in the London prints, that one-third of the whole were native-born British subjects! The news passed from journal to journal, fixing itself, no doubt, in the belief of many an honest Englishman. The commentary upon it is, that Commodore Stewart informed me, that out of his crew, of upwards of seven hundred men, twenty-five would include all of foreign birth. Of these, half were from parts of

Europe other than Britain. I would not be guilty of supposing that errors so gross as the one I mention, could ever be committed by persons having better opportunities of information; but it points to the popular misconception. I fully believe, and this not as an unexamined opinion, that the proportion of native American seamen on board American ships-of-war, will always be found greater than of native British seamen on board British ships-of-war. The relative size of the two navies considered, it is demonstrable indeed, that the United States are far better able to man their's with native American, than the British their's with native British.

The other part of the projet that produced fatal diversity, was in the first article. It ran thus: 'Provided always that nothing contained in this article shall be understood to apply to such natural-born subjects or citizens of either power as may have been naturalized by their respective laws previous to the SIGNATURE of the present treaty.' In place of SIGNATURE, we proposed 'EXCHANGE OF RATIFICATIONS.' To the former, we could not consent. It would have brought with it the consequence of violating our constitution. The obligations of a treaty are not complete until exchange of ratifications. The British plenipotentiaries would not agree to drop their word. The subject was debated until the closing hours of the negotiation, and then fell to the ground. It put the seal to the failure of our efforts. We had offered all that was possible under our laws. We could go no farther.

I pause a moment on the above narrative. I look back, with unfeigned regret, on the failure it records. Perhaps I may be wrong, for I speak from no authority, but am not able to divest myself of an impression that, had Lord Castlereagh been in London, there would not have been a failure. I am aware that he was kept informed of the progress of the negotiation. We had reason to believe that the documents were regularly sent on for his inspection. Still, he could not share in the full spirit of all that passed. He had the European relations of Britain in his hands. Impressment, although in truth a primary concern, could not, at such a season, have commanded all this thoughts. But I know how anxiously he entered into it, before his departure for Aix-la-Chapelle. He saw that the great principle of adjustment had at last been settled; and I can scarcely think that he would have allowed it to be foiled, by carrying too much rigour into details. It is no part of my present purpose to draw the character of Lord Castlereagh; but there was this in him, which his opponents did not deny, and history will award – an entire fearlessness. He knew that a treaty relinquishing impressment, no matter what the terms, would excite clamour in England, come when it would. But having made up his mind to the justice and policy of such a treaty, he would have faced the clamour. And who will say that his wisdom would not have been attested? Seamen, as a race, are short-lived. Had the arrangement been perfected, the lapse of a very few years would have swept away the stock of naturalized British seamen in the United States; whilst the treaty would have remained, a monument of the statesmanship of the minister under whose auspices it would have been concluded.

This subject falling through, others of a maritime nature were withdrawn. It had been agreed that none were to be proceeded with, if we failed on impressment.

The failure to accommodate, this fruitful source of strife, is only postponed, not defeated. If removed in no other way, it will cease, ultimately, through the cessation of the practice as a home measure in England. It cannot endure much longer. Englishmen will get awake to its true nature. It is the remark of a sagacious historian, that nations long after their ideas begin to enlarge and their manners to refine, adhere to systems of superstition founded on the crude conceptions of early years. It is the same with public abuses. The English part reluctantly with those sanctioned by time. But, at length, public scrutiny and the moral sense of the nation, fasten upon them as in the case of the slave-trade. Reason emerges, as from a cloud. Indications are not wanting of this coming change as to impressment. Perhaps no association of men in the kingdom are more likely to form sound opinions on this subject, than the ship-owners of London. This body, at a meeting in September 1818, deliberately condemned the practice. The report of their committee dwells upon its evils, and suggests measures for its entire abolition. There is something if possible more strong. Sir Murray Maxwell, a distinguished officer in the British navy, when a candidate to represent the great commercial interests of Westminster in the House of Commons, made an appeal too remarkable to be forgotten. Addressing himself to assembled thousands round the hustings, he said, that if his opponent could show that he had been 'for fifteen years engaged in promoting a political scheme of such national importance as the one that he (Sir Murray) had been labouring at, he would withdraw from the contest; he meant, *the efforts he had made, in concert with many of his brother officers, to do away the practice of impressment.*' Need I go farther? If the conviction of the impolicy and enormity of this violation of the rights of the subject, this stain upon British humanity, has found its way into the circle of ship-owners and naval officers, is it conceivable that the conviction will stop there? No; it will spread, until echoed by the voice of all Britain.

CHAPTER XXI

THE ENGLISH IN THE AUTUMN – INAUGURATION OF THE LORD MAYOR – DEATH OF THE QUEEN

1818. Whilst the negotiation was going on, its business absorbed attention. Of personal occurrences during its pendency I have little to say. We dined with some of the cabinet ministers and diplomatic corps. On one occasion, a portion of the ambassadors and ministers gratified me by dining at my house, to meet Mr. Gallatin. Some of them had taken a lively interest in the progress of our negotiation. A French philosopher has said, that every day of his life formed a page of his works. I cannot claim this merit, if merit it be. It was not my habit to note down, as a daily routine, the incidents passing around me. I gave myself to the practice according to my feelings and opportunities. During the negotiation, and for the remnant of the year, I scarcely indulged in it at all. Soon after the close of our joint labours, Mr. Gallatin returned to Paris, leaving me to regret the loss of a colleague so enlightened.

In the west-end of London during the autumn, little is seen but uninhabited houses. It brings to mind the city in the Arabian Nights, where everything was dead. The roll of the carriage, the assemblage in the parks, the whole panorama of life, in circles where amusement is the business of life, stops. Pass Temple Bar, and winter and spring, summer and autumn, present the same crowds. Nothing thins them. But the depopulation of the west-end is nearly complete. The adjournment of Parliament is the first signal for desertion. You see post-chaises and travelling carriages, with their light and liveried postilions, issuing from the squares and sweeping round the corners. For awhile, this movement is constant. The gay emigrants find their country-seats all ready for their reception. Thiebault tells us, that the King of Prussia had libraries at several of his palaces, containing the same books, arranged in the same order; so that when going from one to another the train of his studies might not be broken. So the English on arriving at their seats, even if they have several, which is not unfrequently the case, find every thing they want; unlike the châteaux in the provinces of France, which are said to be ill-furnished and bare, compared with the fine hotels of Paris.

The next great egress is on the approach of the 1st of September. That day is an era in England. Partridge-shooting begins. All who have not left town with the first flight, now follow. Ministers of state, even lord-chancellors, can hardly be kept from going a-field. When our conference of the 29th of August was finished, my colleague and I, without reflection, named the 1st of September for the next meeting. '*Spare us,*' said one of the British plenipotentiaries; '*it is the first day of partridge-shooting!*'

The families that flock into the country, generally remain until after the festivities of Christmas, which close with Twelfth-night. Some stay much longer. Cabinet ministers and the diplomatic corps, are among the few persons left in the metropolis, and these in diminished number. The latter are often of the invited guests, when the English thus exchange the hospitalities of the town for those, more prolonged and magnificent, at their country abodes. Field sports are added to them; hunting of all kinds, the fox, the hare, the stag; shooting, with I know not what else, including archery, of the days of the Plantagenets. This last, like the chace, is sometimes graced by the competitions of female agility. But foreign ambassadors and ministers do not always find it convenient to profit of these invitations. If not every day engaged in negotiations, one seldom goes by with those representing countries in large intercourse with England, unmarked by calls upon their time. Like men of business everywhere, they must be at the place of their business to do, or to watch it. But if for the most part cut off from these rural recreations, there is one way in which they partake of the results; I mean in abundance of game for their tables. Amongst the persons to whom mine was indebted throughout the autumn, I must not forget one of the British plenipotentiaries. Let me add, that if not of the same mind with us on all official discussions, they both made us sensible in all ways of their personal courtesy.

The enthusiastic fondness of the English for the country, is the effect of their laws. Primogeniture is at the root of it. Scarcely any persons who hold a leading place in the circles of their society live in London. They have *houses* in London, in which they stay while Parliament sits, and occasionally visit at other seasons; but their *homes* are in the country. Their turreted mansions are there, with all that denotes perpetuity – heirlooms, family memorials, tombs. This spreads the ambition among other classes, and the taste for rural life, however diversified or graduated the scale, becomes widely diffused. Those who live on their estates through successive generations, not speaking of those who have titles but thousands besides, acquire, if they have the proper qualities of character, an influence throughout their neighbourhood. It is not an influence always enlisted on the side of power and privilege. On the contrary, there are numerous instances in which it has for ages been strenuously used for the furtherance of popular rights. These are the feelings and objects that cause the desertion of the west-end of the town when Parliament rises. The permanent interests and affections of the most opulent classes, centre almost universally in the country. Heads of families go there to resume their stand in the midst of these feelings; and all, to partake of the pastimes of the country life, where they flourish in pomp and joy.

In other parts of London, in the vast limits between Temple Bar and the Tower, the crowds, I have said, continue the same. Even here, however, the passion for the country peeps out. Every evening when business is over, the citizens may be seen going to their cottages that skirt the wide environs towards Highgate, Hornsey, Hackney, Stratford, Clapham, Camberwell, Greenwich, and in all directions. I heard a physician call the Parks the '*lungs of London.*' These little retreats, many of them hidden amidst foliage, and showing the neatness that seems stamped upon every thing rural in England, in like manner serve the citizens as places in which to breathe, after the pent-up air of confined streets and counting-rooms. To the latter they return on the following morning to plan operations that affect the markets and wealth of the civilized world.

On the 9th of November I dined at Guildhall. It was the day of the inauguration of the Lord Mayor, Mr. Alderman Atkins had been the successful candidate for the mayoralty. There was the grand procession upon the Thames, and through the streets. I need not give a description of it; for it has been as often described as St. Paul's Cathedral or Westminister Abbey. The dinner was in the large Gothic Hall. There sat down about nine hundred persons. The giants and knights clad in steel, the band of music slowly moving round the hall, the Aldermen in their costumes, the Sheriffs with their gold chains, the Judges in their robes, the Lady Mayoress in her hoop, with long rows of prosperous-looking citizens, presented a novel mixture of modern things, with symbols of the ancient banquet. The lights, the decorations of the hall, and all that covered the tables, gave a high impression of municipal plenty and munificence. The Premier, Lord Liverpool, with Lord Bathurst, Lord Sidmouth, and Mr. Vansittart, as cabinet ministers, were guests. There were many other official characters.

One of the knights wore the helmet which the City of London gave to Henry the Seventh. Its weight was fourteen pounds. The other knight wore the entire armour of Henry the Fifth. It was that of a small man. Lord Sidmouth, who sat near me, remarked, that all the armour of that day and earlier, indicated the stature to be smaller than at present. I thought of what Sir John Sinclair said, at Ormly Lodge. The reasons assigned were, improved agriculture, better personal habits from the greater diffusion of comforts among the people through the increase of wealth science; also, the disappearance of certain diseases, as leprosy and scurvy, and the advancement of medical knowledge, Mr. Vansittart said, that the remains of Roman armour had shown the Romans to be a smaller race of men than the moderns.

After the King, Prince Regent, and members of the Royal Family, had been given as toasts, the Lord Mayor did me the honour to propose my name, that he might make it the medium of cordial sentiments towards the United States. These the company received with applause. In returning thanks I reciprocated the friendly feelings he had expressed.

Before going to dinner we were in the council-room. Among the paintings was a very large one of the scene between Richard the Second and Wat Tyler. Another of that between Mary of Scots and Rizzio; one of the siege of Gibraltar, by

Copley; and other pieces. But I looked with chief interest at the portraits of the naval commanders. Pausing at Nelson's, Lord Sidmouth said, that in a visit he had from him three weeks before the battle of Trafalgar, he described the plan of it with bits of paper on a table, as it was afterwards fought. At Howe's Mr. Vansittart said, that just before his battle with the French fleet, the sailors expressed a wish for a little more grog. Howe replied, 'Let'em wait till it's over, and we'll all get drunk together.' At Rodney's, some conversation took place on the manoeuvre, which he first practised in his victory over De Grasse, of breaking the line. I asked, whether the success of that mode of attack did not essentially depend upon the inferiority of your enemy, especially in gunnery. It was admitted that it did, and that Lord Nelson always so considered it. The Marlborough, Rodney's leading ship, received the successive broad-sides of twenty-three of the French ships of the line, at near distance, and had not more than half-a-dozen of her men killed. My motive to the inquiry, was a remark I once heard from Commodore Decatur of our service, that, in an event, which I trust may be remote, of English fleets and those of the United States meeting, the former would probably change their system of tactics in action. Speaking of naval science in England, Lord Sidmouth said, that it had greatly improved of late years; that Lord Exmouth told him that, when he was a young man, it was not uncommon for lieutenants to be ignorant of lunar observations, but that now no midshipman was promoted who could not take them. He intimated his belief, that naval science generally, was destined to far higher advances than it had yet reached.

After dinner we went into the ball-room, where a ball terminated the festivities.

I should not soon have done if I were to mention all the instances of which I chanced on this occasion to hear of riches among mechanics, artisans, and others, engaged in the common walks of business in this great city. I make a few selections. I heard of haberdashers who cleared thirty thousand pounds sterling a-year, by retail shop-keeping; of brewers, whose buildings and fixtures necessary to carry on business, cost four hundred and fifty thousand pounds; of silversmiths worth half a million; of a person in Exeter Change, who made a fortune of a hundred thousand pounds, chiefly by making and selling razors; of job-horse men, who held a hundred and forty thousand pounds in the Three per Cents; and of confectioners and woollen drapers who had funded sums still larger. Of the higher order of merchants, bankers, and capitalists of that stamp, many of whom were present, whose riches I heard of, I am unwilling to speak, lest I should seem to exaggerate. I have given enough. During the late war with France, it is said that there were once recruited in a single day in the country between Manchester and Birmingham, two thousand able-bodied working men for the British army. It is the country so remarkable for its colleries, iron mines, and blast furnaces. Its surface is desolate. A portion of it is sometimes called the fire country, from the flames that issue in rolling volumes from the lofty tops of the furnaces. Seen all around by the traveller at night, they present a sight that may be called awful. Sometimes you are told that human beings are at work in the bowels of the earth beneath you. A member of the diplomatic corps, on hearing of the above enlistment remarked, that could Bonaparte have known that fact, and seen the whole region of country from which the men came, seen the evidences of opulence and strength in its public works, its manufacturing establishments and towns, and abundant agriculture, notwithstanding the alleged or real pauperism of some of the districts, it would of itself have induced him to give over the project of invading England.

In like manner, let any one go to a lord mayor's dinner; let him be told of the sums owned by those he will see around him and others he will hear of, not inherited from ancestors, but self-acquired by individual industry in all ways in which the hand and mind of man can be employed, and he will be backward at predicting the ruin of England from any of her present financial difficulties. Predictions of this nature have been repeated for ages, but have not come to pass. Rich subjects make a rich nation. As the former increase, so will the means of filling the coffers of the latter. Let contemporary nations lay it to their account, that England is more powerful now than ever she was, notwithstanding her debt and taxes. This knowledge should form an element in their foreign policy. Let them assure themselves, that instead of declining she is advancing; that her population increases fast; that she is constantly seeking new fields of enterprise in other parts of the globe, and adding to the improvements that already cover her island at home, new ones that promise to go beyond them in magnitude; in fine, that instead of being worn out, as at a distance is sometimes supposed, she is going ahead with the buoyant spirit and vigorous effort of youth. It is an observation of Madame de Staël, how ill England is understood on the Continent, in spite of the little distance that separates her from it. How much more likely that nations between whom and herself an ocean interposes, should fall into mistakes on the true nature of her power and prospects; should imagine their foundations to be crumbling, instead of steadily striking into more depth, and spreading into wider compass. Britain exists all over the world, in her colonies. These alone, give her the means of advancing her industry and opulence for ages to come. They are portions of her territory more valuable than if joined to her island. The sense of distance is destroyed by her command of ships; whilst that very distance serves as the feeder of her commerce and marine. Situated on every continent, lying in every latitude, these, her out-dominions, make her the centre of a trade already vast and perpetually augmenting – a home trade and a foreign trade – for it yields the riches of both, as she controls it all at her will. they take off her redundant population, yet make her more populous; and are destined, under the policy already commenced towards them, and which in time she will far more extensively pursue, to expand her an empire, commercial, manufacturing, and maritime, to dimensions to which it would not be easy to affix limits.

On the 17th of November, died the Queen. She expired at Kew Place, after a long illness. The last time I saw her was at an entertainment at Carlton House. There, as at the royal marriage, she had been distinguished by her affability. Going away, gentlemen attendants, and servants with lights, preceded her sedan; whilst the company gave tokens of respectful deference. Now, she had paid the common debt of nature. The event was communicated to me in a note from Lord Bathurst, received the same evening; a form observed towards all foreign ambassadors and ministers.

The Queen enjoyed in a high degree the respect and affection of a very large portion of the inhabitants of Great Britain. For more than half a century, her conduct upon the throne had been to the nation, satisfactory. There were periods when it was said that she had interfered beyond her sphere in public affairs; but besides the obstacles to this under a constitutional government like that of England, however frequent may be the instances in arbitrary governments, there never appears to have been any sufficient evidence of the fact. All agree, that in the relations of private life, her conduct was exemplary; and that the British court maintained in her time, a character of uniform decorum and chastened grandeur.

Her funeral was on the 2nd of December, at Windsor. The body had lain in state for the time usual. The procession moved from Kew. I went there with my sons. The multitude was so great, of carriages, persons on horseback, and foot passengers, that it might be said to form a compact mass from London to Kew, a distance of eight miles. It continued, as long as I looked, to press onward. At night, the road was lighted with torches borne by the military. These, gleaming upon the soldier's helmets, and partially disclosing, now the hearse, then the long solemn procession winding its slow way with its trappings of death, presented a spectacle for the pencil or the muse. The interment took place in the royal chapel of St. George. There, for centuries, had reposed the remains of kings and queens. And there, they had mouldered to dust. Around the vault, seen by dim lights in the Gothic interior, were assembled the Prince Regent, and other members of the royal family, with a few of the personages who composed the funeral train. Canning was of the number – Canning, with sensibilities always quick to whatever in human scenes might awaken moral reflection, or lift up the tone of the imagination.

On the 3rd of December the theatres were re-opened. I went to Drury-lane. The house was crowded, and everybody in black for the Queen. Orders for a court-mourning take in only a limited class; but the streets, as the theatres were filled with persons of all classes, who put it on. Even children wear it, and servants. Such is the usage of the country. The play was 'Brutus, or the fall of Tarquin,' a new tragedy, by Mr. Howard Payne, a young American. I felt anxious for an author who was my countryman, and had the gratification to witness his complete success. When the piece was announced for repetition, bursts of applause followed, and the waving of handkerchiefs.

On the 22nd of the month, accidents occurred all over London, from a remarkable fog. Carriages ran against each other, and persons were knocked down by them at the crossings. The whole gang of thieves seemed to be let loose. After perpetrating their deeds, they eluded detection by darting into the fog. It was of an opake, dingy yellow. Torches were used as guides to carriages at mid-day, but gave scarcely any light through the fog. I went out for a few minutes. It was dismal.

CHAPTER XXII

AMERICANS ABROAD – CASES OF ARBUTHNOT AND
AMBRISTER – OPENING OF PARLIAMENT – ROYAL
SPEECH BY COMMISSION – DINNER AT MR. WELLESLEY
POLE'S – CHESAPEAKE AND SHANNON

January 1, 1819. Twelve of my countrymen dined with me. A
few were residents of London; the remainder, here on their
travels. Some were going to Italy; others had been, or were
going, to France, and other parts of the Continent.

It has been my habit to see my countrymen at my table as
often as in my power. To-day, as generally on these occasions,
we indulged in home topics. Admire as we may what we see
abroad, who among us that has ever left his own country, does
not feel that his warmest affections point to it as a centre?
Though we cannot, in its infancy, claim for it all the monuments of science, letters, and the arts, that are the slow growth
of time, we have already, under each, made rapid progress.
The prospect before us is full of hope; not resting on idle
boast, but the realities of the past. A noble freedom is ours,
resting on the broad basis of equal rights; a freedom fitted for
producing the highest energies and refinements of civilization; yet restrained by constitutional limits; guarded also
against some of the risks of that state by the habits of our
people, who from their origin have been trained to its bless-
ings, and knowing their immense value, will know for ever
how to cling to them. With this, as the ground-work of
national character; with political advantages, the result of
geographical situation; with great agricultural, manufacturing, and commercial capabilities, to what a career of power
and fame, if true to ourselves, may we not look forward! These
are sentiments that Americans meeting in another land,
delight to interchange. The heart has no higher pleasures than
those which the feelings of country inspire. They are exalted
by absence. An American minister abroad, must then be ever

in the experience of his purest social enjoyments, when he sees around him his countrymen as guests.

January 7. Received a note from Lord Castlereagh requesting me to call on him to-day at four, at his private residence. It was dated last night, and indorsed '*Immediate*.' He was confined with the gout. I was shown into a room upstairs, where I found him on his couch.

It was my first interview with him since the negotiation. He expressed his satisfaction at what had been accomplished, with a regret that more had not been done. Of impressment, he said nothing more than that it had gone off on a point unexpected.

He had sent for me on the cases of Arbuthnot and Ambrister. The British Government, he said, had received from Mr. Bagot, their minister in Washington, a copy of the proceedings of the court martial, which had been under full deliberation at a cabinet council.

The opinion formed was, that the conduct of these individuals had been unjustifiable, and therefore not calling for the interference of Great Britain.

Whilst announcing this result he had also to say, that parts of the transaction were viewed as open to exception, whether as regarded some of the operations in Florida, or the conduct of the commanding general, in ordering Ambrister to be executed after the first sentence against him was revoked. He then read me a despatch drawn up to Mr. Bagot, embracing in substance the communication made to me.

I expressed the satisfaction which I was sure my Government would feel at the principal decision, intermingling a regret at the other sentiments with which its disclosure to me had been accompanied.

His lordship then remarked, that it was his desire to hold a conversation with me upon the views of the British Government respecting the Indians along our frontier; but that for the present he would forbear, having reason to expect a communication from me. Here he read part of a despatch from Mr. Bagot, dated the 3rd of December, in which he informs his Government that Mr. Adams had given him to understand that instructions would be sent to me to afford full explanations in relation to the case of these two British subjects.

I replied, that I had actually received such instructions; but as they had only just got to hand, I was not prepared to act upon them. I would be ready at the earliest time he would appoint; on which he named the day after tomorrow. I added, that although the decision to which his Majesty's Government had come, might be considered as anticipating to a certain extent the object of my instructions, I had still a duty of much moment to perform; for that I should ill satisfy the wishes of the President if I suffered the record of the court martial, strong as it was, to be taken as a mere naked record, unaccompanied by elucidations that would serve, I trusted, to place the whole transaction in its right attitude.

Jan. 11. – Called again on Lord Castlereagh. My call had been postponed at his instance, from Saturday until to-day. I felt that the task I had to execute was the more important from the deep sensation which the execution of these individuals had created in England. It was not enough that the act could be technically justified by the strict laws of nations, or sheer rights of war. I felt that it ought to stand on broader grounds; that it ought to be vindicated to humanity no less than justice.

I said to his lordship, that full justice could not be rendered to the United States, if the unhappy occurrence was looked at simply by itself. It was indispensable to consider it in connexion with principles and facts which, for a succession of years, had been interwoven with their history. That it was not my design to enter minutely into this field; but that I should be unable to represent in their true spirit the views, or fulfil the expectations, of my Government, if I did not go into it partially. That it seemed difficult for Europe to understand the precise relations of policy and feeling subsisting between the United States and the Indians. In many respects the misconceptions were fundamental. These Indians were savage, wandering tribes; yet very warlike. Their relations towards the United States were, indeed, so anomalous; there was such an absence of all standards of comparison in Europe, that the rights and obligations of the United States were scarcely perhaps of a nature to be accurately appreciated but by themselves. It seemed a part of their system, more than any other, local and exclusive. The original question of dispossessing the

Indians of their homes, was for the consideration of nations that had gone before us. We had to take them as we found them. The policy and intentions of a nation could nowhere be better read than in its acts of legislation, and habitual conduct. Judged by both, not only would it be found that the United States pursued a just treatment towards the Indians within their territory or along their border, but anxiously sought in all ways to better their condition. They purchased lands from them, only under their own consent. The formed treaties or compacts with them, guaranteeing their rights. Their laws guarded them against the inroads of the whites, prohibited dealings with them by which they might be aggrieved, and in every practicable way sought to diffuse among them the comforts of civilization. But all these just aims had too often failed, and through causes which the United States could not prevent, and sincerely deplored. When peace with the Indians had been interrupted, it was never by the wish of the United States. In the border strife that preceded open hostility, aggression almost necessarily came from the Indian. He lived in the forest. His attack upon the whites was under cover of night, or from his ambush by day. Whole families were surprised and cut off by him. Pursuit could hardly ever reach him, until the tardy force of Government was called out. In this manner the frontier inhabitants had been slain throughout successive generations. But, left to himself, the Indian was not always a dangerous neighbour. If when roused, he took his revenge, he was not desititute of peaceful virtues. He was, moreover, essentially the weaker party. When the Government moved its force, he was sure in the end to be overcome. Hence, if nothing else prevented his incursions, self-interest would be a check, were it not for the intermeddling of others; who, with the double guilt of real enmity to the Indians and the United States, became the party truly responsible for the fate that awaited the former, as well as the butcheries inflicted upon the inhabitants of the latter.

And here, I said, I came to a painful, but indispensable, part of my duty. I was compelled to declare, that my Government, resting upon sufficient proofs, was satisfied, that our Indian wars generally, with the massacres on the frontier always their preludes, had originated in one and the same cause. That they had been produced by British traders, intruding themselves, with evil intentions, among the Indians. To recapitulate the proofs would not be difficult. American history contained them. A single instance might be adverted to. The events of the late war which threw the baggage of General Proctor into the hands of the Americans, had put the Government of the United States in possession of documents to show, that if not all the Indian wars which President Washington had been compelled to wage, the most formidable of them were instigated and sustained on the side of the Indians by British traders. The enormity of such conduct was the more felt in the United States, as it was there alone its consequences were experienced. It was known how explicit had been the refusals of the Government of the United States to admit, under any pretence whatever, British traders among the Indians within their borders; from what motives, might be conjectured from all that I was saying. That his Majesty's Government had disowned all connexion with these agents in their work of death, was well-known. This only exhibited their crimes under a deeper dye, seeing that they persevered in perpetrating them in the name of his Majesty's Government, mocking its justice, abusing its dignity, and misleading the poor Indian but the more fatally by claiming to be invested with its high auspices and support. Here was the fountain of the evil. If any long train of outrages and sufferings along their frontier, could be supposed to affect the sensibilities of a people, it was such as I was obliged to bring into view.

It was under the recollection of them all that the Government of the United States was compelled to regard the cases of Arbuthnot and Ambrister. The necessity of reviewing proofs against them, was superseded by what has passed at our interview on the seventh instant. His Majesty's Government had acquiesced in the reality of their misdeeds, by refusing its avenging arm in their behalf. It only reminded for me to strip their punishment of the features of harshness which, imperfectly understood, it might seem at first to wear. This I could not do more effectually than by declaring it to be the belief of my Government, that it was to these two individuals that the war with the Seminole Indians was to be ascribed. That without their instigation it never would have taken place, any more than the massacres which preceded and provoked it.

As to Ambrister, he had been taken in arms. He had dispensed with the necessity of evidence, by pleading guilty to the charge of leading on the Indians against American troops. And in what light did Ambrister stand? We find him deceiving them by representations which he knew to be untrue; striving to rouse them by artful falsifications of the treaty of Ghent, and unfounded assertions of ill-treatment from the Americans. At another time he is seen applying to the British Minister at Washington, to the British Governor at New Providence, and, indirectly, to the British Government itself, for arms and ammunition for the Indians; drawing on the war by impressions made on their minds that they would be upheld by Britain; and presumptuously usurping the highest official names in Britain, the better to carry on his designs. He was the patron of the Indians, the penman of their petitions, the spokesman at their councils; these were the methods by which he worked upon their passions; these the testimonials of his guilt. It was a guilt to which, in the eye of the Government of the United States, the credulous Indian, whilst perpetrating his worst enormities, was only secondary. It therefore called for the last punishment.

As connected with the general subject of Indian cruelties, I spoke of the massacres of American prisoners during the late war by the tribes associated with the British army. I brought into view those committed after the battle on the river Raisin. On that occasion, American officers, who had surrendered, were scalped and murdered in the presence of British officers, the latter declaring their inability to restrain the ferocity of the Indians. Among the victims was Captain Hart, the brother-in-law of the speaker of the house of Representatives of the United States. The public sensation under such horrors, might be easily imagined. Congress had been forced to pass a law authorizing retaliation on captive British officers, in case of their repetition; the executive of the Union having previously and repeatedly proposed to Great Britain, that neither country should, under any circumstances, employ the Indians as auxiliaries in battle. . . .

I drew to a conclusion by saying, that both of these unhappy individuals had clearly drawn upon themselves their doom.

That towards those who could deliberately become the means of war and bloodshed, the extension of a lenient treatment by the United States, would be to forget what they owed to their own citizens. Long had they borne the evils inflicted by such guilty agents. If a necessary justice had at length, for the first time, held up to public example two of them, there was room for the hope, that, painful as was the example, it might be productive of future good to the cause of humanity. I was directed by the President to say, that whatever deep regret might belong to the occasion, there appeared to be no ground of censure. The commanding general stood high in the confidence of his country, had added to its glory, and was believed on this as other occasions of his life to have been animated only by a sense of the public good. It was scarcely necessary for me to add, that those who mixed themselves up with hordes whose rule of warfare subjected to destruction, with torments, all who fell into their hands, threw themselves out of the pale of those merciful protections which civilized warfare extended to captives. To have allowed these individuals a trial at all, was an indulgence.

His lordship said in the end that he greatly lamented the whole occurrence. It was exciting strong sensibility in England. On this topic he dwelt with some anxiety; giving expression however, for himself, to none other than assuaging sentiments. In this spirit the interview had been conducted and terminated. It may scarcely be necessary to add, that the explanations on my side, were afforded with all the conciliation of manner practicable.

January 14. Received a note from Lord Castlereagh requesting me to call on him. On my arrival he said, that the cases of Arbuthnot and Ambrister were making a deep impression on the public mind; he witnessed it with concern, as he knew not what turn the subject might take when Parliament met; he saw nothing objectionable in the general character of my explanations; on the contrary, that on revolving in his mind all that I said, there were parts which it was rather his desire I would repeat for his more full information. This I did, with the amplifications required. I spoke of the war with the Creek Indians in 1813, and the barbarities at Fort Mimms that provoked it. These, there was much reason for believing, had also been instigated by foreign hands. His lordship requested I would furnish him with a copy of the treaty of peace concluded on that occasion, and a copy of the act of Congress I had mentioned, authorizing retaliation.

January 15. Furnished Lord Castlereagh with a copy of the act of Congress of the 3rd of March 1813, and a copy of the treaty of Fort Jackson, of the 9th of August 1814.

I had expected that he would say something of the views of his Majesty's Government respecting the Indians along our frontier, in pursuance of his intimation on the 9th instant; but he did not. Nor did any further explanations or remarks of a formal nature, pass relative to these executions.

They subsequently became the subject of Parliamentary inquiry. Commentaries that might have been anticipated were made in debate; but Ministers maintained their ground. Out-of-doors, excitement seemed to rise higher and higher. Stocks experienced a slight fall. The newspapers kept up their fire. Little acquainted with the true character of the transaction, they gave vent to angry declamation. They fiercely denounced the Government of the United States. Tyrant, ruffian, murderer, were among the epithets applied to their commanding general. He was exhibited in placards through the streets. The journals, without distinction of party, united in these attacks. The Whig and others in opposition took the lead. Those in the Tory interest, although more restrained, gave them countenance. In the midst of all this passion, the ministry stood firm. Better informed, more just, they had made up their minds not to risk the peace of the two countries, on grounds so untenable. It forms an instance of the intelligence and strength of a Government, disregarding the first clamours of a powerful press, and first erroneous impulses of an almost universal public feeling. At a later day of my mission, Lord Castlereagh said to me, that a war might have been produced on this occasion, 'if the ministry had but held up a finger.' On so slender a thread do public affairs sometimes hang. I retain the belief, that the firmness of Lord Castlereagh under this emergency, sustained by that of his colleagues in the cabinet, was the main cause of preventing a rupture between the two nations.

January 20. Lord Castlereagh gives an official dinner to-day

to the members of the Cabinet and Privy Council, amounting
in all to between thirty and forty. The object is, to agree finally
upon the Prince Regent's speech to Parliament. It is already
drawn up, and will be read by his lordship. This is the custom,
my informant said, every year, the day before Parliament
meets. The office of entertaining the Ministers, and reading
the speech, generally devolves, he added, on the leading
ministerial member in the House of Commons. It had been
for many years in the hands of Lord Castlereagh.

January 21. Parliament was opened. The Prince Regent did
not come in person to the House of Lords. Five Commissioners represented him, viz. the Lord Chancellor, the
Archbishop of Canterbury, the Marquish Camden, the Earl of
Westmoreland, and the Earl of Harrowby. The speech was
read by the Lord Chancellor. It anounced two events, and
only two, in connexion with the foreign relations of the
country. First, that the negotiations of Aix la Chapelle had led
to the evacuation of the French territory by the Allied armies.
Secondly, that a treaty had been concluded with the United
States for the renewal of the commercial convention, and 'the
amicable adjustment of several points of mutual importance
to the interests of both nations.' It stated the trade and
manufactures of Great Britain to be in a most flourishing condition, and that there was a progressive improvement of the
revenue in its most important branches.

January 23. Dined at Mr. Wellesley Pole's. There were at
table, Mr. and Mrs Pole, Mrs Rush, Lady Harvey of Maryland,
Lady Georgiana Fane, Miss Caton of Maryland, the Duke of
Wellington, the Earl of Westmoreland, Lord Fitzroy Somerset,
one of the aids of the Duke of Wellington, Sir Felton Harvey,
another, young Mr. Fane, Mr. M'Tavish of Baltimore, and
Mr. Bouverie.

Conversation was various. Mr. Bagot's probable return
home in May, was mentioned. A frigate was to be sent for him.
I spoke of the satisfaction his diplomatic career had given at
Washington, and from authority, having been directed by the
President to say so to Lord Castlereagh.

Paris and French society were talked of. The Duke of
Wellington and Lord Fitzroy Somerset took a leading share in
what was said. Mention was made of a solemn celebration on

Thursday at the chapel of the French embassy in London, to commemorate the anniversary of the execution of Louis the Sixteenth. The priest read the will of Louis. Lord Fitzroy Somerset, in describing the good accommodations of the house in Paris in which the Duke resided when last there, said it was the same that President Monroe had occupied during his mission to France.

We heard of the exploits of one of the company during the late shooting-season. Eight hundred and twelve partridges, and three hundred and thirty pheasants, were the fruits of his marksmanship. Other exploits of the same nature were spoken of; some that exceeded them. A gentleman was named on whose estate, at the preceding season, three thousand hares were shot by himself and friends; all explained, I might add, by the game monopoly. Something remarkable for numbers in another way, happened to be stated; that Colonel Vivian was one of twenty-six children, and the Bishop of Norwich the youngest of thirty.

Painting became a topic. The collections in France, Spain, and the Low Countries, were familiar to some of the company. My attention was most excited by what was said of a picture of the Black Prince, lately picked up for a few francs at a sale on the Continent. Mr. Pole said there were good grounds for believing it to be an original, formerly of the royal collection in England. The account given was, that James II took it with him to France when he abdicated, since which it had been lost sight of, until traced by chance at this sale. Lord Westmoreland had his doubts, from the circumstances under which James left England. Mr. Pole saw no incompatibility. This turned the conversation to the personal fortunes of that monarch. The picture afterwards gave it a turn to the Plantagenets. Touching upon this part of English history, it was remarked, that the Duke of Wellington had won a battle in Spain on the ground where the Black Prince gained one; that both had fought in the cause of the crown of Spain, one for the restoration of Peter of Castile, the other for that of Ferdinand the Seventh; each Spanish monarch having been ejected by the French. These were close parallels. Another was probably in the thoughts of the company – the fields of Poictiers and Waterloo. All, I believe, would have destined the picture, if genuine, to the ownership of the Duke, as a companion to the colossal statue of Napoleon at Apsley House.

Sir Felton Harvey and Lord Fitzroy Somerset had each lost an arm in the battles of the Duke. The Duke himself had never been wounded. Others of his military suite had been maimed or killed by his side. Sir Felton had been with him in most of his campaigns in the Peninsula. He said to me, speaking of the Duke after dinner, that his self-possession enabled him to sleep soundly on the brink of danger. Often when lying down, under his usual order to be awoke if necessary, he had known him called up repeatedly within a few hours, by the arrival of expresses, and if no movement was required, drop asleep again in a moment. It was such conversation and more, that the evening brought with it.

Of Sir Felton Harvey I subsequently learned an anecdote. It may be in print, but I have not seen it. During one of the battles in Spain, the Duke gave him an order to convey to another part of the field. Half across it, a French officer was seen galloping towards him. Sir Felton had no sword. It was his right arm he had lost; the other held the bridle. But he faced the foe, looking him defiance. As they swiftly drew near, the Frenchman raised himself on his stirrups, his sword uplifted. Discovering his adversary to be defenceless, he brings down his weapon in the form of a salute, and rapidly passes on. Such acts give to war touches of moral beauty, in spite of its evils. After the battle, the restless courtesy of Harvey sought in vain for the chivalrous Gaul. There was too much reason to think he fell. He had made no boast of sparing life, but gave his salute in silence.

January 26. Mr * * * * * called on me. He applied for an interview, stating himself to be _____. It was his purpose to ask information relative to the navy boards of the United States, and other matters pertaining to the civil organization of our marine. He talked a good deal. Sometimes his remarks were more full than the mere desire for information seemed to call. A foolish rumour was in town of Bonaparte's escape from St. Helena, the rumour adding that a fast-sailing American schooner had been in the plot. This led him to speak of the exploits of the American navy. He touched upon them with sufficient complaisance, but wound up with an allusion to the action between the Chesapeake and Shannon. That, on the whole, ought to be considered, he thought, the fairest trial of the naval prowess of the two countries, frigate to frigate. I did not argue with him. He soon left me, after the somewhat singular topics it had been his pleasure to indulge in. It was the first and only time it had been my lot to hear any broached in England not suited to the good feelings of conversation, though, certainly, I experienced no uneasiness.

The Chesapeake, it is true, was captured. The English captain won his prize gallantly; let no American gainsay this. We heard how the achievement was hailed in England; the more, as it had been preceded by a series of encounters terminating differently. But, with whatever satisfaction received there, I cannot think that it equalled the opposite feeling in the United States. I remember (what American does not?) the first rumour of it. I remember the startling sensation. I remember, at first, the universal incredulity. I remember how the post-offices were thronged, for successive days, with anxious thousands; how collections of citizens rode out for miles on the highway, accosting the mail to catch something by anticipation. At last, when the certainty was known, I remember the public gloom. Funeral orations, badges of mourning, bespoke it. '*Don't give up the ship!*' the dying words of Laurence, slain by the first broadside, were on every tongue. His remains were interred at Halifax, with the honours due to a brave foe. But not long did they lie there. When peace came, a vessel, fitted out by American sea-captains, and by these exclusively manned, brought them back to his country. There they rest, under the laurel and cypress; for he too had formerly triumphed over his English adversary, ship to ship. Others may augur the naval destinies of the United States from their victories; I, from the feelings that followed this defeat.

CHAPTER XXIII

DEATH OF THE MARQUIS OF LONDONDERRY – THE
FOREIGN AMBASSADORS AND MINISTERS ATTEND HIS
FUNERAL – MR. CANNING BECOMES FOREIGN
SECRETARY OF ENGLAND – INSTRUCTIONS FOR
OPENING AN EXTENSIVE NEGOTIATION WITH
ENGLAND – INTERVIEW WITH MR. CANNING ON THAT
SUBJECT – CONVERSATION WITH HIM ON THE PLANS
OF FRANCE, AND THE EUROPEAN ALLIANCE,
RESPECTING SPANISH AMERICA – RELATIONSHIP OF
THE UNITED STATES TO THIS SUBJECT – DINNER AT
MR. PLANTA'S – GAME OF TWENTY QUESTIONS

July, 1823. The last preceding memorandum in this irregular
narrative of a public mission, was in January 1819. I cannot
resume its thread, here broken by a chasm of four years,
without alluding to the death of the Marquis of Londonderry,
which happened in August, 1822. He died by his own hand at
North Cray, his country home, in Kent. The event proceeded
from temporary aberration of mind, caused, in all probability,
by his laborious exertions as ministerial leader in the House of
Commons, during the session of parliament which had just
closed; added to toils and solicitudes of scarcely inferior bur-
den upon him, as first minister of the crown for foreign affairs.
His death created a great shock. As a statesman moving largely
in English and European affairs, during the momentous
transactions which preceded and followed the overthrow of
Napoleon, and influencing decidedly some of them, history
has already passed upon his character; and it is no part of my
purpose in these humble and fugitive pages, to discuss it in
those relations. But in relation to that portion of English
statesmanship which has to deal with American affairs, and it
is no unimportant portion, I must appeal to the preceding
pages, to attest the candid and liberal spirit in which he was
ever disposed to regard them. Let those who would doubt it,

consult the archives of the two nations since the end of our revolutionary war, and point out the British statesman, of any class or party, who, up to the period of his death, made more advances, or did more in fact, towards placing their relations upon an amicable footing. His sentiments were all of a lofty kind. His private life was pure, and all who knew him in those relations loved him. In society he was attractive in the highest degree; the firmness and courage of his nature, being not more remarkable than the gentleness and suavity of his manners. He was buried in Westminster Abbey, between the graves of Pitt and Fox. The diplomatic corps all went to his funeral; and not one among them could gaze upon his pall, without having his memory filled with recollections of kindnesses received from him. His personal attentions to them, were shown in ways which appeared to put out of view their coming from an official source, by the impression they made on the heart. Might not each individual of the large assemblage of ambassadors and ministers who were of the funeral train, naturally have felt grief at the death of such a foreign secretary? struck down, as he also was, so suddenly, and in so melancholy a way, in the midst of his high employments, and with apparently so strong a hold upon life and its honours? Nor did I ever see manly sorrow more depicted in any countenance than that of the Duke of Wellington, as he too took a last look at the coffin when lowered down into the vault.

Upon the death of Lord Londonderry, the office of Secretary of State for Foreign Affairs in England, passed to the hands of Mr. Canning – a name also known to fame. He was a statesman and an orator; filling each sphere with powers highly disciplined, whether their exercise was felt on great occasions, or only dazzled on lighter ones. He was the ornament also of private life, in a society refined by age, by education, and by wealth; ascendant in the highest literary circles, and adding dignity to those of rank. His rural residence was at Gloucester Lodge; and his classic dinners at that abode, as the hospitalities of Lord Londonderry at North Cray and St. James's Square, will long be remembered by the diplomatic corps as reliefs along the often anxious path of international business. He too, soon passed away. Raised by his genius to the Premiership, the proud dream, it may be, of his life, he died almost immediately after ascending that pinnacle; the victim, in his turn, of official labours and solicitudes too intense, superadded to those of that stormy ocean where his sway was great – the House of Commons. Britain entombed him also, side by side with those of her distinguished men whose lives were devoted to her service, or her renown.

During the interval of four years and more, which I have passed over, much of public business passed through my hands, and had its completion. I am about to enter upon some account of further negotiations which I conducted with the British government on subjects, some of which still remain unsettled, and have a deep present interest. It has been for the purpose of reaching the point of time when I was first instructed to open these negotiations that I have passed over the intervals mentioned; lest I should extend to undue limits a work, which may already be too long for the reader's patience. Mr. Canning continued at the head of foreign affairs during the full remaining term of my mission.

July 29. To-day I received from Mr. Adams, Secretary of State, five several despatches, each one on a subject in regard to which I am directed to open a negotiation with this Government.

The first bears date the 23rd of June, 1823, and relates to the commercial intercourse between the United States and all the British Colonies in America; England having opened her West India trade to us by Act of Parliament last year, though in a manner which has not proved satisfactory in its practical effects.

The second is dated on the 24th of June, and relates to the suppression of the slave trade.

The third, on the 25th of June; and relates to the unsettled boundary line between the United States and Great Britain, as mentioned in the fifth Article of the Treaty of Ghent.

The fourth, on the 26th of June; and relates to the admission of consuls of the United States in the colonial ports of Great Britain.

The fifth, on the 27th of June; and relates to the fishery on the western coast of Newfoundland.

Instructions are given to me under each of the foregoing

heads, with Mr. Adams's accustomed ability. Documents of various kinds are added; and the first despatch, enclosed a full power to me, from the President, to conclude and sign, on behalf of the United States, any treaty or treaties, convention or conventions, to which the negotiation might give rise.

August 1. I acknowledge the receipt of all the foregoing instructions and documents, and say to the Secretary of State, that whilst I am sensible to the confidence which the being charged with the discussion and settlement of so many and such important subjects manifests in me, I feel the heavy responsibility which it creates.

August 16. On the 4th instant, I addressed a note to Mr. Canning, asking an interview on the subject of the negotiations to be proposed to his Majesty's Government, and he appointed Monday, the 11th, to receive me. When that day arrived, I had not been able, through various interruptions, to give to the whole of my instructions the careful consideration necessary to make me ready in conversation on whatever points might happen to be touched, even on first broaching the subjects to Mr. Canning. I therefore asked a postponement of the interview, and it accordingly went off until to-day, when it was held at the Foreign Office.

I proceeded to mention to him the various subjects in their order; and further told him that I was in expectation of receiving, at an early day, instructions upon certain points of maritime law, which it was deemed desirable for the two nations to discuss and settle at the same time with all the other questions.

He replied, that the number and importance of the subjects, added to the novelty of some of them, to him at first blush, would render some interval necessary before the time and manner of taking them all up, could be determined upon; but that I should hear from him again, as soon as he was able to give due reflection to the whole matter of my communication. He mentioned also, that he was thinking of a short excursion into the country in a few days, and, perhaps, another in September, as his share of relaxation for the season, after his late parliamentary and other fatigues. I put into his hands an informal memorandum of the different subjects, and reported to my Government what passed at this first interview.

The proper object of it over, I transiently asked him whether, notwithstanding the late news from Spain, we might not still hope that the Spaniards would get the better of their difficulties. Pursuing the topic I said, that should France ultimately effect her purpose of overthrowing the constitutional Government in Spain, there was, at least, the consolation left, that Great Britain would not allow her to go farther, and stop the progress of emancipation in the colonies. . . . On my intimating this sentiment, Mr. Canning asked me what I thought my Government would say to going hand in hand with England in such a policy? He did not think that concert of *action* would become necessary, fully believing that the simple fact of our two countries being known to hold the same opinions, would, by its moral effect, put down the intention on the part of France, if she entertained it. This belief was founded, he said, upon the large share of the maritime power of the world which Great Britain and the United States shared between them, and the consequent influence which the knowledge of their common policy on a question involving such important maritime interests, present and future, could not fail to produce upon the rest of the world.

I replied, that in what manner my Government would look upon such a suggestion, I was unable to say; it was one surrounded by important considerations, and I would communicate it to my Government in the same informal manner in which he had thrown it before me. . . .

July 20. Under the present date, I go back a few days in the month in which I re-commence my too-often disjointed narrative, for the sake of speaking of a dinner at Mr. Planta's, recollected with pleasure, probably, by others as well as myself. On the death of Lord Londonderry, Mr. Planta, who had long enjoyed his confidence and esteem, continued his connexion with the Foreign Office, as one of the Under-Secretaries of State. It was in dining with him to-day, that we had Count Lieven, the Russian Ambassador; Count Martin D'Aglie, the Sardinian Envoy; Mr. Canning, Mr. Huskisson, Mr. Robinson, the Chancellor of the Exchequer, Lord Gran-

ville, Lord George Bentinck, Lord Francis Conyngham, Mr.
Charles Ellis, of the House of Commons, and Lord Howard
de Walden.

It would not have been easy to assemble a company better
fitted to make a dinner party agreeable. There was much small
talk, some of it very sprightly. Ten o'clock arriving, with little
disposition to rise from table, Mr. Canning proposed that we
should play 'Twenty Questions.' This was new to me and the
other members of the diplomatic corps present, though we
had all been a good while in England. The game consisted in
endeavours to find out your thoughts by asking twenty questions. The questions were to be put plainly, though in the
alternative if desired; the answers to be also plain and direct.
The object of your thoughts not to be an abstract idea, nor a
mere event, as a battle, for instance, nor any thing so occult, or
scientific, or technical, as not to be supposed to enter into the
knowledge of the company; but something well known to the
present day, or to general history. These were mentioned as
among the general rules of the game, and it was agreed that Mr.
Canning, assisted by the Chancellor of the Exchequer, who sat
next to him, should put the questions; and that I, assisted by
Lord Granville, who sat next to me, should give the answers.
Lord Granville and myself were, consequently, to have the
thought or secret in common; and it was well understood, that
the discovery of it, if made, was to be the fair result of mental
inference from the questions and answers, not of signs passing, or hocus pocus of any description. With these as the pre-
liminaries, and the parties sitting face to face, on opposite
sides of the table, we began the battle.

First question (by Mr. Canning) – Does what you have
thought of belong to the animal or vegetable kingdom?

Answer – To the vegetable.

Second question – Is it manufactured, or unmanufactured?
Manufactured.

Third – Is it a solid or a liquid?
A solid.

[How could it be a liquid, said one of the company, slyly,
unless vegetable soup!]

Fourth – Is it a thing entire in itself, or in parts?
Entire.

Fifth – Is it for private use of public?

Public.

Sixth – Does it exist in England, or out of it?

In England.

Seventh – Is it single, or are there others of the same kind?

Single.

Eighth – Is it historical, or only existent at present?

Both.

Ninth – For ornament or use?

Both.

Tenth – Has it any connexion with the person of the King?

No.

Eleventh – Is it carried, or does it support itself?

The former.

Twelfth – Does it pass by succession?

[Neither Lord Granville nor myself being quite certain on this point, the question was not answered; but, as it was thought that the very hesitation to answer might serve to shed light upon the secret, it was agreed that the question should be counted as one, in the progress of the game.]

Thirteenth – Was it used at the coronation?

Yes.

Fourteenth – In the Hall or Abbey?

Probably in both: certainly in the Hall.

Fifteenth – Does it belong specially to the ceremony of the coronation, or is it used at other times?

It is used at other times.

Sixteenth – Is it exclusively of a vegetable nature, or is it not, in some parts, a compound of a vegetable and a mineral?

Exclusively of a vegetable nature.

Seventeenth – What is its shape?

[This question was objected to as too particular; and the company inclining to think so, it was withdrawn; but Mr. Canning saying it would be hard upon him to count it, as it was withdrawn; the decision was in his favour on that point, and it was not counted.]

Seventeenth (repeated). – Is it decorated, or simple?

[We made a stand against this question also, as too particular; but the company not inclining to sustain us this time, I had to answer it and said that it was simple.]

Eighteenth. Is it used in the ordinary ceremonial of the House of Commons, or House of Lords?

No.

Nineteenth. Is it ever used by either House?

No.

Twentieth. Is it generally stationary or movable?

Movable.

The whole number of questions being now exhausted, there was a dead pause. The interest had gone on increasing as the game advanced, until, coming to the last question, it grew to be like neck-and-neck at the close of a race. Mr. Canning sat silent for a minute or two; then, rolling his rich eye about, and with a countenance a little anxious, and in an accent by no means over-confident, he exclaimed, 'I think it must be the wand of the Lord High-Steward!' And it was – EVEN SO.

This wand is a long, plain, white staff, not much thicker than your middle finger, and, as such, justifies all the answers given.

In answering the ninth question, Lord Granville and I, who conferred together in a whisper as to all answers not at once obvious, remembered that some quaint old English writers say that the Lord High-Steward carried his *staff* to beat off intruders from his Majesty's treasury! When at the twelfth, Mr. Canning illustrated the nature of his question by referring to the *rod of the Lord Chamberlain*, which he said did not pass by succession, each new incumbent procuring, as he supposed, a new one for himself, I said that it was not the Lord Chamberlain's rod; but the very mention of this was '*burning*,' as children say when they play hide-and-seek; and in answering that it was not, I had to take care of my emphasis.

The questions were not put in the rapid manner in which they will be read; but sometimes after considerable intervals, not of silence – for they were enlivened by occasional remarks thrown in by the company, all of whom grew intent upon the pastime as it advanced, though Mr. Canning alone put the questions, and I alone gave out the answers. It lasted upwards of an hour, the wine ceasing to go round. On Mr. Canning's success, for it was touch-and-go with him, there was a burst of approbation, we of the diplomatic corps saying, that we must be very careful not to let him ask us too many questions at the Foreign Office, lest he should find out every secret that we had!

The number of the questions and latitude allowed in putting them, added to the restrictions imposed upon the selection of the secret, leave to the person putting them a less difficult task than might, at first, be imagined; and accordingly, such of company as had witnessed the pastime before, said, that the discovery took place, for the most part, by the time the questions were half gone through – sometimes sooner; and that they had never known it protracted to the twentieth until this occasion. It is obvious that each successive question, with its answer, goes on narrowing the ground of defence, until at last the assailant drives his antagonist into a corner, almost forcing a surrender of the secret. Nevertheless, this presupposes skill in putting the questions; and he who consents to take that part in the game, must know what he can do. It was not until twelve o'clock that we all rose from table, and went up stairs to coffee. So it is that these Ministers of State relax; and it was a spectacle not without interest to see such men as Canning, Huskisson, and Robinson, giving themselves up to this kind of recreation as a contrast in the first, to his anxious labours in the whole field of foreign affairs; in the second, to his speeches on the sugar question, the warehousing system, and on alterations in the tariff; and in the third, to his endless mass of financial questions, during a long and toilsome session of Parliament just ended.

Dining at the Marquis of Stafford's at a subsequent day, this pastime was spoken of; and it was mentioned that Mr. Pitt and Mr. Windham were both fond of it. Lord Stafford said, that the former had once succeeded in it, when the secret was the *stone* upon which Walworth, Lord Mayor of London, stood when he struck down Wat Tyler, in Richard the Second's time; and his impression was, that Mr. Pitt had triumphed at an early stage of his questions.

CHAPTER XXIV

TWO COMMUNICATIONS FROM MR. CANNING, ON
SPANISH-AMERICAN AFFAIRS – STEPS TAKEN UNDER
THEM – FURTHER INSTRUCTIONS ON THE PROPOSED
NEGOTIATION – THIRD COMMUNICATION FROM MR.
CANNING, ON SPANISH-AMERICAN AFFAIRS

August 22. This day brought me an important note from Mr. Canning, dated the twentieth instant, Foreign Office. He informs me, that before leaving town he is desirous of bringing before me in a more distinct, but still in an unofficial and confidential shape, the question opened and shortly discussed between us on the sixteenth instant.

He asks if the moment has not arrived when our two Governments might understand each other as to the Spanish-American Colonies; and if so, whether it would not be expedient for ourselves, and beneficial for all the world, that our principles in regard to them should be clearly settled and avowed. That as to England she had no disguise on the subject.

1. She conceived the recovery of the Colonies by Spain, to be hopeless.

2. That the question of their recognition as independent states, was one of time and circumstances.

3. That England was not disposed, however, to throw any impediment in the way of an arrangement between the Colonies and mother country, by amicable negotiation.

4. That she aimed at the possession of no portion of the Colonies for herself.

5. That she could not see the transfer of any portion of them to any other power, with indifference.

That if the United States acceded to such views, a declaration to that effect on their part concurrently with England, would be the most effectual, and least offensive mode of making known their joint disapprobation of contrary projects. And I am asked, in conclusion, whether I consider that the full power which I had lately received from my Government, would authorize me to enter into negotiation to sign a convention on the above subject; and if not, if I could exchange with him, as the organ of the British Government, ministerial notes in relation to it.

Such was the purport of his communication. It was framed in a spirit of great cordiality, and expressed an opinion, that seldom perhaps at any time among nations, had an opportunity occurred when so small an effort of two friendly Governments might produce so unequivocal a good, and prevent such extensive calamities.

August 23. I replied to Mr. Canning's note to the following effect: I said, that the Government of the United States having, in the most formal manner, acknowledged the independence of the late Spanish provinces in America, desired to see it maintained with stability, and under auspices that might promise happiness to the new states themselves, as well as advantage to the rest of the world; and that, as conducing to those great ends, my Government had long desired, and still anxiously desired, to see them received into the family of nations by the powers of Europe, and especially by Great Britain.

That in other respects, I believed the sentiments unfolded in his note were shared by the United States; because, first, we considered the recovery of the Colonies by Spain to be entirely hopeless. 2. We would throw no impediment in the way of an arrangement between them and the mother country by amicable negotiation, supposing an arrangement of such a nature to be possible. 3. We did not aim at the possession of any of those communities for ourselves. 4th, and last, we should regard as highly unjust, and fruitful of disastrous consequences, any attempt on the part of any European Power, to take possession of them by conquest, by cession, or on any other ground or pretext.

But I added, that in what manner my Government might deem it most expedient to avow these principles, were points on which all my instructions were silent, as well as the power I had lately received to enter upon negotiations with His Majesty's Government; but that I would promptly make known to the

President the opinions and views of which he had made me the depositary, and that I was of nothing more sure than that he would fully appreciate their importance, and not less the frank and friendly feelings towards the United States which their communication to me bespoke.

I immediately transmitted to my Government a copy of the foregoing correspondence; preparing it in quadruplicate, with the request to the Consul at Liverpool to send them off by the earliest ships for New York, or other ports of the United States. . . .

August 30. I have received, and this day acknowledge, the Secretary of State's despatch, of the 2nd of July, relative to the North-west coast of America; his of the 28th of July, relative to maritime questions, and principles of maritime and commercial neutrality; and his of the 29th of July, embracing some general reflections upon the extent and importance of the whole negotiation committed to my hands.

I remark, that having now before me all his instructions, I am fully sensible of the magnitude of the subjects to be treated of; 'of the complicated character' – here using some of the Secretary's own words – 'of the considerations involved in most of them, and of their momentous bearings, in present and future ages, upon the interests, the welfare, and the honour of the United States.' I add the expression anew of the deep sense which I entertain of the President's confidence in committing to my hands negotiations so extensive. . . .

September 1. In writing to the Secretary of State on the importance of the contemplated negotiations, and of the labour of investigation as well as extent of responsibility which it will devolve upon me, I express a wish that the President would be pleased to assign me a colleague. I add, that to associate a colleague with me, would conform to the past practice of our Government, which had always been, on occasions of difficult and complicated negotiations, to employ more than one negotiator; more especially, when the European Power employed more than one. . . .

September 10. Take steps to apprise the deputies of Spanish America in London, of the hostile views of France and the continental Powers, should the arms of the former succeed in Spain. I make no mention of Mr. Canning's name, or any allusion to it, as the source of my information, which information, although it may not be new to these deputies, I impart to put them still more on their guard.

September 12. Take further steps to warn the deputies of the plans of France and the allies, withholding altogether, as before, the source of my information, but letting it be understood that the information is not to be slighted.

September 15. Write to President Monroe, and in continuation of the Spanish American subject say, that Mr. Canning being still out of town, I was giving myself up to investigations which might the better prepare me for taking in hand the various subjects which his confidence had devolved upon me, to discuss and arrange with his Government; that on Mr. Canning's return, I should expect to be invited to an interview, and doubted not but that the whole topic of Spanish American affairs would be resumed between us. That it was still my intention to urge upon him the immediate recognition of the new States by Great Britain; that otherwise our two countries would not stand upon equal ground in going into the measure proposed, we having already acknowledged the new States, but that I would continue to receive, in the most conciliatory manner, new overtures from him; for that my most careful observation in England during my residence, had impressed me with the belief, that the present administration, with Lord Liverpool still at its head, was as favourably disposed towards us as any that could be formed.

CHAPTER XXV

FULL INTERVIEW WITH MR. CANNING, ON SPANISH-AMERICAN AFFAIRS, AND REPORT OF WHAT PASSED – FURTHER INTERVIEW ON THE SAME SUBJECT; AND ON THAT OF THE NEGOTIATION, TO THE OPENING OF WHICH ENGLAND ACCEDES – MR. HUSKISSON AND MR. STRATFORD CANNING, TO BE THE BRITISH NEGOTIATORS – RENEWED INTERVIEW WITH MR. CANNING, ON THE AFFAIRS OF SPANISH AMERICA, AND REPORT OF WHAT PASSED

September 18. Had a full conference with Mr. Canning, at the Foreign Office, in which the subject of Spanish-American affairs was resumed, and the discussion of it gone into at large.

September 19. I reported in the following despatch to the Secretary of State, all that passed in my interview with Mr. Canning, yesterday; relying only upon the substantial fidelity of the report, as it must needs fall short of what is due to Mr. Canning in language, though I endeavoured to recall his own words, as far as I could.

No.331.   'London, September 19, 1823.

SIR, – Mr. Canning returned to town about a week ago, and I had an interview with him at the Foreign Office, yesterday, at his request.

'He entered at once upon the subject of Spanish America, remarking, that he thought it claimed precedence over all others between us, at the present juncture. Military events in the Peninsula seemed every day to be drawing nearer to a crisis in favour of the French arms, and the political arrangements projected afterwards, would, there was good reason to suppose, be immediately directed to the affairs of the late Colonies. . . .

'As to the proposals he had submitted to me, I said, that I

was sure he would himself appreciate the delicacy and novelty of the ground upon which I stood. The United States, it was true, would view any attempt on the part of France, and the continental Alliance, to resubjugate those new States, as a transcendent act of national injustice, and indicative of progressive and alarming ambition; yet, to join Great Britain in a declaration to this effect might lay them open in some respects to consequences, upon the character and extent of which it became my duty to reflect, with great caution, before making up my mind to meet the responsibilities of them. The value of my declaration, it was agreed, would depend upon its being formally made known to Europe. Would not such a step wear the appearance of the United States implicating themselves in the political connexions of Europe? Would it not be acceding, in this instance, at least, to the policy of one of the Great European Powers, in opposition to the projects avowed by others of the first rank? This, hitherto, had been no part of the system of the United States; the very reverse of it had been acted upon. Their foreign policy had been essentially bottomed on the great maxim of preserving peace and harmony with all nations, without offending any, or forming entangling alliances with any. In this broad principle, laid one of my difficulties under his proposals.

'He replied, that however just such a policy might have been formerly, or might continue to be as a general policy, he apprehended that powerful and controlling circumstances made it inapplicable upon the present occasion. The question was a new and complicated one in modern affairs. It was also full as much American as European, to say no more. It concerned the United States under aspects and interests as immediate and commanding, as it did or could any of the States of Europe. They were the first Power established on that continent, and now confessedly the leading Power. They were connected with Spanish America by their position, as with Europe by their relations; and they also stood connected with these new States by political relations. Was it possible that they could see with indifference their fate decided upon by Europe? Could Europe expect this indifference? Had not a new epoch arrived in the relative position of the United States towards Europe, which Europe must acknowledge? Were the great political and commercial interests which hung upon the destinies of the new continent, to be canvassed and adjusted in this hemisphere, without the co-operation or even knowledge of the United States? Were they to be canvassed and adjusted, he would even add, without some proper understanding between the United States and Great Britain, as the two chief commercial and maritime States of both worlds? He hoped not, he would wish to persuade himself not. Such was the tenor of his remarks.

'I said that his suggestions were entitled to great consideration, and that such, and others of the same nature, would probably not escape the attention of my Government, as they had not him. That for myself, speaking only as an individual, I could well conceive that the interposition of an authoritative voice by the United States in favour of these new communities in our hemisphere, would imply no real departure from the principles which had hitherto regulated their foreign intercourse, or pledge them henceforth to the political connexions of the old world. But, I added, that as the questions of the United States expressing this voice, and promulgating it under official authority to the powers of Europe, was one of entire novelty as well as great magnitude in their history, it was for my Government and not me to decide upon its propriety. I was willing to take upon myself all fair responsibility attaching to the station which I held; but here was a conjecture wholly new. It presented a case not seeming to fall within the range of any of the contingent or discretionary duties which could have been in contemplation when I was clothed with my commission as minister to this court.

'He said, that the case being new might serve to account for my not being in possession of previous or specific powers bearing upon it, but that its very nature precluded delay. He had the strongest reasons for believing that the co-operation of the United States with England through my instrumentality, afforded with promptitude, would ward off altogether the meditated jurisdiction of the European powers over the new world. Could higher motives exist to co-operation, and immediately? Let it be delayed until I could receive specific powers, and the day might go by; the progress of events was rapid; the public evil might happen. Why then should the

United States, whose institutions resembled those of Great Britain more than they did those of the other powers in Europe, and whose policy upon this occasion was closely approximated to hers, hesitate to act with her to promote a common object approved alike by both, and achieve a common good estimated alike by both? Such was the drift of his remarks, which he amplified and enforced with his wonted ability. . . .

'The complication of the subject,' said I, 'may be cured at once, and by Great Britain. Let Great Britain immediately and unequivocally *acknowledge the independence of the new States*. This will put an end to all difficulty; the moment is auspicious; every thing invites to the measure; justice, expediency, humanity, the repose of the world, the cause of national independence, the prosperity and happiness of both hemispheres; let Britain but adopt this measure, so just in itself, so recommended by the point of time before us, and the cause of all Spanish America triumphs; the European Congress might meet *afterwards*, if it chose to take so harmless a step.'

He said, that such a measure was open to objection; but asked if he was to understand that it would make any difference in my powers or conduct?

I replied, the greatest difference. I had frankly informed him that I had no *specific* powers to consent to his proposals in the shape in which they had first been presented to me. But that great step of acknowledging the independence of the new States being taken, I would stand upon my general powers as Minister Plenipotentiary. I would be the interpreter of them myself. I had no hesitation in saying, that, under this general warrant, I would put forth, with Great Britain, the declaration to which he had invited me; that I would do so in the name of my Government, and consent to its formal promulgation to the world under all the sanctions, and with all the present validity, that I could impart to it. I had examined all my instructions for years past, bearing, either directly or remotely, on the great cause of these new States; I saw in them all so steady and strong a desire for the firm establishment of their freedom and independence; and if I could thus be instrumental in any degree towards accelerating the acknowledgment of Spanish-American independence, I should feel that I had achieved a positive and great good. Upon British recognition hung, not indeed the final, but perhaps in an eminent degree the *present* tranquillity and happiness of those States.

He said that among the objections to recognizing, at present, was still that of the uncertain condition, internally, of these new States; or at any rate of some of them. He had, for example, sent an agent in January last to Mexico, supposing that Iturbide was at the head of affairs; but by the time he had arrived, a fresh revolution had set up other representatives of the executive authority. The same internal vicissitudes were to be remarked in other of these communities, more to the South.

As regarded the latter topic I replied, that . . . the dilemma thence arising, was not greater than had been witnessed in France during a period of more than twenty years, while her revolution was in progress; than had been seen in Naples more recently, or than was experienced, at the present time, by Great Britain in her diplomatic intercourse with both Portugal and Spain. Had we not seen revolutions and counter-revolutions, royal governments, constitutional governments, and regency governments, succeeding each other, almost day by day, in the oldest countries of Europe? Why then be surprised at changes in the new world? These very changes would be likely to be largely, if not entirely, checked, by the fact of the new States being recognized by Britain. It would tend to give stability to their institutions; and, by breaking down the hopes of the discontented and factious among themselves, become guarantees for their greater internal tranquillity. They had given ample proofs both of military power and political wisdom. Look at Buenos Ayres, which as long back as 1807, could repulse the well appointed legions of even Britain herself. Look at Colombia, who was now laying the groundwork of a confederacy for all Spanish America, and at the same time marching her auxiliary forces into Peru, to uphold the cause of emancipation upon that shore. The independence of all the late colonies of Spain on that continent, was, in fine, the new political element of modern times, and must henceforth pervade the political arrangements of both worlds. Why then should Britain longer forbear to acknowledge this independence? She had already done so in effect, and why should she not in form? What circumstances could be imagined more imperious for hastening this formal recognition, than those now existing; when Spain was seen to be wholly incapacitated from regaining dominion over them, and continental Europe meditating such unwarrantable designs upon them?

'It was thus that I endeavoured to unfold what I suppose to be the views and convictions of the President upon this important subject. Our conversation was a prolonged one, and characterized by the freedom with which I have reported it; in doing which I have sedulously aimed at faithfully presenting all its material points. I do not flatter myself with any sanguine belief that this Government will be prepared to yield to my appeals in favour of immediate recognition; but I am to have another interview with Mr. Canning on a day that he is yet to name, and I can only say that I will be prepared to renew and extend them as opportunities may be afforded me. . . .

'I have the honour to remain, with very great respect, your obedient Servant,

RICHARD RUSH

The Honourable JOHN QUINCY ADAMS,
    Secretary of State.'

September 26. Had another interview with Mr. Canning at Gloucester Lodge, at his request. The subject of our discussions on the 18th instant, was renewed. . . .

He now declared that England felt great embarrassment as regarded the immediate recognition of these new States; embarrassments which, he admitted, had not existed in the case of the United States when they adopted the measure of acknowledging them; and then he asked, whether I could not give my assent to his proposals on a promise by England of *future* acknowledgment.

I replied, that under the peculiar importance of the whole subject, and considering the relation in which I stood to it, I could not feel at liberty to take the step upon any other footing than that of immediate acknowledgment by England. Further conversation passed, though only of a desultory nature, and the interview ended. . . .

November 25. Had a full and final interview yesterday with Mr. Canning at the Foreign Office, on the affairs of Spanish America.

November 26. Report what passed, in the following despatch to the Secretary of State.

'London, November 26, 1823.

'Sir, – I had an interview with Mr. Canning on the 24th instant at the Foreign Office, when he afforded me important information on Spanish-American affairs, which I now proceed to lay before you.

'He began by saying, that our conversation on this subject at Gloucester Lodge, on the 26th of September, having led him to conclude that nothing could be accomplished between us, owing to the ground which I had felt it necessary to take respecting the immediate recognition of the late Colonies by Great Britain, he had deemed it indispensable, as no more time was to be lost, that Great Britain should herself, without any concert with the United States, come to an explanation with France. He had, accordingly, seen the Prince de Polignac, (French ambassador in London), and stated to him that, as it was fit that the two Courts should understand each other distinctly, on the Spanish-American question, it was his intention to unfold the views of Great Britain to him.

'In pursuance of this course, Mr. Canning held several conferences with Prince Polignac in the early part of October, in which each party unfolded the views of their respective governments, and agreed upon the written memorandum or paper which was to embody them.

'This paper, Mr. Canning said, was of a nature which did not leave him at liberty to offer me a copy of it; but he had invited me to the Foreign Office for the purpose of reading it to me, having only since his return from the country last week, exhibited it to the Ministers of the other Powers, and not yet to all of them.

'He accordingly read the paper to me. The points which chiefly arrested my attention as new to me, were, first, that England declares that she will recognise the Independence of the Colonies, *in case France should employ force in aid of their resubjugation*: secondly, in case Spain herself, reverting to her ancient colonial system, *should attempt to put a stop to the trade of Britain with those Colonies*; but it is not said what Britain will do beyond recognising their Independence, her ulterior conduct being left to be shaped, as we may infer, by ulterior events. As regards the form of government most desirable for the Colonies, considered as Independent States, a preference is expressed for monarchy, could it be practicable.

'With the exception of the foregoing points, I recollect nothing material in the paper as regards the policy or intentions of Great Britain, not heretofore made known in my own communications upon this subject.

'To report with the requisite accuracy the views of France from this paper, read over but once to me, I might find a task the more difficult from having had less acquaintance with them beforehand. I am not able, for my own share, to discern the adequate motives for wrapping it up in such secrecy, and have little doubt but that even the public journals of Europe will, before very long, enlighten us with sufficient precision on its whole contents. The London journals of the present week have made some beginning towards it.

'Having said thus much, I will proceed in my endeavours to state the main points of this paper, where it was illustrative of the policy of France.

'It declares that France, like England, considers the recovery of the Colonies of Spain as hopeless.

'It expresses the *determination* (I think this was the word) of France not to assist Spain in attempting their reconquest.

'It expresses the desire of France to see the dispute made up by amicable arrangements between the mother country and the Colonies.

'It disclaims for France all idea of exclusive commercial advantages from the Colonies.

'It knows not what there is to be *recognised* in the Colonies, as independent; France regarding all government there as a mockery.

'It labours to show the necessity of assembling an European Congress to which England should be a party, (which she declines,) to bring about the benevolent end of reclaiming those remote regions from their past errors, and making up the dispute between them and the parent State on terms satisfactory to both, as the policy worthy of both.

'These were the material points of the paper as I recollected them after listening to a single perusal of it. I am sensible that I state some of them in a way to start further questions as to their true meaning; questions which I could myself raise without being able at this moment to solve. The apprehensions of Britain, however, seem to be fully allayed; and it is certain that she does not now anticipate any speedy interruption of the peace of Europe from this cause. The language which France now holds to Britain is obviously at variance with that which her manifestoes breathed when her troops entered Spain in the spring. . . .

'I have the honour to remain, with very great respect, your obedient Servant,

RICHARD RUSH

'Honourable JOHN QUINCY ADAMS,
    Secretary of State.'

CHAPTER XXVI

COURSE OF THE UNITED STATES IN REGARD TO
SPANISH AMERICA – DECLARATIONS OF PRESIDENT
MONROE IN HIS MESSAGE TO CONGRESS, DECEMBER,
1823 – THEIR EFFECT IN EUROPE – REMARKS ON THE
SUBJECT – DINNER AT THE DUKE OF SUSSEX'S: INTER-
VIEWS WITH MR. CANNING ON THE NEGOTIATION –
NORTH-WEST COAST OF AMERICA, THE PROMINENT
TOPIC – ENGLAND OBJECTS TO THE PRINCIPLE OF
NON-COLONIZATION ON THE AMERICAN
CONTINENTS, TAKEN BY PRESIDENT MONROE –
INTERVIEW WITH MR. CANNING PREPARATORY TO
OPENING THE NEGOTIATION

The despatch with which the preceding chapter closed, substantially terminated the correspondence and conferences I
had held with Mr. Canning on the topic, so interesting at that
juncture both to Europe and America, of Spanish-American
affairs. I had further conferences with him; but none
necessary to be recounted, as they made no change in the
course of England.

And now I am to speak of the course of the United States. By
the early transmission of the proposals made to me by Mr.
Canning, in his notes of the latter end of August, the copies of
them, as well as of my reports of our conferences on the whole
subject, arrived at Washington in time to engage the deliber-
ations of President Monroe and his cabinet, before the meeting of Congress in December; and it was very satisfactory to
me to learn that the part I had acted was approved. Although,
in the end, no concerted movements took place between the
two Governments, the communications to me, from the
Secretary of State, in responding to the overtures of Mr.
Canning, were in a high degree conciliatory towards England;
and framed with every just sensibility to the frank and friendly

spirit of those overtures. This I duly made known to Mr. Canning. . . .

November 28. Passed last evening at Count Munster's, Grosvenor Place, where we had most of the diplomatic corps, and other company. My wife says, that Count D'Aglie, the Sicilian Minister, told her, that the late King, George III, in talking once to the Dutch Ambassador, called Holland an *aquatic* Power. The King used the term in good-humour; but the Count added, that the Ambassador did not like it.

November 30. Dined at the Duke of Sussex's, Kensington Palace. Prince Cimitilli, Mr. Roscoe, (author of Lorenzo de Medici), Sir James Macintosh, Dr. Lushington, of the civil law courts; Mr. Denman, Mr. Jekeyll, and others, made the party.

His Royal Highness the Duke uttered sentiments favourable to constitutional liberty with his accustomed frankness and fervour, Mr. Roscoe seconding everything of this kind. The former asked if we had any Tories left in the United States. I said, a few, probably, in their abstract notions of government. Mr. Roscoe asked if they wished re-union with England. I replied that I did not believe there was a single individual in our country who entertained such a wish; we had grown too strong in ourselves. The voluminous and complicated state of the English law became a topic. Dr. Lushington remarked that no man could comprehend it all, and that it called loudly for revision and arrangement. He alluded to the numerous and increasing subdivisions in the profession of the law, as a consequence of the confusion and entanglements of the law itself, and thought it operated unfavourably upon the profession, by tending to cramp the minds of its members, by limiting the range of their professional knowledge.

Cards being spoken of, his Royal Highness said, that the division and numbers of the pack were supposed to have had a connexion among the Egyptians (he gave cards that antiquity) with astronomical science. First, the fifty-two composing the pack, answered to the weeks of the year; next, thirteen of a kind agreed with the fourth part of the year, divided into weeks; then again, four different kinds, answered to the four seasons; and, lastly, by counting up from the ace to ten, then counting the knave as eleven, the queen as twelve, and king as thirteen, you get ninety-one. Four ninety-ones give you three hundred and sixty-four, the number of days, according to some calculations, in the year.

His Royal Highness mentioned that the English Government had a plan for purchasing up the whole slave population of their West India islands, to get rid of slavery in them. This was new to me, and seemed so to others at table. At first blush, I thought it struck all as very bold, if not impracticable.

How far the great West India Emancipation-act since carried into effect by Britain, on the foundation of what the Duke of Sussex then said, will result favourably to the interests of humanity in those islands, does not, as yet, seem to have been ascertained. . . .

December 10. Dined at Mr. Canning's, Gloucester Lodge. Mr. Planta, Mr. Stratford Canning, Mr. Chinnery, and a few others, were the guests.

At dinner, Mr. Canning took less than his usual share of the conversation, leaving it chiefly to his guests. Ships and steamboats formed one of the topics. All agreed that naval science was on the eve of great revolutions, and soon to be carried to a much higher pitch than the present or past ages had witnessed.

At this classic villa of the Foreign Secretary, one of the suite of rooms is the library. We went into it, to coffee, after leaving the dinner-table. The conversation became literary. Washington Irving's Sketch-book was spoken of, and highly recommended. Mr. Canning said it was a work of extraordinary merit; but he preferred the American pieces. In this preference others joined. The 'Dutch Schoolmaster,' and 'Rip van Winkle,' were singled out, as rich in humour. The topic changing, Swift came on the tapis. Several of his pieces were called up, with genuine gusto. Mr. Canning was on a sofa; Mr. Planta next to him; I and others, in chairs, dotted around. 'Planta,' said Mr. Canning, 'pray hand down the volume containing the voyages, and read the description of the storm in the voyage to Brobdignag; seamen say that it is capital; and as true, nautically, as Shakespeare always is, when he undertakes to use sea terms.' Mr. Planta took down the volume, and read the passage. One sentence in it runs thus: 'It was a very fierce storm, the sea broke strange and dangerous; we hauled off upon the lanniard of the whipstaff, *and helped the man at the helm.*' When he was done, all admired the passage, under this new view and commendation of it, which Mr. Canning had given us. He himself said nothing for a few moments, but sat silent; then, as if in a reverie, he uttered, in a low tone, yet very distinctly, the words, '*and helped the man at the helm! and helped the man at the helm!!*' repeating them. It seemed as if the *helm* at the Foreign Office, with all its anxieties, had suddenly shot into his mind, clouding, for a moment, his social ease. His familiar friends of the circle bantered him a little on that fancy. He declared off, however, and only said that it was a fine passage. So passed this agreeable evening in the library at Gloucester Lodge.

December 12. Had an interview this morning with Mr. Canning, at Gloucester Lodge, on the subject of the general negotiation. Learning of my arrival, that he was labouring under an attack of gout, I would have deferred the interview to suit his convenience; but he had given orders for receiving me in his chamber, into which I went, where I found him in bed though anxious to see me. He asked if I still despaired of having a colleague. I said not utterly; but my hope was so slender, that I could not justify it to my duty to ask any delay whatever in bringing on the negotiation, but would be ready at any time. As a further motive to an early beginning I remarked, that perhaps we might then hope to get through with some of the heaviest parts, before the meeting of Parliament in February; after which his own and Mr. Huskisson's engagements in the House of Commons, might be likely to interpose delays to our progress. He informed me, that the instructions on their side were in daily course of preparation, but that he did not now think a beginning could be made with any advantage, on the score of expedition, until after the Christmas holidays, and that these would not be over until after the first week in January. . . .

January 2, 1824. Had an interview with Mr. Canning, at Gloucester Lodge, at his request. His attack of gout had passed off.

The President's message having arrived since our last interview, he referred to that part of it which holds out the principle, that the United States will henceforth object to any of the powers of Europe establishing colonies on either of the continents of America. If I had instructions, he wished me to state the precise nature and extent of this principle. He had not before been aware of it. Suppose, for example, that Captain Parry's expedition had ended, or that any new British expedition were to end, in the discovery of land proximate to either part of the American continent, north or south, would the United States object to Britain planting a colony there? I said, that when such a case arose it might be considered; that I had no instructions on the principle since it was proclaimed in the message, but would be prepared to support it when the negotiation came on. Further conversation passed as to the best mode of dealing with the principle in our approaching negotiation. . . .

January 21. Had an interview with Mr. Canning at the Foreign Office. Mr. Huskisson and Mr. Stratford Canning were present. It was agreed that the general negotiation should be opened, in form, on the 23rd instant, at the office of the Board of Trade.

I then handed Mr. Canning a paper, containing the following list of the subjects:- 1. Commercial intercourse between the United States and the British North-American Colonies, and West India Islands; connecting with these heads, the question of the navigation of the river St. Lawrence. 2. Suppression of the Slave Trade. 3. Boundary Line under the fifth article of the Treaty of Ghent. 4. Admission of Consuls of the United States into the Colonial Ports of Britain. 5. Newfoundland Fishery. 6. Relative claims of the two nations on the North-west coast of America. 7. Debateable questions of maritime law.

Some conversation passed as to the order in which the subjects were to be taken up, when it was agreed that we would begin with the Slave Trade.

CHAPTER XXVII

THE GENERAL NEGOTIATION OPENS – SUBJECT OF
THE SLAVE TRADE FIRST TAKEN UP – DINNER AT THE
DUKE OF SUSSEX'S; AT MR. STRATFORD CANNING'S –
RENEWED INTERVIEW WITH MR. SECRETARY CANNING
ON SPANISH-AMERICAN AFFAIRS – SECOND MEETING
OF THE PLENIPOTENTIARIES ON THE BUSINESS OF
THE NEGOTIATION – DINNER AT MR. PEEL'S –
CONVENTION RELATIVE TO THE SLAVE TRADE AGREED
UPON AND SIGNED – CIRCUMSTANCES WHICH LED TO
ITS DEFEAT

January 23. The negotiation opens at the office of the Board of
Trade, Great George Street, Westminster. The British Plenipotentiaries, Mr. Huskisson and Mr. Stratford Canning, hand
me for inspection their original full power from the King; and
I hand them mine, under the President's autograph, constituting
me the Plenipotentiary of the United States. Theirs, in describing
my appointment, speak of it as having been by the President,
with the consent, and by the authority, of the Senate and *House
of Representatives* of the United States. I pointed out the in-
accuracy, mentioning that the Senate only was associated with
the President in the appointing power; but on their asking if I
thought it material, I said No, being only surplusage; and both
powers being found in due and proper form in all other respects, copies were exchanged, each party attesting his
own.

It having been agreed that the subject of the Slave Trade
should be taken up first, I proceeded to open it on the side of
the United States. After making all such statements and
remarks on the subject as seemed to me necessary to
introduce and explain it, according to the true spirit in which I
had been instructed by my Government to present it, I concluded by reading the entire *projet* of the convention transmitted

to me by the Secretary of State, with his despatch of the 24th of June, 1823.

The British Plenipotentiaries said that they would take the whole into careful consideration. They remarked, that Britain wanted nothing, on her part, to put down this trade, so far as her own subjects were concerned; her laws against it being already effectual, and having put a stop to it as far as laws could. I replied, that such was also the case with the United States; that, for ourselves, we wanted nothing further, and offered this *projet* only to meet the call for a substitute for the British proposals hitherto made to us, but which the United States, under their constitutional system and for other reasons, had been compelled to decline; and also to meet the request expressed in a resolution of the House of Representatives, passed by a vote nearly unanimous, in the winter of 1823. I added, that in the *projet* I had submitted, the first, second, fourth, and ninth articles, were to be considered as embodying principles not to be departed from.

We adjourned at 4 o'clock, to meet again on the 29th.

Immediately after the negotiation was, in due form, opened, the British Plenipotentiaries remarked, in manner altogether conciliatory, that should our labours unfortunately end without any treaties growing out of them, which however they did not wish or mean to anticipate, the failure would at least not disturb the good understanding subsisting between the two nations; a remark to which I cordially responded.

January 25. Dined with the Duke of Sussex, where we had a small party. On rising from table, we went into the rooms containing his Royal Highness's library, in one of which coffee was served. The whole suite was lighted up, enabling us to range through them, and glance at the books. The entire collection was stated to be fifty thousand volumes, chiefly formed by himself within a few years. They are arranged in different rooms according to the subjects. Of theology, there were said to be fifteen thousand volumes, comprising one thousand different editions of the Bible, several of them polyglot editions; his Royal Highness being a good linguist, and fond of biblical learning. The first Bible ever printed with types was in the collection. One hundred and thirty guineas was the price given for it, and it seemed to be prized even beyond that sum by its royal owner.*

January 26. Dined at Stratford Canning's. Mr. Huskisson was there, and requested that our second meeting might take place on the 2nd of February, instead of the 29th instant as first appointed; which was agreed to. Mr. Secretary Canning was of the party, and much pleased with the commencement of our work on the Slave Trade. He had been informed of my *projet* of a convention, called it a promising 'first step,' and one which he hoped would be productive of good fruit in the end.

February 1. Had an interview with Mr. Canning, at Gloucester Lodge, on Spanish-American affairs. I read to him a despatch received from the Secretary of State, dated the 29th of November, 1823, which laid down the principles of my Government on this subject, and gave answers to his propositions and communications to me of last summer and autumn, the basis of which intervening events had changed.

Mr. Canning then mentioned to me the present position of England in relation to this subject; and that it might be known to me the more precisely, he handed me for perusal a despatch which he had prepared to Sir William A'Court, British Ambassador at Madrid, of date so recent as the 30th of January. It was written in consequence of the Ambassador having informed his Government that Spain had again been addressing herself to France, Austria, and Russia, calling on them to hold a congress at Paris, (to which England was *not* to be invited,) for the purpose of assisting Spain in the recovery and establishment of her authority over her colonies in America. I read the despatch entirely through. The substance of it was:-

1. – That England disapproves of the plan.
2. – That she thinks the day gone by for all interference

---

* This liberal-minded and excellent Prince died a year or two ago. He was always attentive to American gentlemen, when afforded opportunities of making their acquaintance. None shared more largely, or better merited, his esteem, than our late Minister to England, Mr. Stevenson; and perhaps I may here add, that when the latter was about to visit Paris in 1837, his Royal Highness, on his own friendly impulse, gave him a letter of introduction to the King; which ardently breathed respect and good-will to the United States, as well as to Mr. Stevenson personally.

towards a settlement of this contest, unless on the basis of the independence of the new States; and that she, England, is willing to mediate between the parties on that basis; *but no other.*

3. – But that she is nevertheless willing that Spain should be allowed special advantages over other nations, England being still content to stand on the footing of the most favoured nation, *after* Spain.

4. – She expresses a desire that Spain should herself be the first among European powers to acknowledge their independence; and that she should do it promptly. The despatch urges this measure strongly, and intimates it to be the intention of England to wait a while longer, in the hope of its adoption.

5. – But that, should Spain refuse to adopt it, or indefinitely put off the recognition of the new states, England will herself recognize them: and that this may even happen in a few months.

Such was this official paper, resolved into its essential points. Mr. Canning said to me, in conclusion, that he had no belief whatever that any Congress would now be held, and before I came away expressed anew his wishes for the auspicious progress of our negotiation.

February 2. The Plenipotentiaries of the two governments met according to appointment, at the same place as before. The British Plenipotentiaries had drawn up the protocol of our first conference, which, with some additions to it which I suggested, was agreed to.

They then went, at large, into the consideration of some of the articles I had submitted on the Slave Trade. They raised objections to some of the provisions, made queries as to others, and were full and free in their general remarks. I replied to them all, under the lights of my instructions, and such others as occurred to me. Many of their objections and difficulties, they admitted, went rather to the details of the plan than its substance; and they said that they would consult more fully with their law-officers, under every anxiety to see all objections satisfactorily removed. We adjourned on this footing, after having been together several hours, agreeing to meet again. . . .

March 6. Dined at Mr. Peel's, Home Secretary of State since

the resignation of Lord Sidmouth. We had nearly all the diplomatic corps, and other guests. In the table ornaments, you saw the alliance of taste with wealth.

The conversation at table, had, as one topic, the reforms in the law, which Parliament has taken in hand, and with which Mr. Peel has had so much to do. In alluding to them this evening, even his incidental and brief remarks told the listener how able he was to look at the law, as a science, through the lights of his general reading in that and other fields; and therefore qualified to take hold of it with a reforming hand, though no professional man.

Prince Polignac, French Ambassador, was of the company. While we were in the drawing-rooms, after dinner, I had conversation with him on the relations between France and the United States. It had not proceeded far, when he alluded to Lafayette's intended visit to the United States, and in a tone of complaint; friendly indeed, but decided. What caused it to be complained of, I asked? how was this possible? 'It was the *invitation* given to him by our Government, and offer to send a frigate over to France to convey him to our shores.' These things it was, he said, which, considering the relations Fayette held to the present Government of France, gave him pain, and would pain others in France. I endeavoured to remove this kind of sensibility in him, by the simple remark, that I thought all France ought to regard the visit in a light precisely the reverse; for that, if it were possible by any single incident, beyond any other imaginable, to revive in the United States the ancient attachment to *Bourbon* France, it would be this very visit of Fayette; whose presence once more among us, after so long an interval, would almost rekindle the enthusiasm of the revolution, recall Washington to us, whose favourite Fayette was, and the times when French hearts and arms were united with our own, while a Bourbon filled the throne of France.

All may do homage to the consistent devotionof such a man as Prince Polignac to his Sovereign, and sympathise with him while a prisoner in Ham Castle; but it is not easy to regard in the same light the clearness of his understanding.

March 13. The Plenipotentiaries met. Full discussions having now been had on the subject of the Slave Trade, and everything agreed upon by the Plenipotentiaries on each side, a convention for the purpose of more effectually putting down the trade by the co-operating naval efforts of both nations, was this day signed and executed in due form, subject to the ratification of the Senate of the United States.

March 15. Under this date I transmit the convention to the Secretary of State, with a despatch giving an account of all the discussions which led to its conclusion. . . .

In ratifying the convention, the Senate excepted from its provisions, the 2nd Article, and a portion of the 7th. They consisted, in the opinion of my Government, of provisions unessential to the great objects of the convention, and need not now be stated, as England herself ultimately yielded them.

But the striking out of a provision from the *first* article, was a measure which proved fatal to the instrument in the eyes of England.

That article commenced thus: 'The commanders and commissioned officers of each of the two high contracting parties, duly authorized, under the regulations and instructions of their respective Governments, to cruise on the coasts of Africa, of *America*, and of the West Indies, for the suppression of the Slave Trade, shall be empowered, under the conditions, limitations, and restrictions hereinafter specified,' &c. &c.

The Senate struck from this article the words, 'of America.'

With the above exceptions, the convention received the full ratification of the Senate; and before the convention finally fell to the ground, Mr. Canning sounded me as to the plan of a qualified restoration of the words struck from the first article, so as to restrict the right of cruising to the southern coast of the United States, as the part alone where slavery was found. I replied at once, that it would be decidedly objectionable, as carrying an appearance, I was sure he could not intend, of our being a divided nation.

England had no solid foundation for complaint at the refusal of the Senate to ratify the convention as signed in London. She knew it to be a fundamental provision of our constitution, that no treaty was finally valid until it be transmitted to the President for his final ratification, '*by and with the advice and consent of the Senate of the United States.'*

Yet, it is not to be disguised that she was disappointed at the result.

I add, in conclusion, on this head of the general negotiation, that President Monroe was prepared to have ratified the convention exactly as I had signed it in London; of which I informed the British Government; and he was pleased to convey to me, in the same despatch in which this was declared, his approbation of the course I had pursued in the negotiation of it.

In the account given in the foregoing of the fate of the Slave-trade convention, only one subject of a complicated negotiation was disposed of. Six others remained, all of importance to the two countries, and some involving interests of humanity not less dear and permanent, and wider in scope, than those involved in the Slave Trade. To treat of such subjects with necessary fulness of investigation, under all the other calls upon the time of the British negotiators and upon my own, (for the current business of the Legation went on,) occupied the remainder of the spring, and two months of the summer; the final conferences running into the closing days of July. Twenty-six formal protocols were drawn up; and the intervals between the meetings at which the matter of them was canvassed and settled, as authentic records of the negotiation, did not pass without toil on the part of the negotiators.

I made detached reports from time to time of its progress, having kept full minutes of everything; but waited until its close for the transmission of a connected Report of the whole, condensed and arranged from those minutes in ways that appeared suited to render the whole intelligible under one view. That Report was dated on the 12th of August, 1824, and was published by Congress. For the share I had in this negotiation, I neither seek nor deserve any award of merit, beyond having faithfully aimed at fulfilling the instructions under which I acted; but let its history duly speak to all American citizens, the merit of the Government of the United States at that epoch.

Let its history convey the just award to that virtuous and honourable man, pure patriot, and wise chief magistrate, James Monroe; whose services and worth ought to be freshened in the eyes of the country. A noble-minded man he was, without a particle of selfishness or ill-directed ambition in his whole nature; a man of Roman mould; honest, fearless, and magnanimous; who, having shed his blood in the war of the revolution, and risked it in that of 1812, the official prop of which he was at the darkest crisis of Mr. Madison's administration, sought, with returning peace, to establish, on the broadest foundations, the relations of peace, and lessen the calamities of future wars, when wars were to come. Let the just award be given to his Secretary of State, Mr. Adams; whose extraordinary endowments and fervent patriotism are stamped upon the instructions I received. I do not republish them, as they would swell too much the bulk of this volume; but their great and enlarged ends, under some views, and profound sagaciousness for his country's interests, under others, will be sufficiently collected, I trust, from my Report.

It will be seen, that the whole subject of our commercial intercourse with the Colonial Empire of Britain, insular and continental, in this hemisphere, which still remains an unsettled subject, has never been put on better foundations for the United States, than were then contemplated; and that our trade and tonnage are in danger of suffering, whenever those foundations are lost sight of. . . .

CHAPTER XXVII

LEVEE AT CARLTON PALACE – INFORM MR. CANNING
OF MY RECALL, AND ASK AN INTERVIEW WITH THE
KING, A TIME FOR WHICH IS APPOINTED – THE MISSION
CLOSES WITH AN AUDIENCE OF LEAVE OF THE KING

April 20, 1825. Attended the levee. Gave Mr. Canning information of my recall, having been invited home by President Adams, to preside over the Treasury Department at Washington. I asked, when I might hope for the honour of an audience of the King, to deliver my letter of recall, and take leave of his Majesty. He appointed the 27th instant.

Mr. Canning congratulated me in friendly terms on the home trust to which I was called, and proposed that we should correspond after I returned to the United States; to which I cordially assented.

I had half an hour's conversation with Sir John Copley,* and the Bishop of London, on our late Presidential election. Both agreed, that its quiet termination, considering the number of candidates in the beginning, (Mr. Crawford, Mr. Adams, General Jackson, Mr. Clay, and Mr. Calhoun,) spoke well for our constitution, and the political habits of the people.

April 23. Dined at Mr. Canning's with all the foreign ambassadors and ministers, it being St. George's day, and the dinner given in celebration of the King's birthday. Mr. Canning was not at table, being suddenly unwell. Mr. Planta and Lord Howard de Walden did the honours of the table for him.

April 27. Had my audience of leave of the King. I said, that having been called home by my Government, I had the honour to deliver to his Majesty a letter from the President, mentioning his intention of recalling me; in delivering which I was

---

* Afterwards Lord Chancellor Lyndhurst.

charged by the President to say, how sincerely it was his desire to maintain, in all respects, the good understanding which had subsisted between the two countries, during the period I had resided at his Majesty's Court.

The King reciprocated fully the President's desire, and thought proper to say that he was sorry I was going away, though, having understood the cause, it was to be expected; and he added other kind words. Lord Bathurst was present at the interview. I thanked his Majesty for the many tokens of kindness with which he had honoured me during so long a residence at his Court. He inquired as to the time of my embarkation, probable duration of the voyage, health of my family, and so on; the conversation lasting fifteen or twenty minutes, when I took my leave.

FINIS.